Governing Mandatory
Health Insurance

Governing Mandatory Health Insurance

Learning from Experience

Edited by

William D. Savedoff
Pablo Gottret

The World Bank

© 2008 The International Bank for Reconstruction and Development / The World Bank
1818 H Street NW
Washington DC 20433
Telephone: 202-473-1000
Internet: www.worldbank.org
E-mail: feedback@worldbank.org

ISBN-13: 978-0-8213-7548-8
eISBN-13: 978-0-8213-7549-5
DOI: 10.1596/978-0-8213-7548-8

Library of Congress Cataloging-in-Publication Data

Governing mandatory health insurance : learning from experience / edited by William D. Savedoff and Pablo Gottret.
   p. cm.
Includes bibliographical references and index.
ISBN-13: 978-0-8213-7548-8 (alk. paper)
ISBN-10: 0-8213-7548-2 (alk. paper)
   1. Insurance, Health—Cross-cultural studies. I. Savedoff, William D. II. Gottret, Pablo E. (Pablo Enrique), 1959- III. World Bank.
   [DNLM: 1. Insurance, Health—Europe. 2. Insurance, Health—Latin America. 3. Mandatory Programs—organization & administration—Europe. 4. Mandatory Programs—organization & administration—Latin America. 5. National Health Programs—organization & administration—Europe. 6. National Health Programs—organization & administration—Latin America. W 100 G721 2008]
   RA412.G72 2008
   368.38'2—dc22

                                                                                    2008013200

Contents

5 Governing multiple health insurers in a corporatist setting: The case of the Netherlands   129

Hans Maarse

6 Governing a hybrid mandatory health insurance system: The case of Chile   161

*Ricardo Bitrán, Rodrigo Muñoz, Liliana Escobar,
and Claudio Farah*

Boxes

Figures

Tables

Foreword

Health is at the center of the global agenda. Indeed, four of the eight Millennium Development Goals that the international community has committed to reach by 2015 are focused on health. Though funding from donors for low-income countries is often specifically directed at the heavy burden of persistent and emerging diseases, such as HIV/AIDS, tuberculosis, and malaria, there is also growing recognition that sustained progress against ill health requires innovation in health systems and better ways to finance them domestically. One of the options for financing that has received increasing attention is mandatory health insurance (MHI).

Efforts to modify health financing through adopting or reforming MHI are not limited to low-income countries. Many high-income countries, such as the Netherlands and Spain, have enacted major reforms in how their systems are financed. In countries that have not pushed through such reforms, the topic is still prominent in public debate and politics, as in the United States. Countries in other regions, such as East Asia, Europe and Central Asia, and Latin America and the Caribbean, are also being motivated by rising health care costs, poor quality of services, or inequities to consider adopting, reforming, or eliminating MHI systems, depending on their particular circumstances.

However, the debates over MHI rarely address how the system will be governed, tending to focus instead on designing the insurance scheme itself, in terms of who will be covered, what benefits will be provided, and whether providers will be contracted or directly employed. Since these design features are likely to change over time, the governance of the system—including the roles of different actors, institutions, and accountability mechanisms—is of much greater importance to the system's sustainability and effective functioning over time than those relatively changeable design features.

This book provides guidance to countries that want to reform or establish MHI by specifically addressing governance. It elucidates the role played by the social, political, and historical context in conditioning how MHI systems are governed and, in turn, how governance structures influence the health insurance systems' performance. The book describes the forms of governance that are associated with success, in particular, the regulatory institutions required to guide the system toward its social goals; the oversight mechanisms that monitor and correct the system; and the internal management of the health insurance institutions themselves. It highlights five governance dimensions—coherent decisionmaking structures, stakeholder participation, transparency and information, supervision and regulation, and consistency and stability—that influence the coverage, financial protection, and efficiency of MHI entities, and show how these operate in particular countries. Detailed analysis of governance arrangements in four countries—Chile, Costa Rica, Estonia, and the Netherlands—provide nuanced lessons for establishing health insurance systems that can truly serve the social goals of improved health, reduced financial insecurity, and greater equity.

Julian Schweitzer
Director, Health, Nutrition, and Population
The World Bank

Acknowledgments

Many individuals contributed to making this book a reality. The country case studies were prepared by country-based experts who have first-hand knowledge of the governance of mandatory health insurance in their respective countries. The Health, Nutrition, and Population (HNP) unit, under the guidance of Pablo Gottret (team task leader), Axel Rahola (currently advisor to the Minister for the Budget, Public Accounts and the Civil Service, Ministry of Finance, France), Birgit Hansl (SASPR), and William Savedoff (Social Insight), conceived and carried out this study. George Schieber, Ajay Tandon, Adam Leive, Valerie Moran, and Emiliana Gunawan assisted in this work. The peer reviewers were April Harding (Center for Global Development), Jose-Pablo Gomez Mesa, Toomas Palu, and Joseph Figueras (WHO-EURO). Cristian Baeza (acting Director of HNP) chaired the review meeting and provided useful comments. Jonathan Aspin (editorial consultant) provided critical editorial support. The report was generously funded by the Government of the Netherlands, through the World Bank–Netherlands Partnership Program.

Country case study authors

Chile—Ricardo D. Bitrán and Rodrigo Muñoz, Bitrán & Asociados
Costa Rica—James Cercone and José Pacheco, Sanigest Health Solutions
Estonia—Triin Habicht, Estonian Health Insurance Fund
Netherlands—Hans Maarse, University of Maastricht, Netherlands

Acronyms and abbreviations

CCSS	Costa Rica Social Security System (Caja Costarricense de Seguro Social)
CTG	Health Care Tariffs Board (College Tarieven Gezondheidszorg)
CTZ	Supervisory Board for Health Care Insurance (College Toezicht Zorgverzekeringen)
CVZ	Health Care Insurance Board (College voor de Zorgverzekeringen)
DIPRES	Public Budget Office (Dirección de Presupuestos)
EHIF	Estonian Health Insurance Fund
EMA	Estonian Medical Association
EU	European Union
FONASA	National Health Insurance Fund (Fondo Nacional de Salud)
GDP	gross domestic product
GES	explicit health guarantees (*garantías explícitas de salud*)
ISAPREs	Health insurance funds (*instituciones de salud previsional*)
MAI	Modalidad de Atención Institucional
MHI	mandatory health insurance
MLE	Modalidad de Libre Elección
NMa	Netherlands Competition Authority (Nederlandse Mededingingsautoriteit)
NZA	Netherlands Health Care Authority (Nederlandse Zorgautoriteit)
OECD	Organisation for Economic Co-operation and Development
SEGPRES	Secretary of the Presidency (Ministerio Secretaría General de la Presidencia)
SHI	social health insurance
SIS	Superintendancy of Health (Superintendencia de Salud)
ZFW	Sickness Fund Act (Ziekenfondswet)

Overview

This book provides guidance to countries that want to reform or establish mandatory health insurance (MHI) with regard to the institutional structures and forms of governance that are most likely to succeed. It specifically aims to identify key differences in how MHI systems are governed and to cull lessons from experience. By describing governance arrangements in greater detail and making the effort to develop institutional variables that can be compared across different countries, the book also contributes to the applied research literature that, if successful, will ultimately link different institutional forms to better and worse performance.

This book does not address the overall merits of MHI. At the same time as many developing countries are trying to adopt MHI systems, countries with long experience—such as Brazil and Spain—are turning away from them. Rather, it begins with the presumption that a country has already considered its options and has decided to reform or adopt an MHI scheme. Consequently, it focuses on providing guidance on the best way to do this.

The following sections give an outline of the chapters in this book.

Defining mandatory health insurance

The definition of mandatory health insurance is quite simple: it is a system that pays the costs of health care for those who are enrolled and in which enrollment is required for all members of a population. It is quite distinct from systems in which health insurance is largely voluntary and from those in which out-of-pocket payments predominate. It is a little more difficult to distinguish MHI systems from those in which government services are provided at little or no cost to the population (for example, the national health services of Malaysia or the United Kingdom), except that in MHI systems the insurance function is generally explicit and provision is often separated from financing. The Some Definitions section in chapter 1 explains this in further detail.

Defining governance

Broad definitions of governance attempt to encompass all the relevant factors that influence the behavior of an organization. For MHI entities, these factors include its relationship to the government, its members, any other payers (such as employers), health care providers, and other insurers (competitors, for example). Narrower definitions of governance look specifically at the "control" mechanisms that are used to hold the entity accountable. These latter definitions are more concerned with such issues as the mechanisms by which board members are elected, the scope and style of government supervision, and the scope of managerial discretion in defining benefits, contribution rates, and negotiating contracts. The Governance Dimensions section in chapter 1 expands this introduction.

The existing literature on MHI systems addresses governance indirectly to the extent that it considers the advantages and disadvantages of affiliation rules, single or plural funds, alternative payment mechanisms, and options for defining benefits and contribution rates. The literature that specifically addresses governance of private corporations and public entities demonstrates the need for attention to ownership, to selection of board members, and to managerial incentives. Additionally, the literature on private corporate governance highlights the importance of capture and responses to multiple principals while the public governance literature emphasizes the emergence of vested interests. It illustrates the tradeoffs that emerge in determining the level of independence and discretion afforded to agencies. Finally, it shows the importance of publicly accessible information to proper oversight and the roles that can be played by different stakeholders, depending on how oversight is structured.

Framework

Numerous frameworks are available for analyzing MHI from the broader literature on health systems and health system performance. The framework here emphasizes the relationships between different actors and focuses on how insurance entities are held accountable to certain agents—such as beneficiaries, governments, or employers. One could call the basis of the framework "accountability through governance" (Figure 1). The section in chapter 1 headed An Analytical Framework develops this idea in depth.

The general rules for good governance are fairly simple: align incentives and make information available and transparent. Achieving this requires a variety of mechanisms, which can be usefully grouped into five dimensions of governance, namely coherent decisionmaking structures, stakeholder participation, transparency and information, supervision and regulation, and consistency and stability.

The choices within each of these five dimensions must also be appropriate to the system's context. Numerous factors condition the effectiveness of governance arrangements, but two particular features make a substantial difference: whether there are multiple competing insurance funds, and the forms of the relationship between the insurance funds and the health care providers.

For this reason it is useful to distinguish four models of MHI, based on contextual factors and distinguished by the existence, or not, of competition and the relationship between insurers and providers. Each of the four case studies

FIGURE 1   Accountability through governance

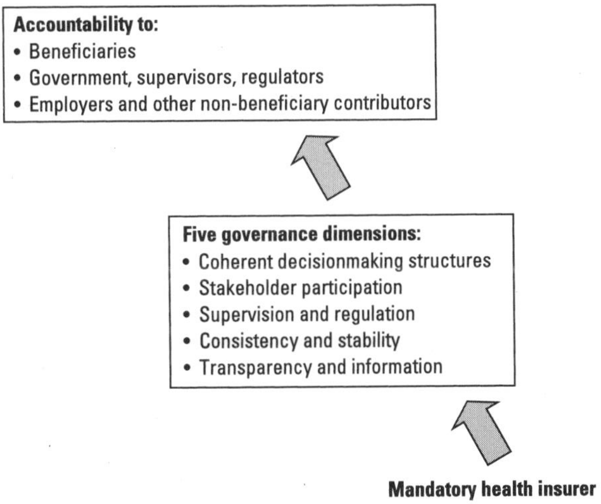

> **Accountability to:**
> • Beneficiaries
> • Government, supervisors, regulators
> • Employers and other non-beneficiary contributors

> **Five governance dimensions:**
> • Coherent decisionmaking structures
> • Stakeholder participation
> • Supervision and regulation
> • Consistency and stability
> • Transparency and information

Mandatory health insurer

in this book represents a different model: direct provision (Costa Rica), single payer (Estonia), corporatist (the Netherlands), and regulated market (Chile). Selected implications of these different models for governance are summarized in Table 1. Other economies for which data are relatively available are also shown in the table.

Other contextual factors that influence the performance of an MHI system include economic variables such as national income level, formality of the labor market, the supply of medical care services, and the depth of financial markets; and political variables such as the capacity for enforcing laws, contracts, and regulations. Any research program has to determine how it will control for these factors for two reasons. First, it is necessary to isolate the policy variable from these potentially confounding factors. Second, controlling for these factors is necessary to judge the generalizability of findings beyond particular contexts.

Dimensions of good governance

The governance of any MHI system encompasses three essential functions: (a) active monitoring, regulation, and guidance to keep the system working toward its broad social goals; (b) the structure for oversight of the system (i.e. its basic objectives, design, and rules and regulations); and (c) the administration of the health insurance institutions themselves. Chapter 2 outlines the features that can sustain dimensions of good governance.

Good governance is fundamental for MHI systems to perform well. The five general dimensions that are used to define good governance for governments, corporations, and financial markets, and that apply equally to MHI systems, are discussed in the following paragraphs.

TABLE 1 Mandatory health insurance models and implications for governance

Model	Economy (case studies in bold)	Number of insurers	Provider payment	Selected implications for governance
Model 1: Direct provision	**Costa Rica** Mexico	Single	Public administration and/or internal contracting	• May have soft budget constraints • Lack of benchmarking information • Risk of capture by providers • Oversight requires political or economic counterweight to the insurer
Model 2: Single payer	**Estonia** Hungary Korea, Rep. of Taiwan, China	Single	Monopsonist negotiating with multiple providers	• May have soft budget constraints • Lack of benchmarking information • Risk of capture by providers • Oversight requires political or economic counterweight to the insurer
Model 3: Corporatist	Germany **Netherlands**	Multiple	Negotiation between representative associations	• Possible to rely on associations for overseeing certain aspects of performance • Need to assure legitimate process for selecting representatives
Model 4: Regulated market	**Chile** Colombia	Multiple	Various forms of contracting providers with different payment-setting processes	• Possible to elicit information about costs through comparative analysis • Possible to rely on shareholders for assuring efficiency • Consumer protection procedures need to be in place • Risk that insurers may "capture" regulator

Coherent decisionmaking structures enable those responsible for particular decisions also to be endowed with the discretion, authority, tools, and resources necessary to fulfill their responsibilities; and to establish consequences (for their decisions) that align their interests with that of the overall good performance of the system.

Stakeholder participation is rooted in the premise that stakeholder views are integral to meaningful governance and should be incorporated during the process of decisionmaking.

Transparency and information ensure that information is available to those who can make decisions—whether financial regulators making sure that insurers have adequate funds to fulfill their obligations, beneficiaries seeking redress for improper treatment, or the general public pressuring government authorities to prosecute misconduct. This entails supporting the rule of law, which requires regulatory authority to be legitimately exercised only in accordance with written, publicly disclosed laws adopted and enforced in accordance with established procedure.

Supervision and regulation are another dimension of governance that can hold insurers accountable for their performance. Such accountability differs from transparency because it involves consequences—reward or sanction—for the performance of the health insurance funds.

Consistency and stability help avoid uncertainty around rule-making and enforcement through time and through periods of political change. If regulations are consistent, people and institutions can make long-term decisions with the assurance that the rules will not change or, at least, will not change arbitrarily.

The governance dimensions enumerated here require greater specificity if they are to be measured and used to assess systems. Chapter 2 describes a set of features that can sustain dimensions of good governance for MHI systems by establishing conditions for effective monitoring, regulation, and guidance (see Table 2.1 in Chapter 2; these features also appear in tabular form in the four case studies).

Each of these features can be measured by an associated indicator to evaluate the degree of conformity with these features of good governance. Applying these to the four case studies demonstrates an effective diagnostic tool for guiding policymakers who want to improve the governance of their systems.

Case studies

The first thing to note about all four cases is that they perform reasonably well in terms of insurance coverage, access to health care services, population health, and financial protection relative to other countries in the world. Still, complaints are aired in the media and legislatures about rising costs (in all four countries, despite widely different levels of spending), waiting lists (particularly in Estonia and the Netherlands), employee absenteeism and evasion (particularly in Costa Rica), and health care quality and equity (particularly in Chile). Chapters 3 through 6 contain the case studies.

The results of applying the indicators associated with the five governance dimensions reveal substantial variability across the cases.

Five dimensions of governance

All four countries perform well with regard to the dimension of *Consistency and stability*, sometimes as a consequence of political deadlock that resists change. Nevertheless, open democratic processes and debates have allowed each country to introduce changes in response to perceived problems without undermining the basic credibility of the system's structure and rules.

Each also performs well on the dimension of *Stakeholder participation*. The highest decisionmaking authorities within Costa Rica's Social Security System (Caja Costarricense de Seguro Social or CCSS) and the Estonian Health Insurance Fund (EHIF) are supervisory boards whose members are selected to represent the interests of organized groups; the sickness funds in the Netherlands also have independent directors serving on supervisory boards; while Chile's national insurance fund responds directly to the President.

The dimension of *Supervision and regulation* had the widest dispersion of performance. In all cases, the MHI system involves a mix of legislative, executive, and independent agencies, and insurers are subject to both internal and external financial audits. But other features vary considerably: the Netherlands regulatory authorities are semi-autonomous entities while the others are more directly managed by their respective governments; private insurers are subject to private sector regulations (for example, labor codes, financial reporting) while the public insurers are supervised by ministries and legislatures.

Surprisingly, the dimension of *Transparency and information* performed relatively poorly. Many MHI beneficiaries still have limited information on their entitlements and rights and, while most countries have consumer protection rules, MHI systems do not seem to have instilled a culture of exercising the right to consumer complaints (as is common in private systems). Nevertheless, issues related to conflicts of interest and consumer protection are of increasing concern: efforts to simplify and standardize information for public dissemination and to widen the range of performance indicators to include measures of health care service quality are, generally, increasing.

Coherent decisionmaking structures was the weakest dimension in all four countries. These are characterized by public ownership—National Health Insurance Fund (Fondo Nacional de Salud or FONASA) and the CCSS—and private ownership (*instituciones de salud previsional* or ISAPREs), and by centralized management (EHIF) and decentralized management (Netherlands sickness funds). At one extreme, the private health insurance funds in Chile (ISAPREs) have the authority to set their own premiums, design the benefits package, and negotiate prices with health care providers. In contrast, Estonia's EHIF does not set its own contribution level, nor does it define the benefits package.

Contextual factors

Competition is an indirect way of holding insurance funds accountable in the sense of creating incentives and pressures to perform well. In the four cases, Chile and the Netherlands have multiple insurers, while Costa Rica and Estonia have just one. The contrasts demonstrate both advantages and disadvantages of competition. *The relationship between insurance funds and health care providers* is also a critical conditioning factor for insurers' performance. The major contrast in these cases is between Costa Rica—which has integrated the insurance and provision functions—and the other three countries—where insurers are separate from providers.

Lessons from governance trends

Which forms of governance encourage the best performance by mandatory health insurers? While the dimensions of governance are important to ensuring accountability, the context of the MHI system is also a critical factor. The four cases demonstrate that the effectiveness of particular governance mechanisms vary in relation to a range of contextual factors—such as presence of competition, relationships between insurers and providers, organization of civil society, effectiveness of political processes, and enforcement of laws. This suggests that the search for better governance mechanisms has to pay more attention to how well the proposed mechanisms "fit" the structure of the health insurance system and its context. Chapter 7 treats these lessons, with regard to context and dimensions of governance, as well as remaining questions for research, in greater detail.

Therefore, the lessons drawn from this book cannot be applied to low-income countries without a number of qualifications. First, the cases presented here are only a small subset of relevant experiences. Second, the countries discussed here all established MHI funds when they had much higher income levels and degrees of economic formalization than is the case in today's low-income countries. Third, these countries are all economically and politically stable, with relatively effective governments, low corruption, and skilled workforces.

Two contextual factors, in particular, appear to condition how governance affects the performance of MHI—the number of insurers and the relationship between insurers and providers. In countries with multiple and competing insurers, external oversight mechanisms can pay less attention to efficiency and management, and focus more on consumer protection, inclusiveness, and preserving competition through anti-trust actions. By contrast, countries with a single health insurer need external oversight mechanisms that make the insurer accountable for integrity, quality, and productivity.

In addition, the relationship between insurers and providers influences the impact of different governance mechanisms. In some countries, this relationship is openly antagonistic, while in others, it is more collaborative. The presence of providers' representatives on the decisionmaking bodies of health insurers or regulatory agencies has different implications under these varied scenarios. In addition, where providers are direct employees of insurers, the character of negotiations and oversight needs to confront issues that arise in civil service codes or labor legislation, while countries where providers are independent of insurers need governance mechanisms that promote transparent and productive negotiations over prices and payment mechanisms.

Dimensions of governance
Coherent decisionmaking structures
The four case studies demonstrate that, with regard to ownership and legal status, mandatory health insurers can function reasonably well as parts of the executive branch (as in Chile), as autonomous public institutions (as in Costa Rica and Estonia), and as nonprofit private entities (as in the Netherlands). If a country has a well-functioning public sector, direct public administration might be the best option. Where the public sector is less effective, autonomous public institutions could be considered, with special attention to assure accountability, avoid capture by special interests, and ensure effective tools for managing personnel.

On the definition of roles and responsibilities, the studies show that many different allocations of decisionmaking powers can function well, but responsibility for making decisions has to be matched with appropriate authority, resources, and managerial discretion. Given the political sensitivity of health insurance, governments are often tempted to intervene in a wide range of financial and managerial decisions. Managing this tendency for undue interference is likely to work better when the respective responsibilities of the government and the insurance schemes are distinct and clear, when independent authorities (for example, courts) can effectively enforce that division of responsibilities, and when each actor has authority and discretion over those decisions for which it is held accountable.

Stakeholder participation

The initial approach to MHI in Western Europe was to explicitly select the members of supervisory boards to represent particular social groups or interests, such as business, labor, government, and beneficiaries. This approach has been criticized for not representing the interests of patients nor adequately controlling corruption and conflicts of interest. An alternative approach is to include representatives from a wider range of actors, as in Estonia. In other cases, countries have chosen to create boards of independent professionals and "experts," as in the Netherlands, or to subordinate the insurers to direct government administration, as in Chile.

Transparency and information

In every country, the number of reports, monitoring agencies, and indicators has increased substantially. This trend appears to be motivated both by a desire to tighten accountability of health insurers and to widen the scope of performance measures. This requires mandatory health insurers to have internal information systems for guiding managerial decisions related to performance; internal audit units; external audits; and regular reports to important stakeholders like legislative bodies, financial markets, and the public.

To be effective, required reports and audits are designed to collect information that is relevant and that can be acted upon.

Supervision and regulation

Unifying supervision for all health insurers—whether public or private, integrated with providers or not—is apparently the best way to assure fairness and efficiency in terms of financial solvency, consumer protection, and equity. While conflicts of interest are in all four cases a matter of concern, they are being addressed. Countries that are creating or reforming MHI should use the opportunity of reforming the health insurance system as a way to introduce measures for addressing conflicts of interest as soon as possible.

Health insurers are, fundamentally, financial institutions and unless they operate according to sound financial principles, they cannot remain solvent or function well. Appropriate financial supervision requires the government to establish minimum capital requirements and reserves, adequate internal controls, external auditing, and timely financial reports to regulatory authorities.

Yet, unlike other financial institutions, health insurers sign contracts that commit them to paying for a service whose quality is not easily monitored or guaranteed. For health insurance to be effective, beneficiaries must be able to reach health care providers in a timely fashion and receive appropriate diagnosis and treatment. Countries need to have mechanisms in place to directly supervise health care providers regarding the quality of services and to verify that health insurers can fulfill their contractual obligations by having negotiated contracts or established payment mechanisms with an adequate number of health care providers in the geographic regions that they serve.

The preceding elements of supervision are part of consumer protection. Good financial supervision reduces the chances that an insurer will go bankrupt when consumers require services. Good health care quality supervision increases the likelihood that consumers will get the services they need when they are injured or fall ill. Beyond these, countries have implemented a number of measures to ensure that consumers have a better understanding of their insurance coverage and responsibilities, that insurers provide good service other than medical care (for example, timeliness and accuracy of payments), and that consumers have ways to pursue their grievances when all else fails.

Consistency and stability

Establishing an open and respected process for changing rules and abiding by them in the early years of a new system also helps establish a reputation for consistency and stability.

When the government has strong credibility, public decision structures for health insurers, written into legislation or even the Constitution, may be the best way of establishing a consistent and stable system. If the government lacks such credibility, autonomous structures, protected by constitutional provisions or anchored in the private sector, may work better.

Additionally, stability can be achieved in a variety of circumstances. When political debates demonstrate broad agreement and support for the health insurance system, legislation and regulatory actions can articulate and implement that consensus. But even in cases where the system is the object of fierce political debates, stability can be achieved by maintaining the deadlock (assuming of course that the current structure is adequate and important changes are not needed).

Clear rules that are judiciously and reliably enforced are the best way for a country to assure consistency and stability for its MHI system. Given that circumstances change over time, clear procedures for modifying those rules are also needed—preferably tailored to the degree of flexibility required.

Contextual factors

Competition

The advantages of scale, simplicity, and equity that come from having fewer insurers are quite strong, and countries that are considering health insurance reforms would be well advised to consider whether consolidating insurers can or should be encouraged. Where countries have a commitment to competition in health insurance markets, they have come to realize that the health insurance market needs to be structured and regulated if normal market mechanisms are going to function well.

Relationship between insurance funds and health care providers

It is extremely difficult to find specific lessons in this regard except to emphasize the importance of this contextual feature. Countries that are designing governance for their MHI systems need to consider the strength and form of health care provider organization and take it into account. This is particularly true for choices regarding stakeholder participation because even without representation on supervisory boards, providers may exert influence in other ways—either politically or by popular appeals.

When designing the governance structures, countries would do well to examine their own experience with labor relations in both the private and public sector, and look for examples that have been more collaborative than confrontational. Using such domestic experiences and examining the current way that providers are organized and relate to insurers may generate ideas for channeling the legitimate interests of insurers and providers in productive directions.

Remaining questions for research

How can countries assure solvency and balanced budgets?

The health insurers studied here have all maintained solvency and balanced budgets, but the causes are not clear. For example, Estonia's EHIF has performed admirably, but in the context of rapid economic growth and a fiscally conservative political system. Without these contextual features, would the EHIF's governance mechanisms have been strong enough to assure solvency and balanced budgets? Every country has to propose governance mechanisms that increase the likelihood of solvency and balanced budgets, but ultimately these are assured only by the dynamics of actual behavior by political and economic actors.

How can countries assure financial protection for the population?

The four countries studied here have achieved universal coverage for their populations with a relatively comprehensive set of health services. However, in many low- and middle-income countries, MHI has not expanded beyond a small subset of the population or provides only limited benefits. Economies that are creating or reforming MHI need to consider the strategy for reaching universal coverage. Will they create specific insurance funds for different population segments and then try to unify them? Or will they begin with universal eligibility and deal with the costs and consequences of trying to provide such wide coverage?

How can countries promote efficiency and raise productivity?

Health care costs will continue to rise as populations become wealthier and demand more services, and as health care technology advances and offers more services and products. None of the approaches to governance of MHI presented here will guarantee that insurers focus on improving efficiency and productivity. Yet every case study country has been concerned with increasing efficiency and productivity as part of its reform efforts. This is another area where countries creating or reforming MHI will have to draw from other countries' experiences, reflect on their own conditions, and experiment with new approaches.

1

Governing mandatory health insurance: Concepts, framework, and cases

William D. Savedoff[1]

> It may be a reflection on human nature, that such devices should be necessary to control the abuses of government. But what is government itself, but the greatest of all reflections on human nature? If men were angels, no government would be necessary. If angels were to govern men, neither external nor internal controls on government would be necessary. In framing a government which is to be administered by men over men, the great difficulty lies in this: you must first enable the government to control the governed; and in the next place oblige it to control itself.
>
> *James Madison, Federalist Papers, No. 51. 1788*

Introduction

Mandatory health insurance (MHI) systems have been established in more than 60 countries, beginning with Germany in the late 19th century. They are generally characterized by a reliance on payroll taxes and some degree of autonomy from the government. As many middle- and low-income countries are considering health system reforms that involve establishing MHI systems or reforming existing ones, questions arise regarding the relationship between how the schemes are structured and function and how well they perform—in terms of population coverage, costs, benefits, and, ultimately, health outcomes. A relatively substantial literature is available on defining benefits, costing services, and creating payment mechanisms with proper incentives for providers. Relatively little is available to provide guidance with regard to how the MHI systems are structured institutionally and governed.

This book seeks to provide such guidance to countries that want to reform or establish MHI with regard to the institutional structures and forms of governance that are most likely to succeed. It specifically aims to identify key differences in how MHI systems are governed and cull lessons from the experiences of a range of countries. By describing governance arrangements in greater detail and making the effort to develop institutional variables that can be compared across different

13

BOX 1.1 *This book*

Mandatory health insurance is governed according to different models. The performance of health insurance funds is influenced by the governance mechanisms that are in place, but also by the way these mechanisms interact with the broader political and social context. Chapter 1 presents definitions, a conceptual framework, and models, and touches on country experiences, with the aim of informing the choices that countries will make when they create or reform MHI systems.

Precise conclusions regarding which governance mechanisms are most effective is not possible at this time because systematic data of sufficient cases to draw such conclusions are lacking. Nevertheless, by identifying and defining relevant institutional indicators and testing them against relevant performance measures, it is possible to both further the longer-term research objectives and to extract more useful information from country experiences.

The four case studies are useful because they provide a catalog of governance mechanisms that have been used in different places. By reviewing these cases, policymakers can see a wider range of options than they may have considered before. Secondly, the case studies show areas of convergence—issues

around which very different countries have adopted similar approaches to difficult problems. For these issues, policymakers would be well advised to consider adopting something similar unless there are very strong compelling reasons to think that they would not function well in the new context. Finally, reviewing the case studies within the broader framework can sensitize policymakers to policy problems which do not have readily apparent solutions, but which must be confronted in one way or another.

The following chapters provide more useful detail on all these points. Chapter 2 discusses efforts to identify and measure institutional dimensions of health insurance governance more precisely, along with its application to four countries. The subsequent chapters present the experiences of Costa Rica, Estonia, the Netherlands, and Chile. The rich institutional detail provided in these chapters shows how much can be learned from considering one's own situation in the light of other countries' experiences with confronting similar problems. The book concludes with a chapter on the lessons that may be extracted from these experiences for low- and middle-income countries today.

---

countries, these studies also contribute to the applied research literature that, if successful, will ultimately link different institutional forms to better and worse performance. (Box 1.1 presents an outline of the book.)

This chapter provides an overview for subsequent analysis of four specific case studies. The early parts of the chapter put MHI into its historical context, by defining key concepts (namely, mandatory health insurance, social health insurance, and governance) and by presenting an analytical framework for the analysis. The last part uses this framework to assess the four cases—Costa Rica, Estonia, the Netherlands, and Chile—and broader data collected on economies like Colombia, the Republic of Korea, and Taiwan (China).

This book is not addressing the overall merits of MHI. In fact, at the same time that many developing countries are trying to adopt MHI systems, countries with long experience—such as Germany, Spain, and Brazil—have actually turned away from it for a variety of reasons (Savedoff 2004; Wagstaff 2007). Rather, this book begins with the presumption that a country has already considered its options and either already has such a system or has decided to adopt one, and therefore focuses on the mechanisms for governing MHI schemes. By cataloging existing mechanisms for governing MHI schemes, and appraising their influence on intermediate outputs, it should be feasible to provide guidance to policymakers who are implementing new schemes or reforming existing ones.

Overview and trends

MHI is not a simple market or government service for several reasons. First, it is a service strongly affected by problems associated with insurance markets (for example, adverse selection, moral hazard) and with asymmetric information (for example, suppliers can "tell" consumers what to buy and normal checks through reputation are ineffective due to infrequent "purchases" and uncertainty over quality). As a result of these features, societies find it very difficult to provide these services efficiently in a way that satisfies all stakeholders.

Second, MHI is a service that has very high visibility ("Voices of the Poor") and, partly in consequence, it plays a central role in national political debates and institutional development.[2] Therefore, it is difficult to analyze MHI without an appreciation for the broader social movements that have shaped it. This section will provide an overview of how MHI evolved and discuss how it is being debated in developing countries today.

Emergence of mandatory health insurance in two regions

Two regions—Western Europe and Latin America—account for the largest share of MHI systems in the world (whether measured by financial flows or beneficiaries). In Western Europe, as early as the Middle Ages, voluntary associations provided their members with assistance in times of medical need. Due, in part, to the limited nature of medical care, most of this assistance was in the form of income support.

By the middle of the 19th century, most Western European countries had numerous associations offering health insurance, with a wide mix of affiliation rules—some on the basis of occupation, others on place of employment, place of residence, or even ethnicity. For example, by 1885 Sweden had dozens of sickness funds covering 10 percent of the population. In 1876 Germany had 5,239 officially recognized regional sickness funds insuring 869,204 people (about 5 percent of the population).

The transformation of these voluntary associations into broad national health insurance systems was driven by the political context, involving struggles between employers, labor groups, and the state. The 19th century process of industrialization transformed European societies and included the growth of organized labor as an important political actor. This threatened political elites who responded in many cases by pursuing "corporatist" policies—that is, political elites sought to channel labor demands through formal associations that would preserve existing power and privileges in return for certain concessions, such as shorter work weeks, unemployment insurance, pensions, and health benefits (Saltman 2004).

This dynamic was important for early citizen-state relations after the creation of Germany as a nation-state under Bismarck, who explicitly enacted MHI in 1883 to co-opt labor demands. Bismarck's legislation effectively knit existing sickness funds into a broader, formally recognized, and publicly supported network of insurance. Universality was not achieved until much later, but the principle of government engagement with employers, workers, and intermediating associations was established.

Different countries followed parallel paths, with MHI emerging as the dominant model in Austria (1887/8), Belgium (1894), Denmark (1892), the United Kingdom (1911), Switzerland (1911), France (1920), and the Netherlands (1941). Assisted by relatively modest medical care costs, rapid economic growth, and formalization of the labor market, Western European countries were able to gradually extend coverage to self-employed and agricultural workers, to dependents, and ultimately to the "non-contributing" population (for example, retirees, the unemployed) and reach "universal" coverage. Benefits were also extended to include a wide range of services from the treatment of acute events to primary care consultations and medications.

In the years following World War II, countries such as Sweden and the United Kingdom would replace the MHI model with a system based on government payment of providers, financed through general tax revenues. Another wave of reforms that replaced MHI with government-funded health care services took place toward the end of the last century after the fall of authoritarian regimes in Portugal (1979), Greece (1983), and Spain (1986). However, in many countries the MHI systems continue to enjoy strong popular support even though they have active discussions about reforms driven by rising costs and concerns over quality of care. Rather than replacing MHI, these countries are experimenting with organizational changes such as requiring consolidation of funds and giving citizens the right to choose their sickness fund. Different countries are also changing their systems' designs by encouraging the wealthy to opt out of the publicly subsidized system, increasing government control over setting contribution rates, introducing selective contracting, or modifying formulas for cross-subsidies.

Latin American countries began to debate and enact MHI systems contemporaneously with Western European developments. However, they did so without the comparable development of voluntary associations, in large part because European conquest and colonial rule had effectively destroyed or marginalized indigenous risk-sharing institutions where they existed. In some countries, notably Chile, Uruguay, and Argentina, European migrants imported many of the insurance forms with which they were familiar. This is the origin of the *Obras Sociales* in Argentina—sickness funds managed by labor unions—and the *Mutualistas* in

Uruguay—many of which were founded as voluntary occupation-based associations. Elsewhere, voluntary associations were relatively small, few and weak.

As Latin American states consolidated at the end of the 19th century, many sought to preserve elite power through adopting Western European political approaches, establishing "corporatist" relations between workers and employers and the state. As part of these political developments, public and formal sector workers were incorporated into social insurance systems. Where previous organizations existed, these tended to take on plural forms—as in Uruguay and Argentina. Where existing health insurance organizations were weak and small, states created large unified entities that provided "social security"—insurance for health care as well as pensions, unemployment, and disability—many of which also established facilities for direct provision of health care.

In contrast to Western Europe, many Latin American countries did not experience sustained economic growth or formalization of the workforce at a pace sufficient to draw in the majority of the population. Chile, Costa Rica, and Uruguay have come closest to universalizing health insurance coverage through social security schemes, while at the other extreme, countries such as the Dominican Republic have less than 10 percent of the population affiliated with MHI. In countries where coverage has not become universal, large disparities have emerged between those covered by MHI and those without; and MHI organizations have acted to preserve privileges for their affiliates even when it required subsidizing deficits with general revenues. In Mexico, for example, the Mexican Social Security Institute (Instituto Mexicana de Seguridad Social) spent about US$125 per affiliated person in 1995 while the health ministry spent the equivalent of less than US$20 per capita on the uninsured population.[3]

The experiences of Western Europe and Latin America show the strengths and weaknesses of MHI as it evolved in the 20th century. In certain contexts, this model appears to have been effective at universalizing health care insurance, while in others it appears to have locked in privileges for a minority. The model has also taken on a variety of forms. In Western Europe, as well as Argentina, Chile, and Uruguay, multiple insurance funds, woven into a nationally regulated system, with arm's-length relationship to providers are the norm. By contrast, in most of Latin America (except those countries noted above), single insurance entities with direct provision of care are common.

Huge global variation in mandatory health insurance

The range represented by Western Europe and Latin America is only part of the international variation across MHI schemes today. For example, in many countries the schemes provide universal coverage while in others they are selective, either because insurance is not offered to all members of the population or because beneficiaries are permitted to opt out of the social health insurance system. This variation in population in terms of coverage sometimes reflects an intentional policy choice, while in others it is an unintended consequence of the system's failure. In many richer countries, wealthier individuals are permitted to "opt out" of public MHI programs (for example, Germany, the Netherlands) and obtain private medical insurance. Meanwhile, in lower income countries, only a relatively small proportion of the population actually receives coverage (the Dominican Republic, the Kyrgyz Republic) despite political goals of universality.

Countries also vary in the number of insurance funds they have. Some countries have a single fund (Estonia, Hungary) while others have a few funds (Chile, the Russian Federation) or a large number of funds (Argentina, Japan, the Netherlands). The variation is even greater because some countries may have a single fund covering a standard health service plan and multiple funds to provide coverage for other health benefits (the Netherlands, Peru).

Beneficiaries are assigned to insurers in many different ways. Sometimes it is on the basis of employment (Mexico), in others geography or age (Japan), or individual choice (Chile, Germany). Sometimes, particular groups of beneficiaries (the wealthy or private sector workers) are offered choices while others are not. Because of these complexities, many questions arise that can only be answered precisely at the level of an individual sickness fund rather than treating the MHI *system* as the unit of analysis.

Competition is a formal and explicit part of MHI systems in many countries, including Argentina, Chile, Colombia, Germany, and the Netherlands, among others. In these systems, it is hoped that allowing individuals to choose their insurer will encourage accountability, improve efficiency, and foster innovation. The degree of regulation varies considerably with some intervening significantly in setting premiums, defining insurance plans, standardizing contracts, and managing risk-compensation funds.

MHI systems also face de facto competition from private voluntary insurers (both for-profit and nonprofit) that may or may not fall under the regulatory authority of the state. When individuals or employers purchase private voluntary coverage, it may indicate the low quality of services or benefits provided by MHI schemes. This is the origin of the so-called "doble afiliación" (double affiliation) that is common in many Latin American countries (for example, the Dominican Republic—Santana 1998). In other cases, it may reflect demands by citizens for more comprehensive coverage—to include the purchase of additional services (such as dental care) or copayments. For example, in France, it became so common for individuals to purchase private voluntary insurance to reimburse their copayments in the public health insurance system that the government eventually agreed to subsidize the purchase of this supplemental coverage for those without means.

MHI schemes often rely on external providers (public or private) for the provision of services to their members. This is the norm in Western Europe where medical professions were relatively well-established at the time that MHI systems were being put in place. Terms for paying providers in such systems are often determined through collective agreements between MHI funds and associations of medical providers. In other cases, terms of payments are established by law or are left to a relatively unfettered market. In some cases, however, MHI schemes rely primarily on their own network of service providers (Costa Rica, Mexico).

The oldest and most mature social insurance funds of Western Europe and Japan are those that offer the most comprehensive benefits packages, including not only a full range of treatments for acute and primary medical care, but also coverage for maternity, income support, and unemployment/disability payments. Benefits packages elsewhere may appear comprehensive on paper, but are often rationed when providers or funds are scarce relative to the demand.

Are existing models relevant?

Pressures to adopt MHI today appear to be driven by a very different political dynamic than the one that drove events in Western Europe and Latin America until the 1980s. In particular, the evolution of MHI in the 20th century was associated with an increasing role of the state in protecting social welfare and regulating society. By contrast, the introduction of MHI today appears more closely related with efforts to restrict the role of the state. This drive is apparent in current or former communist countries—such as China, Estonia, and Hungary—which seek to replace models of centralized provision of medical care with MHI and increase their reliance on private initiative and market institutions. But it is also apparent in countries with "national health service" systems—such as Kenya, Jamaica, and Malaysia—whose governments are concerned with the costs and inefficiencies of direct public provision and seek to effectively "outsource" health insurance coverage to self-financing and autonomous entities.

When low- and middle-income countries propose to adopt or reform MHI systems, the most common goals are to (see, for example, International Labour Office 2001):

- Mobilize funds for health care expenditures—introducing a new "tax."
- Improve insurance—eliminating barriers to utilizing health care services and protecting households against incurring large medical expenditures.
- Improve equity—redistributing income and/or assuring equitable access to medical services.
- Build democratic and participatory institutions—fomenting solidarity and social cohesion; empowering citizens; strengthening civil society organizations.

A priori, it is not clear why MHI would be the best way to address these goals (Savedoff 2004; Wagstaff 2007). Payroll taxes are not necessarily the most efficient to raise funds for the health system, nor is it clear whether MHI systems do a better or worse job of protecting citizens against medical care expenditures

(Xu et al. 2003). Improving equity and building democratic participation can also be fostered by many different forms of civic and social association.

When reasons are given for introducing or expanding MHI, they generally focus on three features: giving contributors a clear stake in the health insurance system, protecting health care expenditures by earmarking funds, and increasing efficiency through competition. Each of these, in turn, should be subjected to empirical analysis to determine whether they hold true, particularly under existing conditions in developing countries.

Given the different political and historical contexts, it is an open question whether these public policy goals can be reached through MHI. First, some countries have supportive economic conditions, with rapid growth and increasing formalization of the labor market, while others are experiencing economic stagnation and the continued presence of large informal sectors. Second, some countries have more propitious institutional contexts than others, particularly in terms of effective governments and prior experience with voluntary health insurance. Third, the demands for health care are much greater and more costly than they were only a few decades ago. Taking lessons from Western Europe and Latin America requires considering how these factors will alter the performance of MHI systems in the future.

Some governments have already adopted MHI systems or are likely to do so in the near future. In these cases, they need to decide how new health insurance entities will be governed and in this regard existing MHI systems provide many lessons. Countries with MHI systems have generated a wide variety of structures for governing MHI entities and these should be instructive in designing governance structures for new reforms.

Some definitions

Mandatory health insurance takes many different forms and is understood differently around the world. Therefore, developing testable hypotheses about the governance of mandatory health insurers requires a clear delineation of these different forms as well as models of how they behave. This section briefly addresses the definition of MHI and explores at greater length a wide range of definitions for the associated concept of "social health insurance."

Mandatory health insurance and social health insurance

The definition of MHI is quite simple: it is a system that pays the costs of health care for those who are enrolled and in which enrollment is required for all members of a population. It is quite distinct from systems in which health insurance is largely voluntary and those in which out-of-pocket payments predominate. It is a little more difficult to distinguish MHI systems from those in which government services are provided at little or no cost to the population (such as the national health services of Malaysia or the United Kingdom), except that in MHI systems

---

BOX 1.2 *Definitions of social health insurance*

Definitions for social health insurance (SHI) tend to fall along a spectrum between (a) a mechanism or instrument for insuring the population against the risks of incurring medical expenses, and (b) an institution that plays a wide range of social roles. Those who see SHI at the narrower end of the spectrum tend to view it as an instrument for achieving specific goals—universal financial protection and access to health care services. To the degree they are concerned about the basis of affiliation, they are oriented toward finding a system of affiliation that maximizes the likelihood of achieving universal coverage. In this perspective, accountability and governance mechanisms are evaluated in terms of how effectively insurers fulfill their mandates to provide financial protection and access to health services for their members.

Those who see SHI more widely and as more of a social process embedded in broader institutions, financial protection, and health care service access are only part of the institutions' goals. The operation of the SHI system is itself seen as a mechanism for linking social benefits into a network that fosters solidarity, builds civic associations, and empowers citizens through participation. This view is particularly prevalent in Western Europe where SHI is seen as "a way of life" (Saltman 2004). Given the origins of SHI in Western Europe and its link with broader corporatist forms of social organization, this is understandable.

These different perspectives are implicit in the characteristics ascribed to SHI. For example, the more instrumental version can view the form of affiliation, the basis for contributions, and the separation of providers and payers as policy choices rather than defining characteristics. On the other hand, a socially embedded view may see affiliation by employment (and consequently a role for intermediating labor representatives), income-based contributions, and separation of providers and payers as core defining features.

---

the insurance function is generally explicit and provision is often separated from financing.

As a category, MHI includes most forms of "social health insurance" (SHI)—a term that is used in a variety of contexts to mean quite different things (Box 1.2). The term is most closely associated with Western European countries whose insurance coverage is modeled on the system established by Bismarck in Germany in the 19th century. However, it is also used to characterize health systems with national integrated providers who are financed by payroll taxes and sometimes applied to nonprofit community-based health insurance programs that are voluntary. Because SHI is the term most frequently used in reform efforts ("national health insurance" is the next most frequent), it is important to understand the range of ways that it is used and understood.

One study identified the following structural characteristics of SHI systems in Western Europe (Saltman 2004):

- Risk-independent and transparent contributions
- Sickness funds are payers/purchasers (not direct providers)
- Universal coverage based on "solidarity"
- Plural actors: beneficiaries, insurers, providers

- A corporatist model of negotiating premiums, payments, and benefits
- Participation by citizens and beneficiaries in shared governance arrangements
- Individual choice of providers.

Western European countries with MHI exhibit some variation within each of these dimensions. For example, beneficiaries elect directors in most countries, but not in France and Switzerland; individuals can choose among sickness funds in most countries, but not in Austria, France, or Luxembourg; and in some countries sickness funds are controlled through legislation, while in others control is exerted primarily through regulation. However, despite these variations, the overall structural characteristics are widely shared. Furthermore, they have been remarkably stable over time despite devastating wars and massive political change.

The problem with relying on these characteristics to define SHI is that they are not present, as a package, in most other countries in the world that adopt systems that are denoted "SHI." For example, SHI systems in Costa Rica and Mexico raise funds through risk-independent contributions via payroll taxes, but there is only one major insurer for those who are formally employed and it provides services directly. In Chile and Colombia, insurance is mandatory and contributions are paid via payroll taxes, but there are no "shared governance arrangements" of the kinds found in Western Europe. In the Republic of Korea and Hungary, the social insurance entity is wholly owned by the government.[4]

The Organisation for Economic Co-operation and Development (OECD) has tried to clarify the distinction between SHI and other kinds of health system. In the guidelines for National Health Accounts, the source of funds—payroll tax—is the first defining characteristic (OECD 2000). But even this leads to some rather problematic terms such as "private social insurance"—that is, cases in which MHI financed with payroll taxes is implemented by private insurance agencies (for example, Switzerland). More recent OECD work has tried to dispel this overlap but it seems unable to clarify the generally inconsistent use of the terms "private" and "public."

If instead, we follow the OECD's lead in recognizing that most systems are "mixed" and that public and private entities can play different roles in the same system, then we can take advantage of the strong and clear distinction between mandatory and voluntary insurance (Figure 1.1). This OECD framework divides MHI schemes into three categories: tax-based, social security, and private. This book focuses on the latter two subcategories of MHI (social security and private) because these are the two categories that are generally presented as options within current "SHI" debates (OECD 2004a).

Rather than arguing over the correct terms or definitions, it would be wise to learn from policy actors which kind of scheme they are proposing and advise them on the basis of a shared definition. The different perspectives on MHI—an instrumental view and a socially embedded view—will be associated to some

FIGURE 1.1   Health insurance schemes

Public health insurance			Private health insurance		
Tax-based	Social security [a]	Private mandatory [a]	Employer-based	Community-rated	Risk-rated
Mandatory health insurance			Voluntary health insurance		

Source: Adapted from OECD 2004b.

a. The focus of this book.

extent with the level of performance measures and the scope of policy levers. It also has implications for which models will be most relevant, as will be discussed in the section *Contextual Factors*. First, though, we turn to the crucial topic of governance.

What is governance?

As with SHI, the meaning of "governance" varies substantially across contexts and researchers. Broad definitions of governance attempt to encompass all the relevant factors that influence the behavior of an organization. For MHI entities, these factors would include its relationship to the government, its members, any other payers (employers, for example), health care providers, and other insurers (competitors). Narrower definitions of governance look specifically at the "control" mechanisms that are used to hold the entity accountable. These latter definitions are more concerned with issues such as, for example, the mechanisms by which board members are elected, the scope and style of government supervision, and the scope of managerial discretion in defining benefits, contribution rates, and negotiating contracts.

The existing literature on MHI systems addresses governance indirectly to the extent that it considers the pros and cons of affiliation rules, single or plural funds, alternative payment mechanisms, and options for defining benefits and contribution rates. (Consider for example, Normand and Weber 1994; Eichler and Lewis n.d.; Carrin and James 2004.) To the extent that the existing literature explicitly examines governance, it tends to be fairly general. For example, Chinitz et al. (2004) contrast structured negotiations, market competition and technocratic planning as mechanisms that are relied upon to govern SHI in Western Europe, but offer relatively little detail about how such things as ownership and supervision influence performance (see also Verdeyen and Buggenhout 2003). Only a few studies provide detailed analysis of specific governance mechanisms, such as the one by Maarse et al. 2005, describing different forms of government supervision.

The literature on governance more generally is much more advanced than that on MHI, and that on governance of private corporations is perhaps the most extensive, having played a role in the advances in principal-agent models and in testing theories on the role of transaction costs (Meckling 1976; Williamson

1999). Principal-agent models focus on the divergence of interests between the principal and the agent under conditions of asymmetrical information (in particular, the principal cannot directly monitor all the agent's actions without cost), and emphasize the value of aligning incentives and distributing risk so as to achieve mutually efficient contracts. Transaction cost models emphasize that individuals behave under *bounded rationality* and with *opportunism*, and therefore "... governance is the means by which *order* is accomplished in a relation in which potential *conflict* threatens to undo or upset opportunities to realize *mutual* gains" (Williamson 1996, p. 12, emphasis in the original).

This literature has shown how features of corporate governance alter the comportment of managers in ways that affect their business performance. These features include: whether a company is publicly traded or privately held, whether managers own significant shares of stock, whether shareholding is widespread or concentrated, whether board membership includes disinterested individuals, whether managers' pay is linked to performance incentives, and systems for electing board members, among others.

Public policymakers have entered the debate because the legal form of corporations is itself a creation of public policy and because there is a public interest in assuring integrity in corporate management. Managers of corporations have discretion so that they can innovate and make decisions flexibly in the interest of improving share value and income; however, this discretion can be abused (sometimes spectacularly as in the recent scandals at Enron and WorldCom in the United States). The public debate over governance of corporations, therefore, seeks ways to ensure that shareholders and employees are protected without interfering excessively in managerial discretion. There is no single answer to reaching this delicate balance, and whatever rules are laid down must be coherent with the broader structure of the legal and financial systems.

This focus on corporate governance has been operationalized in many settings, including in the international sphere, where the OECD has established principles for governance of private corporations. The OECD defines corporate governance thus:

> Corporate governance involves a set of relationships between a company's management, its board, its shareholders and other stakeholders. Corporate governance also provides the structure through which the objectives of the company are set, and the means of attaining those objectives and monitoring performance are determined. Good corporate governance should provide proper incentives for the board and management to pursue objectives that are in the interests of the company and its shareholders and should facilitate effective monitoring.[5]

These international prescriptions are necessarily general. They take on greater specificity when implemented in particular countries (see, for example, Commonwealth of Australia 2003).

The governance of public agencies has many common features with that of private firms. Most of the issues related to balancing discretion with tighter oversight play out in the public sphere as well. But governing public agencies has, in addition, many unique features. A sizable literature has developed on different aspects of governing public agencies, including the identification of problems associated with "capture," multiple principles, and vested interests.

Capture occurs when a public agency, whose mandate is to serve the public in a particular way acts, instead, to further the economic or political interests of a regulated entity.[6] At one extreme are police departments that are corrupted by organized crime and become accomplices in criminal activities. But capture can occur without blatant forms of bribery. The people who are hired to run and manage environmental protection, food safety, or transportation agencies often share similar training and perspectives with those who work in the regulated industry. This may lead them to be more lenient in applying laws than might otherwise be the case.

Capture can occur in MHI systems in several different ways. Health insurers can be "captured" by providers—acting to protect the incomes and jobs of health care professionals over the interests of beneficiaries. In systems with multiple insurers regulated by the government, the supervisory agency itself can be "captured"—acting in ways that benefit the health insurance agencies as against the interests of beneficiaries. The risk of "capture" is lower when decisions are more formulaic, regulators have less discretion, information regarding decisionmaking is publicly accessible, wage scales are comparable to that of the industry being regulated, and restrictions are observed on gifts and on taking jobs with the regulated industry after public service (Ferreiro and Sierra 2001). However, there are tradeoffs that need to be recognized in enacting any of these measures; for example, less discretion can lead to inflexible and inefficient rulings and restrictions on employment in the industry can reduce the pool of applicants to individuals who are not as skilled or knowledgeable about the regulated entities.

Other issues arise when public agencies have more than one mandate and/or are accountable to more than one body. This is analyzed as a principal-agent problem with multiple principals (see, for example, Spiller 1990; Spiller and Urbiztondo 1994). For example, some politicians may be more concerned with protecting the interests of a particular industry that causes pollution while others are more concerned with constituents who value a cleaner environment. In this context, the resulting struggle to influence the behavior of an industry regulator may go beyond a debate over particular measures or regulations to affect decisions over the character of the regulatory agency—with some politicians seeking to protect the regulator from short-term influences and others seeking to subject the regulator to tighter controls. The existence of multiple principals also has implications for the amount and costs of oversight and auditing.

MHI faces similar problems because it is usually structured to serve many "masters" (Box 1.3). It is given the mandate of financially protecting its members from the costs of medical care, but in order to accomplish this, it must satisfy medical care providers' demands for adequate payments and income levels, public

---

BOX 1.3 *Serving many masters*

Pension funds are an example of a public agency that shares some characteristics with mandatory health insurance systems. They are often established as public services or mandatory private funds and have been extensively debated in recent years with regard to whether these systems should be fully funded or pay-as-you-go. But a number of articles also analyze how pension systems are governed, utilizing principal-agent and transaction cost models. For example, one study statistically tested the impact of various governance arrangements on pension fund performance (defined as rates of return on assets and solvency). They find that retiree representation on boards actually reduces returns on assets held by public pension funds in the United States, while there was no measurable difference between those with in-house or external money managers (Mitchell and Hsin 1994). Recent work on pension funds for the World Bank reinforces Williamson's characterization above, defining governance as "the systems and processes by which a company or government manages its affairs with the objective of maximizing the welfare of and resolving the conflicts of interest among its stakeholders" (Carmichael and Palacios 2003, p. 7).

---

demands for lower premiums and solvency, and political pressures to privilege particular constituents—whether defined by geography, class, or illness. In many cases, health care is itself only one of many services that are being provided by the agency. For example, in Brazil, the retirement benefits section of the national social security fund ended up bankrupting the payment of medical benefits during the early 1990s. And in Argentina, premiums paid to the union-controlled social security plans have been diverted instead to political activities or possibly to graft.

Finally, public agencies themselves can develop vested interests, diverting resources toward activities and purchases that preserve their jobs or enhance their incomes or powers. This may be manifested in bloated administrative expenditures, excessive spending on real estate, or investment decisions biased toward capital or high-technology equipment. A variety of mechanisms are often introduced to control such tendencies, for example, establishing a maximum share of revenues that can be spent on administration; however, most efforts at establishing rules can be bypassed through clever accounting or business practices and there is no ultimate guarantee other than through greater transparency and more intelligent oversight. This is a further demonstration of the tradeoffs involved in overseeing public agencies because more rule-bound and detailed oversight can interfere with the need for flexible and intelligent responses to changing circumstances.

In summary, the literature on governance of MHI is quite limited. However, the literature on governance more generally is quite rich. It demonstrates the need for attention to ownership, selection of board members, and managerial incentives in the literature on private corporate governance; and importance of capture, responses to multiple principals, and the emergence of vested interests in the literature on public governance. It illustrates the tradeoffs that emerge in determining the level of independence and discretion afforded to agencies. Finally, it shows the importance of publicly accessible information to proper oversight and the roles that can be played by different stakeholders, depending on how oversight is structured.

An analytical framework

Numerous frameworks are available for analyzing MHI from the broader literature on health systems and health system performance. Many of these studies present frameworks based on functional schemes (Kutzin 2001; WHO 2000). Others have used the flow of funds through a health system as the organizing principle for analysis (La Forgia 1994; Magnoli 2001). Still others emphasize relationships among stakeholders, including government, insurers, providers, and beneficiaries (Preker and Harding 2000; Mossialos et al. 2002; World Bank 2004). This framework follows the third approach since it is more appropriate for analyzing questions dealing with governance.

Consider Figure 1.2 in which three major relationships are highlighted. The insurance entity is *accountable* to certain agents—generally beneficiaries, governments, regulators, and other non-beneficiary contributors such as employers. The entity is also in *competition* with other agents—either formally as in systems with multiple sickness funds or informally with other organizations that people use to insure against the costs of medical care.[7] Finally, the entity has a very important relationship in *how it pays* for provision of care—whether through direct hiring and provision, fee-for-service contracts, capitation, or some combination thereof.

FIGURE 1.2   Three key relationships influencing the behavior of mandatory health insurance entities

Accountability through governance

Beneficiaries   Government   Employers and other
               Supervisors   non-beneficiary contributors
               Regulators

Mandatory health insurer

Forms of payment   **Competition with:**
and negotiation with: Other mandatory health insurers
Providers   Other insurers outside the
                          mandatory system

In what follows, attention will be focused on the accountability of insurers to beneficiaries, government, and contributors, through five governance dimensions (Figure 1.3). These dimensions operate within a context of relationships to competitors and providers. This context will be summarized by grouping countries into four broad models distilled from the range of experiences observed in countries with MHI systems.

Governance dimensions

Many different forms of governance are available to influence the accountability relationships between insurers and their various stakeholders. In the case of private corporations, the governance structure tends to create reasonably direct and separable accountability relationships. A corporation's management is accountable to its shareholders through their selection of board members and decisions with regard to selling or buying equity. It is also accountable to society through government regulation of acceptable environmental, labor, and market behaviors. And its customers hold it accountable with their decisions regarding purchases.

The governance of MHI organizations can be analyzed in terms of similar dimensions, but the actual mechanisms tend to be less direct and overlapping. So, for example, the insurer may have board members representing beneficiaries, employers, and government agencies at the same time that it is subjected to government supervision and regulation, pressured by beneficiaries who may exercise their options to select another fund, as well as negotiating with provider associations on terms of payment and quality of care.

FIGURE 1.3 Accountability through effective governance

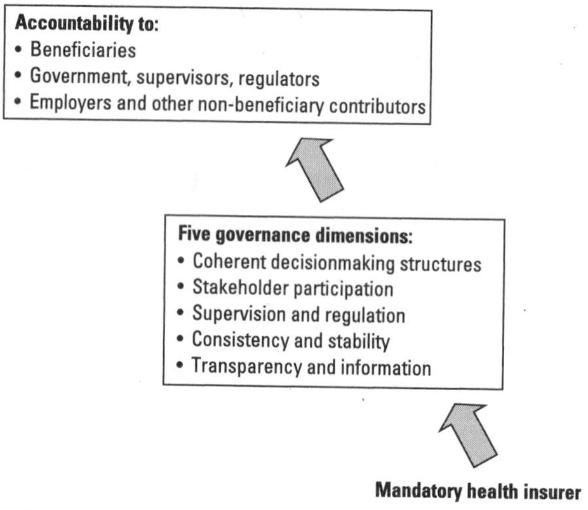

Accountability to:
- Beneficiaries
- Government, supervisors, regulators
- Employers and other non-beneficiary contributors

Five governance dimensions:
- Coherent decisionmaking structures
- Stakeholder participation
- Supervision and regulation
- Consistency and stability
- Transparency and information

Mandatory health insurer

There is no obvious way to frame the governance dimensions needed to achieve accountability, although the general rules are fairly simple: align incentives and make information available and transparent. Many different schemes can be proposed for organizing the analysis, highlighting different dimensions. In this book, we propose the following list: [8]

- Coherent decisionmaking structures
- Stakeholder participation
- Transparency and information
- Supervision and regulation
- Consistency and stability.

Coherent decisionmaking structures are required for an insurer to perform well. This does not mean that decisions should be centralized or decentralized because in a system as complex as MHI, decisions will necessarily be made in many different places—distributed both hierarchically and spatially. Rather, decisionmaking structures are coherent if those responsible for particular decisions are also endowed with the discretion, authority, tools, and resources necessary to fulfill their responsibilities; and if they face consequences for their decisions that align their interests with that of the overall good performance of the system.

This fundamental distribution of decisionmaking authority and resources is generally supported by an explicit legal foundation that establishes the objectives of the system, the roles and responsibilities of different actors (usually government, boards, and management), the rights and obligations of the affiliated population, basic checks and balances, and procedures for amending the law. To be complete this legal foundation needs to include provisions to implement and supervise the system by administrative action and regulation, guided to the extent possible by criteria aligned with the system's objectives.

Two particular elements of the governance structure have implications for the way the rest of the system is structured and performs: ownership and legal status. Ownership is most clearly defined in terms of who has claim to any residual assets of the entity if it were to be dissolved. In private firms, this residual claim is in the hands of shareholders. In publicly owned agencies, this residual claim is in the hands of the government. MHI funds can be configured either way, but are more commonly owned in more complex, even hybrid, ways—with ownership commonly shared among some combination of employers, employees, beneficiaries, providers, and the government. Residual claims are important because they create a strong incentive for the owner to act in ways that will preserve the value of the institution and improve efficiency. When ownership is concentrated, these incentives are expected to work more strongly than when ownership is diffuse. In certain contexts, the government may hold an implicit responsibility for keeping the insurer solvent, creating a situation of moral hazard and leading it to subsidize deficits rather than allowing the insurer to fail. In these cases, the incentives for owners to operate the insurer efficiently are weakened. Although these expectations derive clearly from theoretical models and can be observed anecdotally, few of them have been subjected to rigorous empirical testing.

The legal status of a mandatory health insurer affects the decisionmaking structure because it generally establishes boundaries to what the insurer can and cannot do. For example, its legal status will determine whether it manages its personnel according to civil service or private sector labor codes; whether and under what terms it can be sued. Insurers that are more clearly incorporated as private firms may be held accountable to their members through normal consumer protection laws and proceedings, while insurers that are constituted as public offices may enjoy immunity from certain kinds of legal actions.

The conditions of *Stakeholder participation* are another dimension of governance that seems to affect performance through its influence over the flow of information and accountability relationships. At a minimum, good governance seems to require some opportunity for stakeholders—including owners, but sometimes also including disinterested parties, consumers, employees, or medical care providers—to participate and affect decisionmaking. Representation of consumers' and employees' interests may be indirect—as when insurance agencies are directly operated as part of government—or direct—as occurs in consumer or medical cooperatives. It is common for insurers to be governed by a board of directors, whose members are elected by shareholders, employers, employees, or beneficiaries. This election may be direct or intermediated by unions and employer associations. Terms can be short or long, synchronized or staggered, and terms of office, ethical standards, and compensation also vary. Decisions regarding the mechanisms for selecting and maintaining a board have to consider that each choice has an impact on the degree of independence enjoyed by board members and on the incentives they face in guiding the institution. Participation is also affected by the historical context; in particular, whether the country has a tradition of management through seeking consensus or decisionmaking through adversarial negotiation.

The third dimension of *Transparency and information* plays a critical role in effective governance. Transparency requires, first and foremost, that the basic elements of the system—its legal foundations, procedures, and administration—are clearly stated and disseminated to the public. By explicitly documenting the system's structure, the roles and responsibilities of different actors, and the rights and obligations of the affiliated population, it is possible to know just who can be held accountable for what.

In addition, transparency requires that the system be managed in a way that allows the public and interested parties to know what is being done by whom, from disclosure of conflicts of interest to opening negotiations and decisionmaking hearings to public scrutiny. The forms and frequency of information that are made available to the public can itself promote better performance by ensuring that decisionmakers, at different levels, know they can be held to account.

In general, greater disclosure of information enhances the accountability of insurers; however compiling and publishing information in a readily usable form can be expensive. In most cases, policies try to set standardized information reporting that allows consumers and regulators to hold insurers accountable for making good decisions on a timely basis without creating an undue burden. The standards for financial reporting may be straightforward, oriented toward assuring that insurers have the liquidity to meet their obligations. However, standards for reporting medical care and treatments are currently at a more primitive level of development and appear to be more complex.

Supervision and regulation are another dimension of governance that can hold insurers accountable for their performance. In some countries, insurers operate in a relatively unfettered market and government supervision is restricted to assuring that contracts are fulfilled and that basic fiduciary responsibilities are followed. At the other extreme are countries with laws and/or regulations that establish strict conditions for operation, including standardizing contracts, defining a basic health plan, requiring insurers to accept any applicants regardless of health status, setting premiums, and/or requiring that contracted providers meet quality of care standards.

Government supervision can be conducted through ex ante reviews or ex post auditing. It can be the responsibility of a specific government office, a quasi-government independent agency, or through delegation to a privately constituted entity. The supervisory agent's funding can come directly from government budgets, from taxes on premiums, or as a payment directly from the regulated insurers.

Finally, the fifth dimension of governance is related to the *Consistency and stability* of the system. Mandatory health insurance involves a range of long-term investments and inter-temporal commitments that condition today's decisions on tomorrow's prospects. This dimension is strongly influenced by the political and legal context—governments that have a history of frequently and readily altering policies will have difficulty establishing credible "rules of the game." If the difficulty of establishing consistent and stable policies is primarily a problem within the public sector, a system that establishes independent insurers constituted under a private legal framework may provide greater predictability (Spiller and Savedoff 1998); in cases where public sector governance is effective and private firms face greater uncertainty, a public ownership model might provide greater consistency and stability.

Of course, conditions change over time and rules that are set at one point in time cannot be considered to be completely unchangeable. Rather, transparent mechanisms can establish the conditions under which different rules can be changed. For example, the rules for permitting (or prohibiting) competition in the insurance market are so fundamental that a government should probably have to undertake substantial debate and build wide political support before enacting changes. By contrast, the rules for deciding what benefits are included in a standardized health package need to be more flexible to account for changing technologies, knowledge, productivity, resources, and systemic innovations.

In sum, effective governance of a health insurer depends upon five dimensions of good governance. While the literature and experience provide numerous ideas about the advantages and disadvantages of different arrangements within these categories, most of these "lessons" are actually hypotheses that require empirical testing. Furthermore, the way these dimensions function will vary considerably depending on contextual factors, primarily whether insurers are subject to competition and the kinds of provider payment arrangements they are engaged in. The next section turns to these factors.

Contextual factors

As noted earlier, the governance dimensions discussed above are critical but they do not exhaust the factors that influence an insurer's behavior. Notably, two aspects—the existence of competition and the relationship with providers—will have substantial impact. Reviewing the dynamics of MHI systems suggests that these two aspects—the number of competing insurers and the way an insurer pays providers—appear to play a crucial role. In this regard, four distinct models can be proposed, each of which presents particular advantages and challenges with regard to establishing effective accountability mechanisms (see Table 1.1 on page 34, and Box 1.4).

The first of these models is a single dominant insurer with a substantial capacity for direct provision of medical and health care services—denoted here as a "direct provision" model. The dominant form of setting payments and allocating resources is through normal public sector arrangements, including internal contracting. This can be found in Mexico and Costa Rica, where the major mandatory health insurers, the Mexican Social Security Institute and the Costa Rica Social Security System (Caja Costarricense de Seguro Social or CCSS) respectively, own and operate health facilities. The determination of contribution rates and benefits is formally in government hands; however, the effective coverage of services is determined by how efficiently the insurer can apply its funds. Hence, the primary challenges faced in these systems relate to efficient public administration. For example, Costa Rica has addressed problems of rising costs and inefficiency by experimenting with "Management Contracts"—creating an explicit statement of responsibilities for its health facilities which are subject to review, discipline, and budgetary consequences—with uncertain results (Abramson 2001).

A second model also has a single dominant insurer, but in this case, health care provision is separate and generally plural. These systems, denoted "single payer," are found in many Eastern European and Central Asian economies such as Hungary and Kyrgyz Republic, as well as Jamaica, the Republic of Korea, and

Taiwan (China). In such cases, the insurance agency may have autonomy but it is directly and actively supervised by the government and its representatives, who tend to be engaged regularly or be consulted in determining benefits, negotiating budgets, and setting premiums. The relationship with providers can be quite limited, acting effectively as a passive third-party payer, or quite extensive, engaging in detailed negotiations with providers and their representative associations.

The third model includes multiple insurers who may or may not be competing with one another for clients. It is characterized by a structured form of bilateral bargaining between insurers and providers through their respective associations. This will be denoted as the "corporatist" model. It is found in much of Western Europe and exemplified by Germany where associations of sickness funds negotiate with provider associations at the federal level to establish ground rules and parameters for regional negotiations that determine contributions, payments, and benefits. This is also found in Japan where the Ministry of Finance apparently sets prices by fiat, when in fact its discretion is limited by parameters negotiated between the sickness funds, the government, and providers (Campbell and Ikegami 1998).

The fourth model can be described as "regulated competition," and is found in countries like Chile and Colombia. Like the corporatist negotiation model, these systems have multiple insurers but the process of determining benefits and payments is highly decentralized and lacks the intermediation of the corporatist systems. In Chile, for many years, insurers were free to set their own premiums, define individualized benefits packages, and establish exclusive contracts with particular providers. Recent reforms have restricted what insurers can do, but their options are formulated by the government rather than a tripartite negotiation. In Colombia, competition has also been introduced with substantial regulation, including a formula for determining contributions and a legally mandated

---

BOX 1.4 *A "fifth" model*

A fifth model could be proposed—stressing the relationship between the health insurer and its beneficiaries—but we refrain from doing that since, at present, this relationship does not seem to dominate in any country with MHI. It certainly plays a role and may be more important in cases where health insurance entities are relatively small associations. For example, mutual associations organized by consumers appear to behave differently than those organized as medical cooperatives in Uruguay (Labadie 1998). It may also be relatively more important in systems with voluntary private insurance, as in the United States, but even in these cases beneficiaries tend to have a very limited role in defining the terms of insurance contracts, either through exit or voice. Some of the *mutuelles* of Western Africa might fit this beneficiary-led characterization or they may be better described as following the "corporatist negotiation" pattern. This requires further investigation. If anything, MHI systems more commonly channel beneficiary interests through a variety of representative agents—whether labor unions, consumer advocates, elected representatives, or government officials.

TABLE 1.1 Mandatory health insurance models and implications for governance

Model	Economy (case studies in bold)	Number of insurers	Provider payment	Selected implications for governance
Model 1: Direct provision	**Costa Rica** Mexico	Single	Public administration and/or internal contracting	• May have soft budget constraints • Lack of benchmarking information • Risk of capture by providers • Oversight requires political or economic counterweight to the insurer
Model 2: Single payer	**Estonia** Hungary Korea, Rep. of Taiwan, China	Single	Monopsonist negotiating with multiple providers	• May have soft budget constraints • Lack of benchmarking information • Risk of capture by providers • Oversight requires political or economic counterweight to the insurer
Model 3: Corporatist	Germany **Netherlands**	Multiple	Negotiation between representative associations	• Possible to rely on associations for overseeing certain aspects of performance • Need to assure legitimate process for selecting representatives
Model 4: Regulated market	**Chile** Colombia	Multiple	Various forms of contracting providers with different payment-setting processes	• Possible to elicit information about costs through comparative analysis • Possible to rely on shareholders for assuring efficiency • Consumer protection procedures need to be in place • Risk that insurers may "capture" regulator

minimum package of benefits. Yet, within these constraints, insurers are free to negotiate many different kinds of contracts with health care providers (Ferreiro and Sierra 2001).

The importance of these different models is illustrated in Table 1.1. In cases where a single insurer directly provides care, it is difficult to leave the insurer's corporate structure to chance. For example, it may be advisable to include consumer, employee, and even government representatives (from, for example, the Ministry of Health) on the board of directors to ensure that their interests are taken into consideration since they have no alternatives in the marketplace. By contrast, in a system with multiple insurers—such as regulated competition—the specific composition of boards could be more flexible, and left to the determination of each firm, because consumers and employees are not wedded to a particular firm and can express dissatisfaction by leaving.

Similarly, assuring that a single insurer is governed properly requires mechanisms for negotiating benefits, payments, and premiums with an institution that has weak incentives to control costs or improve service. By contrast, insurers in competitive systems may have stronger incentives to control costs and improve service, but they also have incentives to use marketing and advertising to gain advantage in ways that do not necessarily reflect better quality care or financial protection. Hence, in these multiple insurer systems, oversight needs to grapple not only with assuring financial solvency and appropriate medical care, but also consumer protection.

Other contextual factors that influence the performance of a mandatory health insurer include economic variables such as national income level, formality of the labor market, the supply of medical care services, and the depth of financial markets; as well as political variables such as the capacity for enforcing laws, contracts, and regulations. Any research program has to determine how it will control for these environmental factors for two reasons. First, it is necessary to isolate the policy variable from these potentially confounding factors. Second, controlling for these environmental factors is necessary to judge the generalizability of findings beyond particular contexts.

* * *

In sum, the proposed framework is based on relations: *accountability through effective governance structures* and *contextual factors*, especially competition among insurers and insurers' relationships with providers (particularly payment approaches). It proposes focusing attention on which governance structures—namely coherent decisionmaking structures; stakeholder participation; transparency and information; supervision and regulation; and consistency and stability—are most effective in improving the performance of mandatory health insurers. Hypotheses regarding the particular mechanisms that are most relevant, important, and effective can be generated with reference to the literature on principal-agent models and transaction cost models.

However, the focus on governance dimensions cannot ignore the impact of widely differing MHI contexts. To manage this, four models are proposed—direct provision, single payer, corporatist, and regulated market—that distinguish systems with single insurers from those with many insurers, and distinguish those with corporatist forms of negotiating benefits and payments from those with more decentralized and market-like mechanisms. The research strategy would be to compare the performance of different accountability mechanisms after controlling for these core institutional differences—such as competition and payment negotiation as summarized by the four models—and to control for environmental factors such as income levels and political systems that influence the generalizability of any findings.

Four case studies

It is not yet possible to conduct an exhaustive study of which forms of governance perform best, largely because institutions are so multifaceted, the number of "observations" available to us (i.e. countries and insurance funds) is relatively small and the literature has not yet converged on precise definitions for relevant variables and how to measure them. Furthermore, governance mechanisms interact with other social institutions and, therefore, the performance of any particular mechanism is likely to vary across contexts. Nevertheless, it should be possible to move this research agenda forward by investigating specific cases within the proposed framework, and using the examples to help refine variables, concepts, and questions. In the process, we can learn from the experiences of these countries, seeing how societies have addressed their dissatisfactions with health insurance fund performance by reforming them. The resulting lessons for low-income countries that are introducing or expanding MHI funds then come in several flavors: problems that can be foreseen and avoided, opportunities that other countries struggled for but which the newer countries can seize from the start, and qualifications regarding how context can trump even the best-laid plans.

This section discusses four detailed case studies—Costa Rica, Estonia, the Netherlands, and Chile—that were informed by the preceding framework and questions. It draws out the main contrasts and findings from these experiences and notes their generalizability with reference to other cases—including Colombia, the Republic of Korea, and Taiwan (China)—for which more limited data was collected.

The main four cases presented here were selected because they each represent one of the four models identified earlier. Costa Rica's MHI system is characterized by a single insurer, the CCSS, that directly manages its own network of health care provision, making it a clear representative of the first model. Estonia's MHI system is comprised of a single national insurance scheme—the Estonian Health Insurance Fund (EHIF)—which purchases and reimburses health care provided to its affiliates. Thus, Estonia's system represents a single payer model.

The Netherlands and Chile both have MHI systems that include multiple insurers, some public and others private. Though they were selected initially as representatives of the third and fourth models ("corporatist" and "regulated market"), recent developments have eroded the value of the distinction between these two models.

In the Netherlands, insurance funds developed largely independent of government, emerging from social and political processes of bargaining and consensus-building, suggesting the corporatist model; however, recent reforms have moved it squarely in the direction of a regulated market.

Chile has the earliest MHI legislation of these four countries, enacted within a corporatist vision of social organization, but its current system also reflects reforms from the early 1980s that sought to establish a competitive health insurance market. Today, Chile's MHI system is dominated by the National Health Insurance Fund (Fondo Nacional de Salud or FONASA)—which covers almost 70 percent of the population. Political negotiation plays a significant role in defining health care packages, prices, and relationships with health care providers. Competition continues with private health insurers—called ISAPREs, from the term *instituciones de salud previsional*—but their market share has actually declined in recent years, to less than 20 percent of the population.

The first thing to note about all four cases is that they perform reasonably well in terms of insurance coverage, access to health care services, population health,

TABLE 1.2   General characteristics of case study countries

	Costa Rica	Estonia	Netherlands	Chile
First mandatory health insurance law (year)	1941	1991	1941	1924
Insurance coverage (% of population, public/private where split), 2000–03	100	95	63/35[a]	68/17
Gross national income per capita (US$, 2004)	4,470	7,080	32,130	5,220
Population (million, 2004)	4.3	1.3	16.3	16.1
Life expectancy at birth (male/female, years, 2004)	75/80	66/78	77/81	74/81
Under-5 mortality rate (per 1,000 live births, 2002)	13	8	5	9
Total health expenditure (per capita, US$, 2004)	290	463	3,442	359
Out-of-pocket share of total health expenditures (2004)	20.4	21.3	7.7	24.3
Births attended by skilled health personnel (%, 2001)	98	100	—	100
Ranking on Transparency International Corruption Perceptions Index (2005)	51	27	11	21

Sources: WHO, *World Health Statistics,* 2006; World Bank, *World Development Indicators 2006*; and Transparency International, *Global Corruption Report 2006.*

— Data not available or not applicable.

a. Two percent had another type of insurance (military, prisoners) or no insurance at all.

and financial protection relative to other countries in the world (Table 1.2). Over 90 percent of the population is formally affiliated with an insurer in all four countries, and access to many health care services is close to universal, as well. For example, professional birth attendance is close to 100 percent in all four countries. The four countries also rank high in population health status with average life expectancies well above 70 years and child mortality rates below 15 per 1,000 children under the age of 5. Out-of-pocket expenditures range from 8 percent of total health spending in the Netherlands to 24 percent in Chile, which is only a very rough indication of the degree of financial protection, but still much better than most developing countries (Xu et al. 2003).

This is not to say that people are entirely satisfied with these systems. To the contrary, complaints are aired in the media and legislatures about rising costs (in all four countries, despite widely different levels of spending), waiting lists (particularly in Estonia and the Netherlands), employee absenteeism and evasion (particularly in Costa Rica), and health care quality and equity (particularly in Chile). The problems are real and legitimate, but they also need to be placed in context. In lower income countries like Bangladesh and Nigeria, insurance coverage rarely surpasses 10 percent and professional birth attendance is a mere 13 percent and 35 percent, respectively. Even in many middle-income countries, universal health insurance is still a distant dream, evasion is common, and costs are high.

In considering the generalizability of these experiences to low-income countries, it is important to recognize that all four countries have reasonable economic and political stability, rank high on general governance indices, and have substantial resources—Costa Rica is the least wealthy, but still enjoys a per capita annual national income of US$4,470. The countries also range in size from the smallest, Estonia (1.3 million people) and Costa Rica (4.3 million people), to Chile and the Netherlands, which each have about 16 million people.

Given that these health insurance funds perform reasonably well despite widely varying forms of governance, it is unlikely that a single form of governance is the "right" approach. Rather, we need to analyze the variation in governance mechanisms from two different angles. First, we need to catalog the differences so that low-income countries that are implementing MHI can see the full range of approaches that have been tried. Second, we can identify ways in which countries converge on solutions for common problems. Ultimately, we need to analyze how particular governance mechanisms emerge from and interact with their context so that the appropriateness of particular approaches can be better assessed before they are rejected or adopted.

Governance and contextual factors

The governance mechanisms discussed earlier vary substantially across the cases. For example, mandatory health insurers range from wholly public entities to private for-profit firms in ways that strongly affect their decisionmaking structures. Chile's national insurance fund (FONASA) is a wholly government-owned and operated agency. The single national insurance funds in Costa Rica and Estonia are autonomous and cannot declare bankruptcy. In this sense, the state can be considered the ultimate residual claimant, but legally the insurance funds are obligated to maintain financial solvency. The sickness funds in the Netherlands are nonprofit firms, whose legal status is akin to private firms and whose members have formal ownership; they enjoy full autonomy. At the other extreme, the private insurers in Chile (ISAPREs) and the Netherlands (voluntary funds) are generally owned by shareholders and have the legal status, and obligations, of other kinds of private financial firms.

One common hypothesis is that ownership should affect *Coherent Decisionmaking structures*, particularly with regard to financial solvency, yet these cases suggest that ownership is not sufficient in itself. The four countries here include experiences of deficits and surplus in both private and public funds. In both the Netherlands and Chile, some private health insurance funds have gone bankrupt. In Estonia and Costa Rica, diffuse public ownership has, perhaps, been counterbalanced by other mechanisms to focus management's attention on keeping expenditures roughly in line with revenues. In Estonia, efforts have been made to separate what might be considered commercial from political risks.[9] The EHIF board has authority to use one set of reserves when expenditures exceed revenues; the government has authority to use another set of reserves and is obligated to compensate the EHIF when it intervenes to change policies.

Other economies—such as the Republic of Korea, Mexico, and Taiwan (China)—have experienced greater difficulties with maintaining fiscal balance in national insurance funds. For example, the Republic of Korea enacted a special subsidy to its National Health Insurance Corporation that is supposed to end in 2006. In Latin America, the Mexican Social Security Institute has increasingly relied on subsidies from the federal government to balance its books. In this regard, the four case studies may not be representative.

Decisionmaking is also affected by the insurer's legal status—particularly as it concerns the insurer's ability to manage personnel. The staff of public insurance funds in Chile and Costa Rica are contracted as public functionaries and managed accordingly. But the variation in performance suggests that legal status alone cannot explain differences. Productivity in Costa Rica has declined over the years, and is manifested in high rates of employee absenteeism. While the constraints of civil service laws are often cited as obstacles to better personnel management in the CCSS, those same laws are the direct consequence of bargaining between the government and unions. In Chile, staff of FONASA and the public health services are also hired under civil service codes, but productivity appears to have improved and absenteeism is not a significant problem. The contrast between these two cases suggests that the nature of political association and bargaining has more of an influence on performance of staff than legal status, per se.

Stakeholder participation in these four MHI systems varies substantially. The highest decisionmaking authorities within Costa Rica's CCSS and Estonia's EHIF are supervisory boards whose members are selected to represent the interests of organized groups—employers, employees working in formal jobs, and the government. The sickness funds in the Netherlands also have supervisory boards, but they are largely "self-perpetuating," that is, the current board members solicit nominations and then select new board members to fill vacant or expiring posts. Meanwhile, Chile's national insurance fund, FONASA, has no board at all. Its director is appointed by the president of the republic and enjoys cabinet-level status, but operates within the executive branch of government in close contact with, and reportedly subordinate to, the minister of health.

None of these arrangements is unique. Tripartite representation on supervisory boards is quite common and is found in countries that have relatively old SHI institutions, including Colombia, Germany, and Mexico. However, more recent health insurance funds have also included employer and employee representatives in their supervisory boards. For example, four of the thirteen directors who oversee PhilHealth—a national health insurance plan created by the Philippines in 1995—are chosen to represent labor, employers, the self-employed, and "overseas workers." Self-perpetuating boards of nonprofit insurers are, perhaps, less common but can be found in countries like Argentina and Uruguay. Taiwan, China's single insurance fund, the Bureau of National Health Insurance, is an agency of the executive branch, in a fashion similar to Chile.

In the two cases with tripartite representation, Costa Rica and Estonia, boards have focused quite narrowly on financial matters, with significantly less attention to other matters that concern beneficiaries, like the quality of health care services. It is not clear how much interest representation contributes to this financial focus, though workers' and employers' representatives do have clear interests in constraining expenditures to keep contribution rates from rising.

The existence of different representatives on supervisory boards does not appear to have provided sufficient oversight, transparency, or pressure to reveal and deal with conflicts of interest or corruption. Decisions regarding investments and allocations are reported to be influenced in both countries by providers who serve on boards, and in Costa Rica, a massive corruption scandal involving the executive president, board members, Congressional representatives, and a former president of the republic led to the resignation of the entire board of the CCSS. But other forms of selecting board members or governing funds are not without their problems. In the Netherlands, the government has criticized sickness funds for paying salaries to board members and managers that are considered to be excessive. In Chile, the lack of a board means that concerns over conflicts of interest meld with general problems and critiques of public sector management.

Transparency and information seem to play increasingly important roles in all four cases, though some appear to be more open and sophisticated in dissemination than others. Information reporting requirements are significant in all four countries. Generally, insurance funds are required to report annually on their finances and performance to their boards or other supervisory authorities, with more frequent reports going to financial supervisory authorities on a monthly or quarterly basis. Estonia has set particularly rigorous reporting requirements for the EHIF, linking expenditures to performance at departmental or unit levels.[10] In Chile, FONASA submits its annual report to Congress, while performance indicators are reported to the Ministry of Finance, and financial and accounting reports go to the Controller-General's Office (Contraloría General de la República de Chile). Estonia and Chile are also taking advantage of modern communications technology by posting financial and performance data on the Web.

Supervision and regulation in these cases involves a mix of legislative, executive, and independent agencies. In Estonia, the EHIF is subject to strong government oversight, with direct involvement of major ministries, despite its legal autonomy. The Ministry of Finance, Ministry of Social Affairs, and Parliament all play strong roles in defining major policies that limit the EHIF's scope of action, and in monitoring its performance, with particular attention to its finances and to measurable indicators like waiting times. The EHIF is also audited at three levels: it has an internal audit office, an independent external auditor appointed by the supervisory board, and the State Audit Office (that audits all public agencies).

Until recently, Chile's FONASA was supervised much like the EHIF. It is subject to strong government control, particularly from the Ministry of Health and the

Ministry of Finance. In addition to its own internal auditing unit, it is also subject to external audits by the Controller-General's Office. Chile created a Superintendancy of Health (Superintendencia de Salud or SIS) in 2004 (operational from 2005) that supervises all public and private health insurers. The role and authority of the SIS are much clearer with regard to private insurers than to FONASA.

Like Chile, the Netherlands recently reformed its system to unify supervision of public and private insurers. Prior to the reform, private insurers were hardly regulated at all, while the sickness funds were intensively supervised by a specific supervisory agency that addressed the legality of all funds' actions under the sickness fund law. However, as a consequence of the recent reform, all health insurance funds are now subject to a single authority—a new agency, The Netherlands Health Care Authority (Nederlandse Zorgautoriteit or NZA), created specifically to supervise and regulate health insurance funds. In the Netherlands, the health sector regulatory agencies are not part of the government, rather their direction is in the hands of appointees who are selected to represent different groups, but are increasingly chosen for technical and professional expertise.

In Costa Rica, the Ministry of Health is legally responsible for supervising the CCSS, but the CCSS enjoys substantial autonomy, controls its own finances, and has independent political support. This compromises the Ministry of Health's ability to hold the CCSS accountable. As in Chile and Estonia, the CCSS is subject to several levels of government audits, internal and external. Internal auditing is conducted by an office within the CCSS which, nevertheless, is functionally tied to the country's national Controller-General (the Contraloría General de la República) and follows its regulations. The Internal Audit Office (Auditoría Interna de la CCSS) conducts audits of managerial processes, finances, use of data, health care delivery, and medical care quality. Annual external audits are conducted by an auditing firm, contracted through open bidding by the board of directors.

It is not clear whether one form of supervision is better than another. What is apparent from these cases, however, is that supervisory functions are becoming more uniform, more explicit, and encompassing a wider range of functions. On this latter point, all four countries have established audit systems to assure transparency in financial accounting. They have also addressed issues of financial solvency, particularly with regard to nongovernmental insurance funds. Attention to the quality of care, to consumer protection, and to other performance measures is less consistent, but becoming more common.

The character of regulation also varies considerably as a function of the insurance funds' degree of independence (Table 1.3). At one extreme, the private insurance funds in Chile (ISAPREs) have the authority to set their own premiums, design benefits packages, and negotiate prices with health care providers. The Superintendancy's responsibility is only to ensure that the ISAPREs comply with general legislation and with the specific provisions of their contracts. This

TABLE 1.3 Decisionmaking authority by country and issue

Issue	Costa Rica CCSS	Estonia EHIF	Netherlands (pre-2006) Sickness funds	FONASA	Chile (pre-2005) ISAPREs	Voluntary funds
Contribution levels	BoD	Parliament	MoF	MoF	Management	Management
Payments to providers	BoD, Providers	Government		MoH	Management	Management
Benefits package	BoD, CEO (Courts)	Government	MoF	MoH	Management	Management
External auditor	Controller-General	Controller-General	Private CPAs	Controller-General	Private CPAs	Pension and insurance chamber
Internal auditor	Yes	Yes	Yes	Yes	Yes	Yes

Sources: Case studies in Chapters 3 through 6.

Note: BoD = board of directors; CEO = chief executive officer; CPA = certified public accountant; MoF = Ministry of Finance; MoH = Ministry of Health.

includes provisions defining rules for setting and changing prices, solvency requirements, and assuring that a minimum benefits package is being effectively covered. By contrast, Estonia's EHIF does not set its own contribution level, nor does it define the benefits package. With more authority vested in the Ministry of Finance and the Ministry of Social Affairs, and in Parliament, government regulation is characterized by direct oversight and decisionmaking authority.

Consistency and stability characterize all four systems. Though the Chilean system was established first, its significant reform in the early 1980s made a clear structural break with the past. Nonetheless, the evolution of Chile's MHI system since the return of democracy in the early 1990s demonstrates how a relatively open political process can alter the rules of the game without undermining general confidence in the system by most stakeholders, including public sector agencies, private insurers, providers, and beneficiaries. Costa Rica appears to have a very consistent and stable system, but one which is, for this very reason, criticized as inflexible and incapable of addressing many of its problems. Estonia's national insurance fund has a relatively short history, but appears to enjoy the benefit of a supportive political structure that makes credible commitments while maintaining flexibility through political participation, particularly in its Parliament. The Netherlands also enjoyed substantial consistency in its legislative and regulatory framework over a long period of time, making significant reforms only rarely and after substantial debate and discussion.

These five dimensions of governance do not, in themselves, explain the performance of the insurance funds. They do, however, demonstrate how each country has chosen to empower and constrain the funds, balancing autonomy and dependency, to encourage solvency, efficiency, and good service. The fact that all four countries continue to revise and reform these accountability mechanisms also demonstrates that this balance is difficult to achieve, that pragmatic approaches are needed, and that standards and goals evolve over time.

The two contextual factors that underlie the four system models vary across the country cases by design. Competition is a factor in Chile and the Netherlands, while Costa Rica and Estonia have single payers. The relationship between payers and providers is close in Costa Rica's integrated system and between Chile's public insurance fund and its public providers; by contrast, the relationship between payers and providers is much less direct in Estonia and the Netherlands.

Competition is an indirect way of holding insurance funds accountable in the sense of creating incentives and pressures to perform well. In the cases here, Chile and the Netherlands have multiple insurers while Costa Rica and Estonia have just one, and the contrasts demonstrate both the advantages and disadvantages of competition. For example, Estonia appears to have reaped impressive gains in administrative efficiency by merging its many insurance funds into a single entity. Costa Rica, too, has relatively low administrative costs, but it has also experienced substantial declines in the productivity of health care services.

In Chile and the Netherlands, where insurance funds do compete, it is apparent that "sorting" occurs—with certain funds attracting wealthier or healthier members. This can be problematic if it is left untended; however, in both cases, regulations have addressed this by establishing standard minimum benefits packages, constraining price setting and the ability to end contracts, and requiring enrollment of any applicant. Also, both countries created compensatory financial flows—through general revenues in Chile and through levies on insurance funds in the Netherlands—to promote solidarity between wealthier and poorer residents and between healthier and less healthy ones. The Netherlands' recent health reform eliminated these levies but built solidarity into the structure of premiums paid by the insured—basing part of the contribution on income.

The Chilean case suggests that competition between the public and private sectors may have spurred innovation in both directions. For example, the private sector voluntarily created a high-cost coverage plan when it was criticized for "dumping" its most critically ill members on the public sector. In the other direction, FONASA adopted electronic reimbursement after it had become widespread among ISAPREs. In the Netherlands, private insurers were also put under pressure to expand coverage and reduce premiums when the sickness funds entered the voluntary market—even to the extent of threatening their solvency.

In both Chile and the Netherlands, the existence of separate regulatory frameworks for insurers who are in competition with one another produced serious problems. Ultimately, this led them to unify the regulatory framework so that it would apply equally and fully to both public and private insurers. The existence of separate regulatory frameworks in each country was due to historical factors, mainly the different origins of private and public insurers. For countries with incipient and multiple forms of health insurance, there is a strong message here that a unified approach to supervision and regulation is warranted.

The relationship between insurance funds and health care providers is a critical conditioning factor for health insurance fund performance. The major contrast in these cases is between Costa Rica—which has integrated the insurance and provision functions—and the other three countries—where insurers are separate from providers. Costa Rica has effectively utilized this integration of insurance and provision to universalize access to basic health care services, but it does not seem to be reaping the benefits of integration in other ways (as demonstrated by high absenteeism and declining productivity). On the management level, providers are paid salaries according to explicit civil service codes, and management discretion over personnel is constrained by those same codes. The CCSS is experimenting with "management contracts" to approximate a separation of responsibilities between payer and provider, but with limited effect. Ultimately, the management of this integrated system appears to be conditioned by bilateral negotiations between the CCSS and the medical professional unions, and is, therefore, heavily politicized.

In Chile, Estonia, and the Netherlands, the arms-length relationship with providers has occasioned some experimentation with performance and selective contracting, but much of it is incipient, ineffective, or limited. The most common innovation is to move away from fee-for-service payments and to introduce case-based payments (like diagnosis-related groups) for a subset of diagnosed conditions. In Estonia, explicit negotiations between the EHIF and providers over prices and volumes of services take place within the broader framework of the government's budget and revenue projections. In the Netherlands, a similar process occurs. Chile can be seen as a hybrid in some ways because private health care providers are largely paid on a fee-for-service or case-based system, while public health care providers are salaried as in Costa Rica. Chile's public sector is also experimenting with different approaches to management, including decentralization of budgets, changes in discretionary authority at local levels, and the introduction of performance budgeting.

Endnotes

1. The author gratefully acknowledges the support, suggestions, and comments from Pablo Gottret, Axel Rahola, and Birgit Hansl. The authors of the case studies, James Cercone, José Pacheco, Ricardo Bitrán, Rodrigo Muñoz, Hans Maarse, and Triin Habicht, also provided important insights to this work along with key information. Any remaining errors are the author's responsibility.

2. "Voices of the Poor," a World Bank study examining poverty from the perspectives of the poor themselves, interviewed over 60,000 individuals in 60 countries around the world.

3. Author's calculations from National Health Accounts data and publications of the Mexican Social Security Institute.

4. One resolution would be to reserve the term SHI for systems that share these characteristics with Western European countries, but this creates two problems. It ignores the commonalities between Western European MHI systems and others; and it artificially limits the

range of design alternatives available to policymakers. It is also worth noting that all the organizations discussed in this book are members of the International Social Security Association and consider themselves to be *social* health insurance.

5. Definition of Corporate Governance from the Preamble (p. 3) of OECD 2004b.

6. See Laffont and Tirole 1993, Chapter 11 for an overview of theories and application of the concept of "capture."

7. For example, the Social Security Institute of the Dominican Republic has a monopoly in public provision of mandatory health insurance coverage to formal sector workers. Nevertheless, its care is so little valued that many employers negotiate parallel contracts with private health care insurers called "Igualas" (see Santana 1998).

8. Numerous schemes have been proposed for analyzing governance. This list draws from Preker and Harding 2003; World Bank 1996 and 1997; Williamson 1996; and the author's own experiences.

9. The EHIF Board has authority to use the "cash reserves" and "risk reserves." A third "legal reserve," not less then 6 percent of the annual budget, is set aside and can only be used by order of the government.

10. This is part of a broad effort to improve public sector performance, called the "balanced scorecard."

Reference list

Abramson, W.B. 2001. "Monitoring and Evaluation of Contracts for Health Service Delivery in Costa Rica." *Health Policy and Planning* 16(4):404–11.

Campbell, J.C., and N. Ikegami. 1998. *The Art of Balance in Health Policy Maintaining Japan's Low-cost, Egalitarian System.* Cambridge, U.K.: Cambridge University Press.

Carmichael, J., and R. Palacios. 2003. *A Framework for Public Pension Fund Management.* Washington, D.C.: World Bank.

Carrin, G., and C. James. 2004. "Reaching Universal Coverage Via Social Health Insurance: Key Design Features in the Transition Period." World Health Organization, Geneva.

Chinitz, D., M. Wismar, and C. Le Pen. 2004. "Governance and (self-)regulation in Social Health Insurance Systems." Chapter 6 in R.B. Saltman, R. Busse, and J. Figueras, eds., *Social Health Insurance Systems in Western Europe.* Maidenhead and New York City: Open University Press.

Commonwealth of Australia. 2003. "Public Sector Governance. Better Practice Guide: Framework, Processes and Practices." Vol. 1. Australian National Audit Office, Canberra.

Davis, C. 2001. "Reforms and Performance of the Medical Systems in the Transition States of the Former Soviet Union and Eastern Europe." *International Social Security Review* 54(2 and 3):7–56.

Eichler R., and E. Lewis. n.d. "Social Insurance Assessment Tool." Management Sciences for Health, Boston, MA, http://www.lachealthsys.org/documents/siat_tool.pdf.

Ferreiro Yazigi, A., and L.A. Sierra. 2001. "El Papel de las Superintendencias en la Regulación de Seguros de Salud: los Casos de Chile, Argentina, Perú y Colombia." Pan-American Health Organization, Washington, D.C.

ILO (International Labour Office). 2001. *Social Security: A New Consensus.* Geneva.

Kutzin, J. 2001. "A Descriptive Framework for Country-level Analysis of Health Care Financing Arrangements." *Health Policy* 56(3):171–204.

La Forgia, G.M. 1994. "First Steps Toward Health Reform: Analyzing and Redirecting Financial Flows. A Review of Reform Proposals in Colombia and The Dominican Republic." Inter-American Development Bank, Washington, D.C.

Labadie, G.J. 1998. "Regulation and Performance of Health Cooperatives in Uruguay." Chapter 7 in W.D. Savedoff, ed., *Organization Matters: Agency Problems in Health and Education in Latin America*. Washington, D.C.: Inter-American Development Bank, pp. 253–85.

Laffont, J-J, and J. Tirole. 1993. *A Theory of Incentives in Procurement and Regulation*. Cambridge, U.K. and London: MIT Press.

Maarse, H., A. Paulus, and G. Kuiper. 2005. "Supervision in Social Health Insurance: A Four Country Study." *Health Policy* 71(3):333–46.

Magnoli, A. 2001. *National Health Accounts in Latin America and Caribbean: Concept, Results, and Policy Uses*. Washington, D.C: Inter-American Development Bank/INDES.

Meckling, W. 1976. "Theory of the Firm: Managerial Behavior, Agency Costs and Ownership Structure." *Journal of Financial Economics* 3:305–60.

Mitchell, O.S., and P.L. Hsin. 1994. "Public Sector Pension Governance and Performance." NBER Working Paper No. W4632, Cambridge, MA.

Mossialos, E., A. Dixon, J. Figueras, and J. Kutzin. 2002. *Funding Health Care: Options for Europe*. Buckingham, U.K. and Philadelphia: Open University Press.

Normand, C., and A. Weber. 1994. *Social Health Insurance: A Guidebook for Planning*. Geneva: World Health Organization.

OECD (Organisation for Economic Co-operation and Development). 2000. *A System of Health Accounts*. Paris.

———. 2004a. *OECD Principles of Corporate Governance*. Paris.

———. 2004b. "Proposal for a Taxonomy of Health Insurance: OECD Study on Private Health Insurance." Paris.

Preker, A.S., and A. Harding. 2000. "The Economics of Public and Private Roles in Health Care: Insights from Institutional Economics and Organizational Theory." Report No. 21875. World Bank, Washington, D.C.

Preker, A.S., and A. Harding. 2003. *Innovations in Health Service Delivery: The Corporatization of Public Hospitals*. Washington, D.C.: World Bank.

Saltman, R.B. 2004. "Social Health Insurance in Perspective: The Challenge of Sustaining Stability." Chapter 1 in R.B. Saltman, R. Busse, and J. Figueras, eds., *Social Health Insurance Systems in Western Europe*. Maidenhead and New York City: Open University Press.

Santana, I. 1998. "Social Security and Private Prepayment Plans in the Dominican Republic." Chapter 5 in W.D. Savedoff, ed., *Organization Matters: Agency Problems in Health and Education in Latin America*. Washington, D.C.: Inter-American Development Bank, pp. 183–214.

Savedoff, W. 2004. "Is There a Case for Social Insurance?" *Health Policy and Planning* 19(3):183–184.

Spiller, P.T. 1990. "Politicians, Interest Groups and Regulators: A Multiple-Principals Agency Theory of Regulation, (or "Let Them Be Bribed")." *Journal of Law and Economics* 33:65–101.

Spiller, P.T., and S. Urbiztondo. 1994. "Political Appointees vs. Career Civil Servants: A Multiple-Principals Theory of Political Institutions." *European Journal of Political Economy* 10(3):465–497.

Spiller, P.T., and W. Savedoff. 1998. "Governmental Opportunism and the Performance of Public Enterprises." Inter-American Development Bank, Washington, D.C.

Verdeyen V., and B.V. Buggenhout. 2003. "Social Governance: Corporate Governance in Institutions of Social Security, Welfare and Healthcare." *International Social Security Review* 56(2):45–64.

Wagstaff, A. 2007. "Social Health Insurance Reexamined." Policy Research Working Paper 411. World Bank, Washington, D.C. January.

WHO (World Health Organization). 2000. *The World Health Report 2000. Health Systems: Improving Performance*. Geneva.

Williamson, O.E. 1999. *The Mechanisms of Governance*. London: Oxford University Press.

World Bank. 1996. "Bureaucrats in Business: The Economics and Politics of Government Ownership." Policy Research Report. Washington, D.C.

———. 1997. *World Development Report 1997: The State in a Changing World*. Washington, D.C.

———. 2004. *World Development Report 2004: Making Services Work For Poor People*. Washington, D.C.

Xu, K, D.B. Evans, K. Kawabata, R. Zeramdini, J. Klavus, and C.J. Murray. 2003. "Household Catastrophic Health Expenditure: A Multicountry Analysis." *The Lancet* 362(9378): 111–7.

2

Good governance dimensions in mandatory health insurance: A framework for performance assessment

B. Hansl, A. Rahola, P. Gottret, and A. Leive

Introduction

The governance of any mandatory health insurance (MHI) system encompasses dimensions and features that guide the relationships between the health insurance institutions and those who supervise and influence them—often including legislators, government agencies, contributors, and beneficiaries. This chapter examines the elements of good governance as they apply to five important governance dimensions—coherent decisionmaking structures; stakeholder participation; transparency and information; supervision and regulation; and consistency and stability.

As a first step to classifying and eventually analyzing MHI governance, this chapter expands on the prior discussion by proposing a set of features for each dimension that describes the character and quality of MHI governance in a particular country (Table 2.1). These features are not meant as unidimensional measures of progress toward good governance because, as discussed in Chapter 1, each feature of governance interacts with features of the MHI system itself. For example, the appropriate level and kind of supervision will be very different in a system with multiple insurers than one with a single payer.

In addition, by proposing a set of specific indicators, we hope to develop a more objective institutional description of the features, and take preliminary steps to operationalize such diagnostics by applying the resulting framework to the case studies: Costa Rica, Estonia, the Netherlands, and Chile. As a result, it should be possible to demonstrate the kinds of analysis necessary either to design new governance mechanisms or improve existing ones.

Good governance dimensions of mandatory health insurance

Good governance is fundamental for MHI to provide financial protection to the covered population in a sustainable manner. It is difficult to attribute causality

TABLE 2.1   Dimensions, features, and indicators of good governance in mandatory health insurance

Dimension	Features	Indicators
Coherent decisionmaking structures	1. Responsibility for MHI objectives must correspond with decisionmaking power and capacity in each institution involved in the management of the system.	Yes/No Examples: • The institution responsible for the financial sustainability of the system must be able to change at least one of the parameters on which it depends (e.g. conditions of affiliation, contribution rate, benefits package, ability to act a strategic purchaser, or tariffs). • The institution in charge of the supervision of sickness funds has the capacity to fulfill its responsibilities (i.e. it has enough skilled staff, it has access to the necessary information, and legal texts give it the authority to fulfill its role vis-à-vis sickness funds).
	2. All MHI entities have routine risk assessment and management strategies in place.	Yes/No Example: • Clear regulations on MHI entities' continuous risk assessment and risk management are in place. • Strategies are in place, i.e. MHI entities follow and analyze the evolution of expenditures and contributions. • MHI entities have the capacity to manage risks, i.e. to take corrective action in order to ensure the financial sustainability of the system by modifying some of the parameters influencing it (contribution rate, composition of the benefits package, etc.).
	3. The cost of regulating and administering MHI institutions is reasonable and appropriate.	Yes/No Example: • Maximum administration costs for MHI entities are set in legal texts or regulations. • Administrative costs are monitored by the regulator. • Provisions for covering the costs of the MHI regulator are stipulated in legal texts. • Before new regulations are put in place a cost-benefit assessment is conducted.
Stakeholder participation	4. Stakeholders have effective representation in the governing bodies of MHI entities.	Yes/No Examples: • Governing bodies of regulatory oversight and institutional governance (board of directors, oversight body) have representatives of government agencies, regulatory bodies, MHI entities, unions, employers' organizations, beneficiaries, providers, and independent experts. • Representation is effective, i.e. different stakeholders' views are considered in decisionmaking.

(continues)

TABLE 2.1   Dimensions, features, and indicators of good governance in mandatory health insurance *(continued)*

Dimension	Features	Indicators
Transparency and information	5. The objectives of MHI are formally and clearly defined.	Yes/No Examples: • Objectives are stated in a high-level legal text (e.g. the Constitution or a law). • Objectives are publicized and easily accessible to the public. • Objectives are clearly defined and easily understandable.
	6. MHI relies upon an explicit and an appropriately designed institutional and legal framework.	Yes/No Examples: • Main characteristics of the system are defined in legal texts (coverage, benefits package, financing, provision, regulatory oversight, and institutional governance). • The framework is appropriate given the country MHI context (i.e. it is not too restrictive, considers special local circumstances, and does not ignore important parts or players in the system). • The status and responsibilities of each different MHI institution in the system are clearly defined and transparent.
	7. Clear information, disclosure, and transparency rules are in place.	Yes/No Examples: • Explicit disclosure regulations exist in the law or regulations of the law. • Business activities, ownership, and financial positions are regularly disclosed (i.e. the rules are followed). • Beneficiaries have access to the financial information of sickness funds.
	8. MHI entities have minimum requirements in regard to protecting the insured.	Yes/No Examples: • Consumer protection regulations exist in law, including consumer information, and independent mechanisms for resolution of complaints, appeals, grievances, and disputes. • The insured can obtain timely, complete, and relevant information on changes in benefits or premium, coverage length, etc. • Consumer complaint mechanisms exist and are being used.

(continues)

TABLE 2.1   **Dimensions, features, and indicators of good governance in mandatory health insurance**
(continued)

Dimension	Features	Indicators
		• Appeals and grievance mechanisms exist and are being used.
		• Independent dispute resolution mechanisms exist and are being used.
Supervision and regulation	9. Rules on compliance, enforcement, and sanctions for MHI supervision are clearly defined.	Yes/No Examples: • Rules on compliance and sanctions are defined in legal texts. • Corrective actions are imposed, based on clear and objective criteria that are publicly disclosed. • Adequate capacity for the execution of these functions is provided. • Cases of rule violation and subsequent actions by the regulator are publicized.
	10. Financial management rules for MHI entities are clearly defined and enforced.	Yes/No Examples: • Financial standards for MHI entities are defined in legal texts or regulations. • Clear financial licensure/market-entry rules are defined (minimum capital requirements). • Ongoing reserve and solvency requirements are defined. • Regulations of assets and financial investments are defined. • Audit (internal and external) rules are defined. • Rules for financial standards are enforced.
	11. The MHI system has structures for ongoing supervision and monitoring in place.	Yes/No Examples: • Clear nonfinancial licensure/market entry rules are defined. • Insurance product filing/registration is defined and regulated. • Adequate on-site inspections and off-site monitoring are in place. • Ongoing financial reporting rules are defined and provided information is accurate and timely. • Clear market exit/dissolution rules are in place.

(continues)

TABLE 2.1 Dimensions, features, and indicators of good governance in mandatory health insurance
(continued)

Dimension	Features	Indicators
Consistency and stability	12. The main qualities of the MHI system are stable.	Yes/No Examples: • Objectives have remained substantially the same in the recent past. • Fundamental characteristics of the MHI system (e.g. benefits package, rules for affiliation, contribution requirements, basic protection rights for the insured, and basic institutional requirements for operators) are defined in law. • The law has remained substantially the same in the recent past (i.e. independent of political elections or economic crises).

between financial protection and the extent of health coverage and governance or any other determinant. However, the importance of governance for the sustainability and growth of financial institutions as well as for Mandatory Health Insurance institutions has been well documented in the literature (Brunetti and Kisunko 1997; Chong and Calderon 2000; La Porta et al. 1997; Litan et al. 2002; Greg 2006; Hsiao 2005). The governance literature has developed general dimensions that are used to define good governance for governments, corporations, and financial markets and which also apply to MHI. They generally fall within five dimensions of governance, as given in the first paragraph of this chapter.

These dimensions are rather broad and require greater specificity than presented in Chapter 1 if they are to be measured and used. The following section presents a number of features, and their related indicators, that have been used in the governance literature because they are believed to contribute to good governance. Within each dimension, these indicators can be assessed jointly to provide a rating that can be useful for assessing the importance of that dimension in contributing to the overall governance structure of a country and be one input, among many, to analysis and design. Some of these features and related indicators may actually contribute to different governance dimensions, but we have sought to include them in the category to which we consider are most directly relevant.

Coherent decisionmaking structures

In order to be coherent, decisionmaking structures require those responsible for decisions to possess the discretion, authority, tools, and resources to fulfill their responsibilities. The structures must also establish consequences for decisions that align incentives with achieving good performance of the overall system. Explicit legal foundations generally support institutionalizing such incentive-compatible constraints.

Ownership and legal status are two key elements that affect the way the system is structured and performs. Ownership can provide incentives for the owner to act in ways that support achieving the principal goals of good population coverage and financial sustainability at the lowest possible cost. Legal status often determines boundaries for what the insurer is allowed and prevented from doing. It also limits the personal boundaries of liabilities and responsibilities of owners and managers of the insurance entity. The legal foundation also has implications for ensuring all actors in the system have the tools necessary to reach the objectives assigned to them.

For instance, if the law makes insurance funds responsible for the financial sustainability of the system, they must be able to change at least one of the parameters on which it depends, such as conditions of affiliation, contribution rate, benefits package, ability to act as a strategic purchaser, or tariffs. Otherwise the sharing of responsibilities between the different players is not consistent and does not permit effective governance of the system. This is critical for MHI since governments often create insurance funds and assign them ambitious objectives in order to improve the management of the system, while at the same time retaining the authority to make key decisions given the political sensitivity of the subject.

The following indicators describe some features of coherent decisionmaking structures that affect the quality of governance:

Feature Number 1. Responsibility for MHI objectives must correspond with decisionmaking power and capacity in each institution involved in the management of the system

If the different players, mainly the state and the insurance funds, do not have the tools to reach the objectives assigned to them, the sharing of responsibilities between the different players is not coherent and does not permit effective governance of the system.

Feature Number 2. All MHI entities have routine risk assessment and management strategies in place

The supervisory authority requires MHI institutions to continuously recognize the range of risks they face and to assess and manage them effectively. Having risk assessment strategies implies that MHI institutions closely monitor trends in the amounts and composition of health expenditures and MHI revenues, with the analytical capacity to understand and respond to changes that might jeopardize the system. The capacity to manage these risks means that the insurance funds can take corrective action to ensure the financial sustainability of the system by modifying key parameters, such as the contribution rate, or the composition of the benefits package.

Feature Number 3. *The cost of regulating and administering MHI institutions is reasonable and appropriate*

Efficient governance achieves its goals at a cost, in terms of administration costs and the costs of complying with the regulations, that is proportional to the benefit.

Stakeholder participation

Stakeholder participation influences the flow of information and accountability relationships of the actors within the system. The representation of stakeholder interests can be functional or dysfunctional depending on which groups it includes and in what proportion; beneficiaries, employers, and medical professionals each often bring different perspectives regarding cost containment and financial sustainability versus service provision. To be successful, representation should attempt to achieve inclusiveness, participation, and consensus orientation.

Inclusiveness is rooted in the premise that stakeholder views are integral to meaningful governance and should be incorporated during the process of decisionmaking. *Participation* emphasizes the broad involvement of constituents in the direction and operation of MHI systems and strives to create opportunities for a broad range of stakeholders to have access to and make meaningful contributions to decisionmaking. *Consensus-orientation* refers to a process of achieving agreements in decisionmaking that requires serious treatment of every stakeholder's considered opinion. For example, on the different levels of MHI governance it would be advantageous if decisionmaking authorities seek to engage stakeholders who are both directly and indirectly affected. This would include representation and participation of different interest groups, like health care providers and the insured in consultations or standing committees on the nature and diversity of MHI products and covered services. Stakeholder engagement is a dynamic process which likely strengthens trust in the MHI system, and in turn, fortifies credibility.

The following indicator describes one feature of stakeholder participation that affects the quality of governance:

Feature Number 4. *Stakeholders have effective representation in the governing bodies of MHI entities*

Stakeholder participation in decisionmaking strengthens trust in the MHI system and in turn, fortifies credibility. Having representatives of unions and employers' organizations in the governing bodies is also consistent with the nature of MHI, which is financed through employers' and employees' contributions. The payers should have some say in decisions.

Transparency and information

Transparency is a means to hold public decisionmakers accountable and to control corruption. There is less opportunity for authorities to abuse a system in their own interest when laws, rules, and decisions are available for everyone to see, when critical meetings are open to the public, and when budgets and financial statements may be reviewed by anyone. In this way transparency is a necessary condition for feedback *before, during,* or *after* a decision or action. Transparency includes, for example, that MHI regulatory rules are generated openly, creating a level playing-field. All regulations should also be clear, simple, and user friendly. Any other decisionmaking regarding the regulations, such as compliance and enforcement, should also follow a transparent process that limits discretionary actions. The rule of law requires that regulatory authority is legitimately exercised only in accordance with written, publicly disclosed laws adopted and enforced in accordance with established procedure. This is intended to be a safeguard against arbitrary governance.

The following indicators describe some features of transparency and information that affect the quality of governance:

Feature Number 5. The objectives of MHI are formally and clearly defined

They are stated in a high-level legal text, either the Constitution or a law. These objectives are valid over time and guarantee continuity of the MHI system.

Feature Number 6. MHI relies upon an explicit and appropriately designed institutional and legal framework

Explicit means that the main characteristics of the system are defined in legal texts. Adequate institutional arrangements include the composition and status of the institutions[1] and some degree of flexibility to respond to eventual challenges and changes.

Feature Number 7. Clear information, disclosure, and transparency rules are in place

MHI entities must disclose relevant information on a timely basis in order to give stakeholders a clear view of their business activities and financial position.

Feature Number 8. MHI entities have minimum requirements in regard to protecting the insured

The requirements include provision of timely, complete, and relevant information to those who are insured.

Supervision and regulation

Another mechanism to hold insurers accountable is through supervision and regulation. It is important that supervisory and regulatory arrangements are consistent with the structure of the MHI system. While it is important for the behavior of institutions to be transparent, it is necessary for them to be answerable and responsible for their actions in order to achieve accountability. Visibility is important for supervision and the presence of consequences—reward or sanction—for the performance of the health insurance funds is key to regulation.

The following indicators describe some features of supervision and regulation that affect the quality of governance:

Feature Number 9. Rules on compliance, enforcement, and sanctions for MHI supervision are clearly defined

Corrective actions are imposed, based on clear and objective criteria that are publicly disclosed. Adequate capacity for the execution of these functions is provided.

Feature Number 10. Financial management rules for MHI entities are clearly defined and enforced

MHI entities have to comply with standards for establishing adequate technical provisions and other liabilities.

Feature Number 11. The MHI system has structures for ongoing supervision and monitoring in place

This includes adequate reporting (on-site and off-site) in order to evaluate the condition of each MHI entity and the whole system.

Consistency and stability

Consistency helps to avoid uncertainty around rule-making and enforcement through time and through periods of political change. If regulations are consistent then people and institutions can make long-term decisions with the assurance that the rules will not change or, at least, will not change arbitrarily. *Stability* is of particular importance for MHI systems because insurance necessarily entails commitments over time, because MHI must be financially sustainable over generations, and access to health care and financial protection has to be maintained in the face of political change or economic downturns. Of course, there are times when slavish adherence to consistency would forego important opportunities. For example, Korea experienced such strong economic growth between 1977 and 1989 that it was able to extend MHI coverage abruptly to almost the entire population. But such exceptions are limited.

The following indicator is one feature of consistency and stability that affects the quality of governance:

Feature Number 12. The main qualities of the MHI system are stable

The fundamental characteristics that define the MHI system (such as benefits package, rules for affiliation, contribution requirements, basic protection rights for the insured, and basic institutional requirements for operators) should persist in the long-run. One way to at least partially achieve this objective is to establish these characteristics in the law to make them less easy to modify. An orderly and legitimate process for reviewing and changing these provisions, if effective, can flexibly respond to changing circumstances while reinforcing the basic stability of the system.

Methodology: Measuring MHI governance performance

The framework developed in the previous sections can be used to qualitatively measure MHI governance performance along the five dimensions. Based on information available for indictors linked to each feature, an assessment of the importance of each dimension in the governance structure can be formed. As Table 2.1 above shows, fairly detailed and specific information on a country's MHI system is required to compile the information for the indicators and subsequent ratings of the features and dimensions. Once that information is compiled, the indicators are assessed for each dimension. Dependent on the countries' MHI performance under the indicators, the individual features can be rated and aggregated to rate the dimension. After ratings are constructed for each of the five dimensions, the results can be displayed in a five-dimensional radar graph to conceptualize the relative significance of each dimension (Figure 2.1).

For example, if a country's MHI system performs very well in terms of *transparency and information*, features one to five should have high ratings assigned to them. Higher ratings can be graphically depicted as locations that are farther away from the center of the radar graph. The actual ratings depend on the quality of the provided indicators for the MHI governance system. Table 2.1 lists as possible determinable indicators the MHI objectives that need to be stated in a high-level legal text (such as the Constitution or law), be publicized and easily accessible to the public, and be clearly defined and easily understandable. If all indicators imply excellent clarity on MHI objectives in a country, then on that given scale the highest rating can be assigned for feature one.

FIGURE 2.1   **Example for mandatory health insurance governance performance assessment**

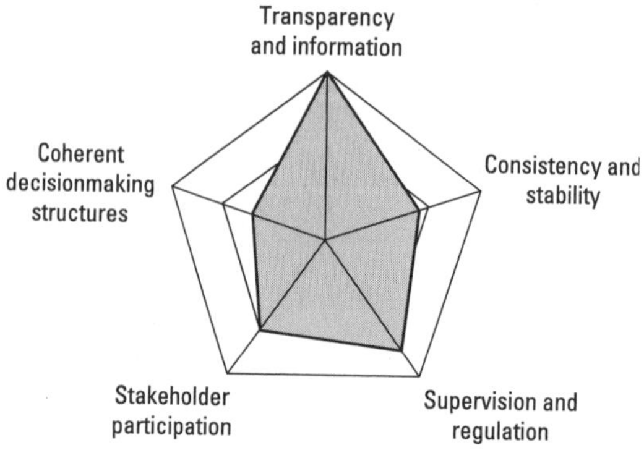

Combining the assessments for all five features under the dimension *transparency and information* would yield its final rating. For a perfect rating under any dimension, the location on the radar graph for that dimension would be on the pentagon's perimeter.

For the given example, *Transparency and information*, the location on the perimeter of the radar graph displays the maximum rating. In the example shown, the particular country does not perform as well on the four other dimensions, especially *Coherent Decisionmaking Structures* and *Consistency and stability*. The interpretation of these results can only be meaningfully explained with specific information from each country. Thus, general recommendations based on the nature of MHI governance arrangements of well-performing countries have to be considered with caution. In summary, this methodology provides a useful first step to quickly conceptualize the MHI governance performance of a country by identifying particular issues or problems that can orient subsequent and more comprehensive analyses.

Results: MHI governance assessment in four countries

An assessment of MHI governance performance was conducted for the following four countries: Costa Rica, Estonia, the Netherlands, and Chile. Each country has had successful MHI governance performance. A comprehensive table with explanations for the indicators for each feature and dimension were compiled, for all four countries, using the country expertise of the case study authors (Table 2.1 above). While the ratings should be given an ordinal interpretation rather than a cardinal one, the experts used scorecards as a simple mechanistic tool to value how well the country had performed on each dimension as a way to estimate the relative importance of each dimension in MHI governance for that particular country. The aim is, ultimately, to develop indicators that can be monitored over time in order to assess and constructively improve MHI governance performance.

This method is useful to analyze how well an MHI system in a country performs in one dimension relative to other dimensions, and thus helps identify areas where additional improvements should concentrate. The values of indicators are based on country expert opinion and, as a result, are largely subjective. The methodology is useful to evaluate governance of MHI in one country and can be useful to assess progress if it is carried out over time, but it should not be used to compare governance arrangements across countries.

The following four sections summarize the main information from each country's table in radar graphs, with some selected background information. A fifth section compares the performance of all four countries.

Costa Rica

Costa Rica performs very well in two of the five dimensions, namely *Consistency and stability* and *Stakeholder participation* (Figure 2.2). With regard to *Consistency*

FIGURE 2.2   Costa Rica mandatory health insurance governance performance assessment

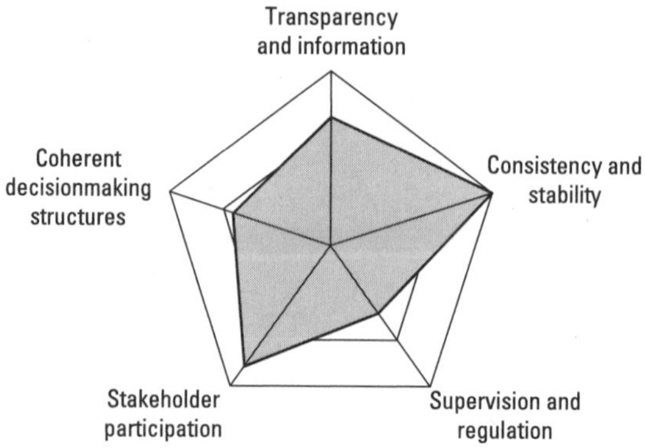

and stability, the objectives of the health insurance system have remained unaltered since the creation of the system in 1941. The Constitutive Law (Ley Constitutiva) of the CCSS has been basically the same since its promulgation in 1943, with only few amendments, and the main components of the MHI system remained unaltered. For example, the package of benefits stayed practically the same and changed only when the Constitutional Court forced the CCSS to include particular treatments (such as AIDS antiretrovirals) as part of the benefits. The core legislation for the basic drugs list dates from 1989, and is another example of the stability of the system. *Consistency and stability* is also evident at the management level—since 1974 only two executive presidents did not complete their term, one because of death and the other because of a corruption scandal.

In terms of *Stakeholder participation*, the board of directors—which is the main body for regulatory oversight and institutional governance—is a tripartite body with representatives from employees, employers, and government. Within each group the range of key stakeholders, including medical doctors, is ample and diverse. However, some experts felt that, despite the balance of powers in the board of directors, clients were underrepresented.[2]

The weakest dimensions were *Supervision and regulation* and *Coherent decision-making structures*. The low rating for *Supervision and regulation* is driven, in part, by the evidence that, in spite of explicit legal competencies to sanction individuals and organizations that fail to comply with their responsibilities, such sanctions are rare in practice. Situations covered by the legislation are either obsolete or lack specificity, and associated sanctions are not clear and objective. Furthermore, most of the supervisory regulations are applied ex post, with little provision for preventing such problems in the first place. In cases where sanctions are clearly defined, the penalty is inadequate. For instance, those who evade their responsibility to make social security contributions, if caught and punished, are assessed fines of US$350 irrespective of the size of the unpaid debt. Also, even if the sanction is correctly specified, administrative problems and processes tend to complicate the work of the institutions. For example, in the CCSS, the number of supervisors is quite small for monitoring more than 6,000 firms. In order to shut down a defaulted company, the judicial process may take more than two years. Publicized scandals are mostly the result of mass media investigations and not the outcome of institutionalized mechanisms to prevent and detect corruption.

Other aspects of *Supervision and regulation* have similar weaknesses. For example, financial management rules with respect to reserves clearly assign responsibility to the board of directors. Nevertheless, the law is vague with respect to how these reserves should be managed and what kinds of investments are permitted. For "ongoing supervision and monitoring," the CCSS has created specific departments for on-site and off-site inspections, such as the Procurement Department and the Medical Management Department. However, the capacity to effectively carry out inspections is limited by the amount of resources allocated to these activities, by the weak scope of responsibilities and powers defined by law, and by the low priority given to inspection activities by the CCSS. Finally, financial information is provided to the public via Web sites, but both financial and clinical data generally lag by a year or more.

Regarding the dimension of *Coherent decisionmaking structures*, the CCSS has the power to alter contribution rates, implement new health plans, and redefine the package of benefits and essential drugs. In fact, according to experts, the board of directors of the CCSS has such power that its regulations have the same effect as an Act approved by Congress. In other words, the board of directors is not tied to most regulations that affect the performance of other similar autonomous institutions. Despite these comprehensive decisionmaking powers, the CCSS lacks routine risk assessment and management strategies. It has no permanent program or capacity to analyze and manage risk, although it tracks the evolution of revenues and expenditures and has a department of Actuarial Studies and Economic Planning.

Relative to the other dimensions, *Transparency and information* performance is average. The code of ethics for CCSS personnel adopted by the CCSS board in 1999 attempted to establish standards of conduct. However, the code has failed to prevent some major scandals in the areas of, for example, purchase of medical services at inflated prices, procurement of medicines and equipment, provision of private training courses and medical research, construction of hospitals, and management of the CCSS pensions system. There are limited provisions to address conflicts of interest and check the power of the executive president and board of directors. These issues became especially apparent in 2004 when almost US$9 million from a Finnish loan was used for bribes and other illegal payments.

Estonia

Estonia's MHI system seems to be well governed and performs well to very good on all five dimensions (Figure 2.3). It performed best with regard to *Consistency*

FIGURE 2.3 Estonia mandatory health insurance governance performance assessment

FIGURE 2.3 Estonia mandatory health insurance governance performance assessment

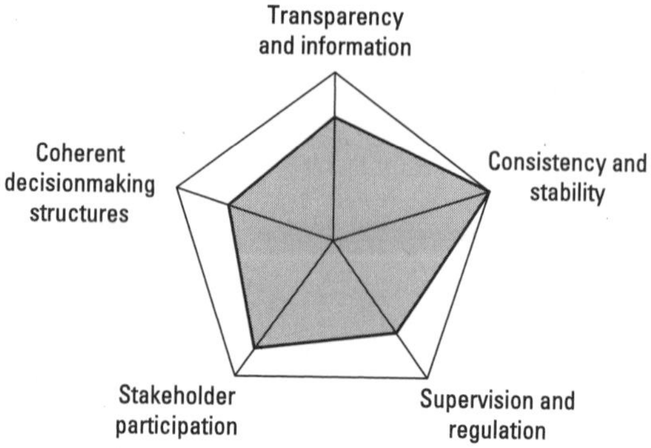

and stability, receiving the maximum rating due to the ongoing commitment to its original objectives and basic values and principles. While the establishment of the current health insurance system in 1992 was a very radical change, the system since then has not been changed significantly. For example, the contribution rate has remained at 13 percent since it began, and there have been only minor changes in entitlement rules. Legislative changes have largely focused on developing the system further. Moreover, changes in political power have not unduly influenced important characteristics of the health insurance system.

Stakeholder participation performed nearly as well. Stakeholders are represented in the governing bodies of the Estonian Health Insurance Fund (EHIF) in ways that appear quite effective. The highest body of the EHIF is the tripartite supervisory board with 15 members: five representatives chosen by the government, five by employers, and five by beneficiaries. Although provider representatives are not explicitly included in the EHIF's supervisory board, they play an important role in decisionmaking because all questions related to the benefits package and contract conditions are negotiated with provider associations. Providers' involvement is important to the EHIF and progress is measured by provider satisfaction surveys, which currently are conducted every year. In 2006 the general satisfaction with partnership with the EHIF was quite high—76 percent of contracting partners considered it very good or good.

Supervision and regulation is one of the slightly weaker areas, largely because sanctions and corrective actions are not generally applied, despite rules allowing for them. For this reason, it is difficult to assess the quality of corrective actions, the capacity for execution of these sanctions and actions, and whether they would be publicized or otherwise publicly discussed.

Estonia scores well for *Transparency and information* for several reasons. Financial management rules for the EHIF are quite explicit and the system has good structures for supervision and monitoring. In addition, financial performance of the EHIF is monitored quarterly by the supervisory board. In addition to financial information, quarterly reports include an overview of EHIF performance in terms of strategic objectives and yearly action plans. All quarterly reports are publicized on the EHIF's Web page and those who have no access to the Internet can get this information on request in hard copy. (Beneficiaries also have the right to get more detailed information on themselves from the EHIF's database, for example, treatment costs.) The EHIF's annual report is more detailed and audited by an external auditor; it is also public, and has gained the best public reporting award for four consecutive years.

However, there is room for improvement on *Transparency and information* because consumer protection is relatively weak. Currently there is no separate patient/insured protection legislation other than the Law of Obligations, which regulates all contractual relationships. According to insured satisfaction surveys (annual population-based surveys), beneficiaries' awareness of their rights and of changes in health insurance system (benefits, copayments, etc.) is relatively limited. Also, beneficiaries have the right to put their complaints to the EHIF, but procedures are not established or clear. If the EHIF receives a complaint and no agreement is reached, then the complaint goes directly to an administrative court according to general procedures. However, the number of court cases is limited and this is uncommon.

A *Coherent decisionmaking structure* is another important dimension for Estonia. Given the impact of different decisionmaking bodies, the creation of separate financial reserve accounts is potentially useful. The financial reserve fund of the EHIF is accessible to the supervisory board for covering normal commercial risks and management problems associated with managing the EHIF. The additional reserve can be released only by the government and is meant to cover the costs of government decisions affecting EHIF finances. In addition, the consolidation of health insurance entities may make operational performance more efficient, particularly for smaller populations. Estonia appears to have substantially reduced administrative costs by consolidating 22 regional insurers into a single fund covering the country's entire population of 1.3 million.

The Netherlands

Governance of MHI in the Netherlands is rated quite high. It scored well in most of the governance dimensions. The score was highest for *Consistency and stability*, followed by *Supervision and regulation* (Figure 2.4). Although the institutional and legal framework of MHI legislation was substantially reformed in 2006, the broad objectives and instruments of legislation for the MHI system have remained substantially the same since the 1960s (even though less fundamental changes did occur, such as the extension of the population covered and the benefits package). MHI has remained unaffected by political changes.

FIGURE 2.4   The Netherlands mandatory health insurance governance performance assessment

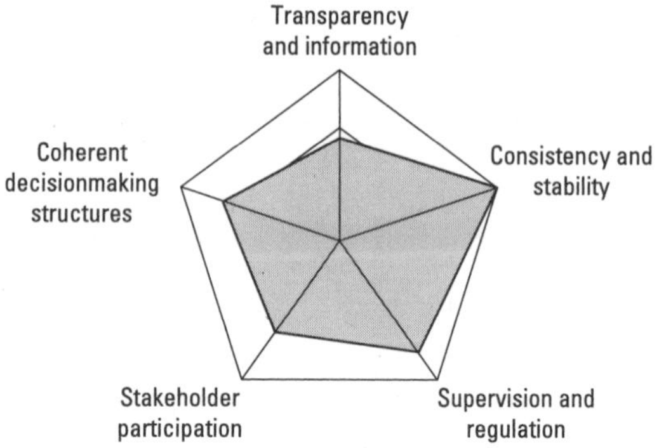

With regard to *Supervision and regulation,* rules on compliance and sanctions are clearly defined in legal texts and the Supervisory Board for Health Care Insurance has imposed corrective actions (mainly financial). All regulatory agents publish annual reports with information on cases of rule violation and subsequent actions.

For *Transparency and information,* the Netherlands performs less well because disclosure rules regarding business activities, ownership, and finances were not in place until recently. A new disclosure arrangement states that each health insurer (or provider) must annually publish information on the salary of its chief executive. Frequent efforts are made to measure the performance of health insurers and provider organizations, and to disclose information to the general public through the Internet. In addition to formal information requirements, a number of social actors, including citizen groups and the press, play a role in reporting information, such as the salaries of chief executives of sickness funds, as they do for other public and semi-public institutions. The Netherlands also has consumer protection regulations related to consumer information, responsibilities, grievance procedures, and appeal mechanisms. However the complaints and appeals mechanisms are relatively weak and rarely used. An ombudsman exists, and the insured have the right to appeal decisions made by their sickness fund to this officer.

Stakeholder participation was good. In the past, representatives of employers, unions, provider, and insurers sat on the semi-public independent agencies that regulate the sector. However, recent reform of these bodies has put an end to this "representative model." At present, their boards consist of independent experts, appointed by the minister of health. Reporting to the board are usually various working groups. Stakeholders often have representatives in these working groups and such representation is generally effective. Also, there is a tradition in the Netherlands of decisionmaking by consensus and shared responsibility. Thus, for example, the minister of health is expected to negotiate with interest groups when problems arise, rather than acting unilaterally.

Regarding *Coherent decisionmaking structures,* improvements in efficiency may not be achieved, despite the existence of multiple competing health insurers, if fundamental pricing and service decisions are imposed by the government. The Netherlands' recent health reform seeks to structure competition so that health insurers will suffer financially for poor management but not for insuring a disproportionately high-risk population. The government has the authority to regulate the benefits package but there is flexibility by insurers to complement packages. The supervisory authority is independent and periodically assesses the risk borne by insurers.

Chile

The assessment of Chile's MHI governance performance included both FONASA and the private health insurers (ISAPREs). Although the two kinds of insurers are quite different, they both operate within the context of a single MHI system. Therefore, the assessment for each dimension was made on the basis of information for both types of insurers, and a combined rating was then given. Generally the ISAPREs are regulated much more comprehensively than FONASA. Consequently the overall results are more variable than in the other three countries (Figure 2.5).

The divergence between the two systems can be illustrated with *Supervision and regulation,* in regard to rules on compliance, enforcement, and sanctions. The Superintendancy of Health (SIS) has no power to sanction the public insurer, FONASA, if it fails to meet its obligations; the SIS has the right to audit FONASA's activities, but not to directly impose sanctions; there is no information regarding corrective actions based on clear and objective criteria for FONASA that are publicly disclosed; and finally, no rule violations have been documented in the case of FONASA.

In contrast, SIS has substantial authority to impose sanctions on the ISAPREs—specific regulations govern their oversight and imposition; sanctions

FIGURE 2.5 Chile mandatory health insurance governance performance assessment

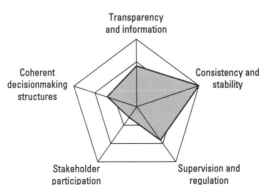

take the form of legislative investigations against the institution involved; the new laws allow SIS to impose financial sanctions on ISAPREs; the SIS Web site publishes the sanctions imposed on private insurers, as well as the cause of the sanction and the fee levied; and finally, SIS publishes the sanctions imposed against ISAPREs on its Web page and in other media.

Chile's MHI governance system performs very well in terms of *Consistency and stability*. For FONASA and the ISAPREs, the system's basic objectives have remained the same. Fundamental characteristics of the MHI system, including the minimum benefits package, contribution requirements, and basic institutional requirements for operators, are defined in different laws. The current system was established in 1981, and legislators have since sought to improve it: in 2004 a reform process was initiated, including new laws and new rights that apply to all beneficiaries, regardless of the insurance system, but changes have largely related to expanding the rights and benefits of the insured.

The *Transparency and information* dimension was good, although objectives of the system are not always clearly defined and easily understood by beneficiaries. For example, a SIS opinion survey shows that just over 20 percent of beneficiaries feel that they have enough information, 60 percent feel that they have little information, and the rest feel that they have none. The differences between FONASA and ISAPREs in this regard are small. The legal framework is adequate given the local context, even though key players and beneficiaries did not help establish the framework. Consumer complaint mechanisms exist for both ISAPREs and FONASA, but only the private system has a culture of consumer complaint. The regulatory agency periodically publishes data regarding the nature and rates of complaints for each of the ISAPREs, usually in the form of a ranked list. No complaints data are available for FONASA.

For other MHI governance dimensions there is also room for improvement, especially *Stakeholder participation*, which is very weak. FONASA's stakeholders do not have direct representation in the institution's supervision. Since FONASA reports directly to the government, through the Ministry of Health, no representatives from unions, employers, beneficiaries, or providers meet in an oversight body. FONASA does have 14 user committees (participatory bodies of patient associations and beneficiaries), but these are advisory and have no power to impose or vote on decisions. Similarly, the SIS is a technical body appointed by the government and has no representatives from unions, employers, beneficiaries, or providers. ISAPRE boards of directors are generally chosen by shareholders, leaving beneficiaries, employees, and providers without explicit representation.

Coherent decisionmaking structures are the weakest dimension in the case of Chile. The ISAPREs have, over time, been able to risk-select the insured population, forcing the transfer of higher risk to the realm of FONASA. Recent changes in regulations imposed explicit health guarantees (*garantías explícitas de salud* or

GES) on all health insurers, but it is uncertain that this change will affect existing risk selection.

Summary

So far, the focus of this book has been on developing an analytical framework for the assessment of MHI governance performance based on five dimensions of good governance and features that should apply to the main components of MHI governance. Four countries with MHI systems were assessed with regard to their adherence to these features through a standardized set of indicators. The results revealed that they perform well with regard to *Consistency and stability* and *Stakeholder participation*. More widely, the findings also suggest that once countries choose MHI to finance their health care systems, they remain supportive over long periods of time.

The dimension of *Supervision and regulation* had the widest dispersion of performance, while *Coherent decisionmaking structures* was the weakest dimension for all countries. This was probably due to an inherent trade-off between this dimension and the *Consistency and stability* dimension.

Surprisingly the dimension of *Transparency and information* performed relatively poorly. Many MHI beneficiaries still have limited information regarding their entitlements and rights and while consumer protection rules exist in most countries, MHI systems did not instill a culture of exercising the right to consumer complaints as it is common in private systems.

This framework of five governance dimensions is useful in the context of analyzing MHI and understanding the dimensions that are most important to successful MHI governance. It can function as a practical self-assessment tool for MHI governance systems and can encourage them to put the developed features of well-governed MHI systems into practice. Still, general recommendations based on the nature of MHI governance arrangements of well-performing countries have to be considered with caution. In all cases, this methodology requires a deep understanding of each country's MHI system.

Endnotes

1. For example, an independent regulatory agent would seem important when insurers and providers include institutions of the public as well as private sector.

2. The creation of community boards was an attempt to include users in the decision-making process, to incorporate citizens' views on local health problems, and to help providers in the implementation of better clinical and administrative processes.

Reference list

Brunetti, Ayno, and G. Kisunko. 1997. "Institutional Obstacles to Doing Business: Region-by-Region Results from a Worldwide Survey of the Private Sector." Policy Research Working Paper 159. World Bank, Washington, D.C.

Chong, A., and C. Calderon. 2000. "Empirical Tests of the Causality and Feedback Between Institutional Measures and Economic Growth." *Journal of Economics and Politics* 12(1):69–81.

Greg, S. 2006. "Regulated Competition in Social Health Insurance: A Three Country Case Comparison." *International Social Security Review* 59(3).

Hsiao, W. 2005. "Social Health Insurance for Developing Nations." Harvard University School of Public Health.

La Porta, R., F. Lopez-de-Silanes, A. Shleifer, and R. Vishny. 1997. "Legal Determinants of External Finance." *Journal of Finance* 52: 1131–1150.

Litan R., M. Pomerleano, and V. Sundarajan. 2002. "Financial Sector Governance: The Roles of the Public and Private Sector." World Bank, Washington, D.C.

3

Costly success: An integrated health insurer in Costa Rica

James Cercone and José Pacheco

Editors' introduction

Costa Rica's mandatory health insurance (MHI) system has its origins in the creation of the Costa Rica Social Security System (Caja Costarricense de Seguro Social or CCSS) in 1943. Coverage is mandatory and universal, with only a single insurer, the CCSS, responsible for both health insurance and health care provision. Created as a public independent agency, the CCSS enjoys substantial—but not complete—autonomy. Oversight is primarily in the hands of a supervisory board comprising representatives of employers' associations, labor unions, and the government.

Costa Rica's MHI system has been very stable for more than half a century, and the commitment to incorporating the entire population in a single system has been unwavering. Though the independence of the CCSS has served Costa Ricans well, it has also contributed to a number of problems, including declining productivity and rising costs in the health care system and incidents of high-level corruption. Costa Rica is addressing these challenges with a variety of initiatives, including management agreements, information systems for improved transparency, and—possibly—changes in the composition of the supervisory board.

This case study confirms some common views about governing MHI systems, but contradicts others. It shows that:

- *Strong political commitment to universal coverage from a broad spectrum of politicians can make an MHI system effective at expanding access, delivering services, and providing financial protection, but not necessarily at maintaining productivity and quality of care.*
- *Integrating financing and provision of health care can have a negative impact on costs, productivity, and quality of care if the dynamic between management and labor is dysfunctional.*
- *While representation can improve a mandatory health insurer's performance, it can also be problematic. In Costa Rica, representation of employers and labor unions on*

the CCSS board of directors has neither contained costs nor improved performance. Furthermore, the presence of representatives of health care providers may be an obstacle to improved performance if they resist certain management reforms.

- *Autonomy from the government and a hard budget constraint do not always lead to efficiency. The management of Costa Rica's MHI has substantial autonomy and incentives to improve productivity, yet it has not staffed important positions (e.g. a Medical Controller or adequate numbers of supervisors), tolerates a fragmented information system, lacks clinical guidelines, and has been unable to fully implement its system of management agreements with health care facilities.*

- *A lack of special provision for addressing conflicts of interest and a lack of appropriate checks on the power of the executive president and board of directors of the CCSS allowed a major scandal to erupt. The existing regulations and code of ethics have been inadequate for preventing individuals with conflicts of interest from sitting on the board.*

- *Even organizations with substantial formal autonomy may actually be highly constrained. The scope of decisionmaking power in the CCSS is significantly curtailed by the labor unions that represent health care professionals—when they resist management reforms—and by the Constitutional Court—when it voids efforts to set priorities and to limit the provision of certain services or drugs.*

- *Reliance on payroll taxes for revenues can lead to financial difficulties when economic growth is slow or, as in recent years, the labor market has become increasingly informal.*

The trajectory toward universal coverage

An early commitment to health insurance

The Costa Rica Social Security System (Caja Costarricense de Seguro Social or CCSS), started operating in 1943 to oversee both the financial management and provision of health services. Initially, the entity lacked autonomy and its reserve funds were directly managed by a special board, on which no member of the CCSS sat. These features created problems and the original Act was reformed in 1943 to give the institution significant autonomy, the power to govern itself, and the right to manage its own funds.

The CCSS was originally created to protect workers against risks arising from illness, maternity, and labor injuries. Over the following decades, the mandatory health insurance (MHI) scheme gradually expanded. In 1961 Congress established universal health insurance for workers and their families and, in 1975, extended health insurance to cover farmers and peasants. In 1978 the CCSS created the voluntary health insurance scheme for independent workers. In 1984 it created a special scheme, funded by the government, to cover indigent people (representing 12 percent of the insured population in 2003). Figure 3.1 depicts the historical trend graphically.

In addition to expanding its coverage, the CCSS and the Costa Rican health system have changed how health care services are managed. Most recently during

FIGURE 3.1　**Evolution of health insurance coverage in Costa Rica**

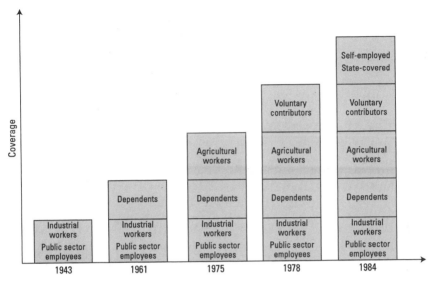

Source: Prepared by Sanigest.

the 1990s, different governments promoted health sector reforms (particularly after 1993) that included four basic changes in the MHI system. First, an institutional reorganization consolidated provision of health care under the CCSS and gave the Ministry of Health the role of stewardship and regulation. Second, it made financial changes, increasing the contribution rates and combating evasion. Third, it modernized its management of providers, decentralizing many functions and introducing management agreements (*compromisos de gestión*) to relate performance to budgets. Finally, it redesigned its model of care, creating a comprehensive network of local health teams to provide primary care and serve as gateways for access to the health system.

Today, the CCSS is the only entity in charge of managing and organizing MHI in Costa Rica. It currently covers 90 percent of the population and offers a broad package of services. The provision of health services is based on the principles of solidarity, universality, unity, equity, and egalitarian conditions of access. Although the entire population is covered by health insurance, the share of people directly contributing to the system has been decreasing and today amounts to only 53 percent of the economically active population.

The current context

Costa Rica has a population of 4.3 million people, which has been growing at 2.4 percent a year for the last 15 years. Over time, the CCSS has contributed to significant improvements in health conditions. Today, life expectancy is nearly 80 years and the infant mortality rate is now close to 9 deaths per 1,000 live births.

In the last 15 years, Costa Rica's economy and labor market have experienced trends that affect the performance of the CCSS. First, though Costa Rica is an upper-middle-income economy with a gross domestic product (GDP) per capita of US$4,500 in 2005 (US$10,100 in purchasing power parity terms), the pace of growth has slowed, affecting CCSS revenues, which depend on payroll contributions from employers and employees. Between 1991 and 2005, GDP per capita grew at a moderate 2.4 percent a year and per capita real disposable income grew at 2 percent a year. In the six years to 2005, this rate fell to just 1 percent a year.

Rising unemployment and informalization of jobs have also reduced the number of formally affiliated individuals; and the slow growth of real wages has limited the CCSS's revenue stream. Costa Rica has enjoyed relatively low formal unemployment rates relative to neighboring Latin American countries; however, the rate rose from 4.6 percent in 1990 to 6.5 percent (approximately 185,000 unemployed individuals) in 2004. Different sources estimate the rate of informal unemployment to be between 33 percent and 42 percent of the labor force (ILO and Estado de la Nación Web pages). Of immediate concern to the CCSS, because it affects revenues, is the slow growth of real wages, which grew at an average of 0.65 percent a year between 1984 and 2004, approximately one-fourth the average GDP growth rate. By 2004 the real minimum wage was only 13 percent higher than in 1984. Some of this is due to the decline in real wages of 3 percent between 2000 and 2004.

Though the CCSS is the only authority providing health insurance and health care services in the public sector, the private sector for health care services has expanded significantly in recent years. During the 1990s, the share of medical staff in the private sector increased from 10 percent to 24 percent. Despite almost universal coverage for health care services provided in CCSS facilities, household surveys show that around 30 percent of the population uses private health services at least once a year. Many of these private services are provided by doctors who are also CCSS employees but are permitted to operate private practices.

Governance of CCSS

In Costa Rica, "autonomous entities" account for a large share of public institutions. These entities were created by the Constitution of 1949 as a way to provide government institutions with political and administrative autonomy from the executive branch. The CCSS was established as a "fully autonomous" organization, the first of these entities in the country.

The Law of the CCSS was issued in 1943 and revised in 1949 during discussions on a new Constitution. Article 73 of the 1949 Constitution clearly states that "administration of social securities will be the responsibility of an autonomous institution called CCSS Costarricense de Seguro Social." In 2000 a reform to the Law of the CCSS reaffirmed the autonomy of the CCSS, such that (in theory at least— see below) the board of directors has enough freedom to take decisions related to governance, coverage, financing, and the organization of health care services.

Although the CCSS is an autonomous institution with technical, administrative, and functional independence, it has important relationships with other entities, particularly the Controller-General of the Republic (Contraloría General de la República), the Ministry of Health, and the Ministry of Finance.[1] The Controller-General, for example, supervises the CCSS with regard to financial, and employment and salary, issues, while the Ministry of Health supervises it in terms of health issues. The supervisory role of the Controller-General is relatively strong, but that of the Ministry of Health is relatively weak. In general, the CCSS has no incentive to follow any recommendation issued by that ministry, so the ministry's power to change any CCSS board decision is limited.

In administrative terms, the CCSS is organized around three levels: central or national, regional, and local. The central level represents the political, normative, controlling, and financial level of the system. At this level, key authorities draw up the National Health Plan; formulate strategies, programs, and plans; and organize the necessary budgets. At the regional level (seven medical regions and five financial regions), the system adopts and implements health programs defined at the central level and manages the budget allocated for those purposes. The regional level coordinates, supervises, and trains local human resources. Finally, the local level consists of hospitals and primary care facilities.

The local clinical structure of the CCSS is organized around three levels of care. Primary care comprises 104 health regions, each one with a basic team of integral care (known by the Spanish acronym, EBAIS). The second level has clinics and regional hospitals, and they specialize in providing curative services to the population. Finally, tertiary care services provide highly complex and specialized services.

Government oversight

In 2000 a reform to the Law of the CCSS reaffirmed the autonomy of the CCSS from the executive branch, except in those areas related to employment and salary policies. Derived from what the General Law for Public Administration states in articles 99 and 100, it is clear that the executive branch cannot set goals and policies for the CCSS. The interrelationship between the two organs is only a "relation of confidence," which is not compatible with direct orders or instructions. According to this law, it is clear that the CCSS has the right to accept or reject requests from the executive. However, it is also clear that on financial matters, policies for employment and salaries must be followed (a practical example of this is the necessary approval of the CCSS budget by the Controller-General).

Other than this relation of confidence, there is no institution that explicitly provides oversight to control the CCSS. However, as seen in the following pages, the Controller-General, the Constitutional Court, and health sector labor unions all limit its autonomy, de facto.

Executive president of the CCSS

Since 1974 autonomous institutions have been managed by "executive presidents," appointed by the president of the republic through the cabinet. Executive presidents are the chief executive officer of the institution, responsible for all internal activities, and act as the president of the board of directors. They are also in charge of coordination with the government and legal representation of the institution. The executive president is appointed for a four-year term that coincides with the term of the president of the republic; no specific academic background or experience in the health sector is required. Government representatives are appointed by the executive, and they cannot be a part of the ministries or be ministry-related delegates. Removal of the executive president is the responsibility of the cabinet.

Article 6 of the Law of the CCSS defines (somewhat vaguely) the conditions necessary to be executive president of the CCSS and (in greater detail) the responsibilities involved. For the former, the executive president should have recognized experience in the field and good knowledge of the CCSS; for the latter, he or she is required to oversee implementation of the board of directors' decisions, as well as ensure coordination within the institution and with other government institutions. Forbidden to work as a freelance professional, the executive president is a full-time employee paid a flat salary of approximately US$4,500 per month, an amount that may be considered low given the responsibilities of the post and the size of the institution. However, despite the low salary, stability has been a major characteristic: from 1974 to 2006, all but one executive president completed their term (González 2006). The one resigned due to the "Finnish loan scandal" (see "Code of Ethics and Anti-corruption" below).

The executive president is a political figure, acting as a chief executive officer with a high degree of decisionmaking independence, except for the financial guidelines that fall mainly under the responsibility of the Ministry of Finance. Also, because the CCSS is part of the health sector, the executive president represents the CCSS in the Health Sector Council, a collegiate body responsible for deciding on health and health service policies. Decisions issued by the Council have limited power and are not binding on the executive president, although they may represent a solid input for discussion and his or her future decisions.

Board of directors

Since 1943 the managerial and governing structure of the CCSS has seen relatively few changes; however, some of these changes had a significant impact on the composition of the board of directors. Although the tripartite structure of the board has remained unaltered since its creation, several government interventions have reformed its composition. Key changes were mainly oriented to modifying the number of representatives per party and the head of the board. Most of the people consulted during the research for this case study agreed that the board's stability strengthens the system, given the significant representation granted to a wide range of social groups. Although not all key stakeholders are members of the board (there is no user representative, for instance), the core of the interested parties have a seat.

The government has full discretion to elect its two additional board members (the third one is the executive president). The process to elect representatives from employers and employees is similar. In the case of employers, the three representatives are nominated in a democratic process administered by the Costa Rican Association of Chambers and Associations of Private Companies (Unión Costarricense de Cámaras y Asociaciones de la Empresa Privada). This will guarantee balanced representation from industry, agriculture, and commerce. By law, the executive power must respect the election and should appoint those elected.

Three members representing employees are elected in a democratic process as well. Three groups—cooperatives, solidarity movements, and labor unions—have the right to nominate a member to the board. In three separate processes, each group organizes a special session in which a list of candidates is presented. The members of the plenary vote on competing candidates and elect the representative.

Responsibilities of the board of directors are established in Article 14 of the Law of the CCSS. In general they are as follows: guiding the CCSS; controlling CCSS operations, as well as authorizing and approving requests from affiliates; approving CCSS investments; complying or appealing legal compensation or settlements; appointing managers and chief auditors of the CCSS; and approving the annual budget before sending it to the Controller-General for final approval.

Internal and external auditing

The auditing function is under the responsibility of the Internal Audit Office of the CCSS (Auditoría Interna de la CCSS). It has functional ties with the Controller-General, and operates according to its own laws and regulations. Since 1999 the Internal Audit Office has focused on six areas of interest, including operations, financial, computing, hospital and clinics, decentralized offices, and medical audits.

Role of other institutions in CCSS decisions

Table 3.1 summarizes the influence of different political and social institutions on CCSS decisionmaking, and depicts the concept of "bounded" autonomy in a clear way. Higher-level political actors, like the national president and Congress, have only a limited impact. The role of the country's president is limited to appointing the executive president and nominating the other two members of the board. For its part, Congress has no influence in any of the areas shown. Neither the executive president nor the board is accountable to Congress.

Internally, the executive president and the board have strong influence in all areas. Providers also play a major role in practically all areas.

Other institutions such as the Controller-General and the Constitutional Court play a role in some key areas like wages, budget, purchasing, and internal

TABLE 3.1   Influence of different parties on CCSS decisions

Decisionmaker	Nomination of board members	Nomination of executive president	Level of financing	Package of services	Regulation	Capital investments
President	++	++	–	–	–	–
Constitutional Court	–	–	+	++	–	–
Congress	–	–	–	–	–	–
Ministry of Health	+	–	–	+	+	–
Ministry of Finance	–	–	+	–	–	+
Controller-General	–	–	+	–	+	+
Board of Directors	+	–	++	++	++	++
Executive President of CCSS	–	–	+	++	++	++
Ombudsman	–	–	–	+	–	+
Providers	+	–	–	+	+	++

Decisionmaker	Price setting	Contracting	Procurement	Quality improvement	User protection	Salaries and directors' fees
President	–	–	–	–	–	–
Constitutional Court	–	–	+	–	++	–
Congress	–	–	–	–	–	–
Ministry of Health	–	–	–	–	+	–
Ministry of Finance	–	–	–	–	–	++
Controller-General	–	–	–	–	–	++
Board of Directors	++	++	++	+	+	+
Executive President of CCSS	++	++	++	++	++	+
Ombudsman	–	–	–	+	++	–
Providers	++	++	++	++	+	++

Source: Prepared by Sanigest International.

Note: CCSS = Costa Rica Social Security System.

++ = strong influence; + = moderate influence; – = no influence.

administrative processes. Resolutions issued by these two institutions have to be implemented by the CCSS.

The Controller-General, for example, as the most powerful supervisory entity of Costa Rica, has extensive power to force changes or to disallow decisions, and it frequently uses this power. For instance, it is entitled to approve or reject the CCSS budget. In addition, it is the final approval body for any investment project (especially if private firms are involved), for drug purchasing, and for acquisition of medical equipment. Finally, it is entitled to recommend changes in the internal processes of the CCSS, in areas such as contracting, purchasing, and planning. Although most of the Controller-General's resolutions may be considered "suggestions," the CCSS ultimately has an incentive to follow them because it generally only receives final approval if it does so.

The other institution that strongly constrains the CCSS is the Constitutional Court, through decisions that force the CCSS to provide particular services or medications (Box 3.1). Despite the absence of an explicit right to health as a human right in the country's Constitution, some articles are closely related to the issue and the CCSS board must adhere to the resolutions of the Constitutional Court. By forcing the CCSS to cover certain services and medications, it is in effect depriving the CCSS of control in defining its coverage. This increases financial risk for the CCSS and makes planning difficult.

Relation to providers

In the mid-1990s, the CCSS board introduced regulatory instruments called management agreements. They define, for instance, the primary health care services to

---

BOX 3.1 *Resolutions of the constitutional court*

Resolution 5024-06. On the supply of a drug for treatment against breast cancer. The petitioner indicated that her doctor, at the Hospital Calderón Guardia, prescribed her a medicine called trastuzumab, which proved to be very effective in treating her breast cancer. Despite the prescription and the importance of the medicine to her, the CCSS did not supply the drug despite the fact that the CCSS itself highly recommends its use. The Constitutional Court accepted the petition and ordered the CCSS and the Hospital Calderón Guardia to immediately supply trastuzumab to the patient. The cost of a 12-week course of treatment with trastuzumab monotherapy is approximately US$9,000.

Resolution 5023-06. No provision of drugs. The petitioner charged the CCSS with not providing him, *in a timely manner,* with the medications against primary biliary cirrhosis. The Constitutional Court accepted the petition and ordered the executive president of the CCSS, the Director of the Hospital San Juan de Dios, and the pharmacy director of the same facility to (a) supply, immediately, the prescribed medication and (b) adopt the necessary urgent measures to purchase enough

Ursodiol 300 mg in order to avoid further drug shortages.

Resolution 5934-97. Provision of antiretroviral therapy. The petitioner, diagnosed with HIV/AIDS, pointed out that the only way of improving his quality of life was to use antiretroviral therapy, a medicine not provided by the CCSS. The benefits were multiple, including a general status of well-being, the possibility of going back to his work and studies, and living longer. The petitioner argued that the antiretroviral was key for restoring his former condition, but the treatment was "catastrophic" for his current economic situation. He also argued that, as a contributor to the CCSS, he had the right to receive the most appropriate drugs, otherwise his right to a healthy life had been eroded. Articles 21, 33, 50, and 73 of the Constitution were used for supporting his argument. The petitioner requested adequate antiretroviral therapy from the CCSS. The Constitutional Court accepted the petition and forced the CCSS to provide him with antiretroviral therapy.

Source: Constitutional Court of Costa Rica.

be supplied by providers throughout the country. One of their weakest points is the absence of explicit sanctions against providers. Providers negotiate and report performance results to the purchasing unit of the CCSS. Even if the providers do not achieve the negotiated "score," the unit cannot apply sanctions, such as a reduced budget or wage penalty. Another structural problem militating against sanctions is the way in which hospital directors are appointed: they are appointed for life, which is a huge check on the managerial prerogatives and decision space of the CCSS central administration.

Health sector unions

Approximately six labor unions have a direct relationship with the CCSS, the most prominent being the Sindicato de Profesionales en Ciencias Médicas (SIPROCIMECA) and the Unión Médica Nacional. Historically, labor unions have had a large influence inside the CCSS. They have a seat on the board, and so are directly involved in decisionmaking. (A clear example of this power is the Law on Medical Incentives No. 6836 of 1982.)

Absenteeism and private practice are two major issues in human resource performance, and indirectly, a measure of the power of the labor unions and doctors in the system. The post-1993 health reforms explicitly made reducing absenteeism one of the core policy objectives. However, despite increased autonomy to manage human resources and the importance of the topic on the reform agenda, absenteeism seems not to have declined (Garcia-Prado and Chawla 2006).

Private practice is very common and current regulations permit it, yet this public-private mixture is a channel for corrupt practices. It is relatively common for doctors to charge an informal copayment to patients for "jumping" the waiting list of the CCSS and receiving medical care in public facilities (especially for highly complex treatment). These so-called *biombos* have been uncovered and condemned by the media and political actors, but only partial solutions have been applied.

Code of ethics and anti-corruption

In 1999 the CCSS board of directors approved a code of ethics for CCSS personnel at all levels, with the aim of establishing norms of conduct. However, the code has failed to prevent some major scandals in the areas of, for example, purchase of medical services at inflated prices, procurement of medicines and equipment, provision of private training courses and medical research, construction of hospitals, and management of the CCSS pensions system (Transparency International 2005).

A major corruption case—known as the Finnish loan scandal—hit the CCSS in 2004 when its executive president, together with a former president of the country, directors, and staff of one of the leading pharmacies, were charged by the General Prosecutor. The formal accusation described a situation in which the CCSS was granted a US$39 million loan from the Government of Finland for modernizing hospitals. However, preliminary investigations point to the possibility that at least US$8.8 million was used for bribes and other illegal payments.

System performance

The CCSS performs well in three areas that are the main objectives of the MHI system: coverage, financial protection, and access/equity. Those areas are strongly supported by a solid legal framework, and the institution has a long tradition of policy implementation in those areas. However, in the areas directly managed by the central level, such as contributory coverage and administrative efficiency, performance is weak (or at least the indicators show some deterioration over time). Finally, in those areas where providers play the main role and the central level monitors/controls the performance of providers, the results are mixed (good in productivity, poor in quality and cost control). This may suggests that major gains had more to do with reorganizing providers and expanding primary care than with changes in the way in which the CCSS behaved as an insurer, despite the institutional changes introduced in the CCSS in the post-1993 reforms (e.g. the creation of a purchasing unit).

Coverage

Over 10 years, the population covered by primary health care services increased very fast (Figure 3.2). Before 1995, the traditional primary health care model[2] was eroded and the share of the total population with physical access to a primary health care facility (one less than 30 minutes away) fell from 46 percent of the

FIGURE 3.2   Population covered by the primary health care program, 1990–2003

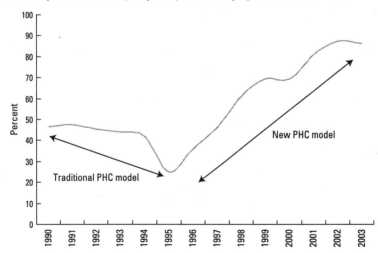

Source: Costa Rica Social Security System.

Note: PHC = Primary Health Care.

population (1990) to only 25 percent (1995). The new model that accompanied the health reforms implemented from 1994 strengthened the role of primary care by establishing basic teams of integral care (EBAIS) throughout the country. In terms of population covered by these teams, the rate jumped from 36 percent in 1996 to 69 percent in 2000, and to 86 percent in 2003.

Financial protection

Evidence from national surveys suggests that the system is financially protecting the population, especially poorer groups. The household income and expenditure survey (INEC 2006) estimated that households allocate 2.6 percent of their income to health spending, or 4.1 percent of current, noncapital spending. Most of the households' health expenditures go to specialist/hospital services and drugs, and such expenses affect urban households (5.1 percent of their income) more than rural families (3.6 percent).

Between 1988 and 2004, health expenditures increased more rapidly than total spending. However, the burden of out-of-pocket health spending primarily affected wealthier households, and that for the poorest quintile of the population actually fell—from 2.1 percent of income in 1988 to 1.8 percent in 2004, when the corresponding share for the wealthiest quintile was 6.6 percent, or 3.7 times as high as for the poor.

The system also protects most age-vulnerable groups (children under 15 and adults above 50) as evidenced by the higher rates of health service use in those two groups. For ambulatory and hospitalization services, there is a greater incidence of service use by the retired population. Rural areas, generally poorer than urban regions, also benefit more in terms of health service use.

Access and equity

Access to health services was studied using information on constraints to access. According to the health module of the 2001 household survey, 9.5 percent of those interviewed said that they had not received medical care because there were no appointment slots available. This implied that for 2001, close to 17,000 people did not receive any care due to limited system capacity; that is, it was a supply-side problem.

From the demand side, one of the key barriers to accessing health care services was lack of money. Almost 10 percent of the respondents not having access to health services said that money problems were the main barrier to access. This is particularly important in rural areas, where the costs associated with paying a visit to a health facility in the capital (hotel, transportation, and food) place a heavy burden on family spending.

Economic constraints affect rural and poorer areas more than urban regions. In the three regions with the highest poverty incidence rates, financial restrictions affect more than 15 percent of those without adequate access to care, while in those regions where poverty is lower, economic factors account for less than 5 percent of those with problems of access.

Finally, public health spending is the most progressive of all the social sectors in Costa Rica, with the poorest families receiving a larger share of resources that their share of the population.

Efficiency and cost control

Administrative costs have averaged 3.6 percent of total expenditures in the CCSS since 1990. In any given year, administrative outlays have not exceeded 4 percent of total costs, suggesting that the Costa Rican system performs relatively well compared to other mature MHI systems, which reportedly have average administrative costs of 4.2 percent of total expenses, ranging from 2 percent in Japan to 6.6 percent in Switzerland (WHO 2004).

Clinical efficiency, as indicated by utilization and productivity rates, is relatively good. For instance, the average length of stay has declined by 12 percent since the early 1990s, while the bed turnover rate has increased by 30 percent and the occupancy rate by 5.5 percent.

The positive results in average length of stay (Figure 3.3) were driven mainly by the decline observed in surgery. A more strategic role of ambulatory surgeries was the main factor in this. Consequently, average length of stay in Costa Rica is low compared, for example, to countries of the European Union (EU), where the average length of stay was 8.5 days in 2004.

FIGURE 3.3   Average length of stay in the hospital, 1990–2004

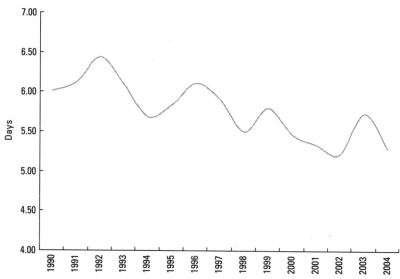

Source: Costa Rica Social Security System.

In contrast to administrative costs and clinical efficiency, productivity has declined and unit costs have therefore increased. Measuring productivity by the number of external consultations per hour of medical work demonstrates this, with a steady decline from 1990 (3.55 consultations per hour) to 2004 (3.30 consultations per hour). During the early years of this century, productivity was 5 percent lower than in the 1990s (see Figure 3.4).

Unit costs have worsened more sharply. Costs per consultation and per discharge have both increased in real terms over the last 15 years, by 10 percent and 39 percent, respectively. The significant increment observed in the cost per discharge may have several explanations. First, an input-based budgetary system is used, in which funds allocated to the hospital system increase according to inflation and resources, not according to outcomes. Second, the level of discharges tended to decline over time. Between 2000 and 2004, hospital discharges per 100 habitants fell by 4 percent. The case-mix structure of the system also changed and moved toward more costly activities. Surgeries, for example, which represented 25 percent of hospital discharges in 2000, now represent 33 percent. Chronic patients, formerly with an average length of stay of 52 days, now stay for 70 days on average. Other cost drivers, such as laboratory examinations and drug prescriptions per discharge, have also risen over the years.

Quality of care and patient satisfaction

Quality of care can be analyzed in three main areas: on the one hand, higher mortality rates and deteriorating conditions of patients operated on; and on the

FIGURE 3.4 External consultations per hour, 1990–2004

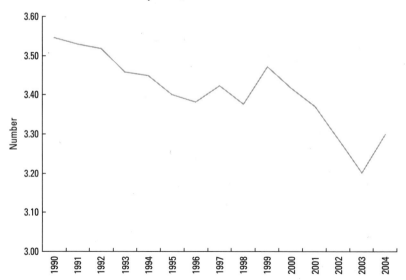

Source: Costa Rica Social Security System.

other, increasing prenatal consultations. Both hospital and postoperative mortality rates increased, the latter significantly so, to 2.3 times the level of 1990. But two indicators showed significant progress: the number of prenatal consultations per birth and the rate of first-time consultations. The former indicator increased by 2.4 times relative to 1990, and the latter by 10 percent.

Effect of governance on performance

The link between governance and performance has not been explored in Costa Rica in the literature before. The conclusions presented here are, therefore, the result of questions asked of key staff of the CCSS and others.

Does the current governance model contribute to the achievement of the objectives of the CCSS?

In general, the current legal framework governing the CCSS is broad and solid, and provides enough tools to achieve the core objectives of the institution—coverage, financial protection, and (to a lesser extent) efficiency. Additionally, the composition of the board of directors allows for representation of the three contributory groups (workers, employers, and government) while consumers are weakly represented. Yet even though board members are elected through a democratic process and act as a collegiate group, there is a potential risk of a particular group favoring its own membership.

The existing structure of the MHI and the definition of financial protection as an explicit objective of the board have yielded positive benefits. Some recent decisions, like the establishment of a new financial management system—the Centralized System of Collection (Sistema Centralizado de Recaudación or SICERE)—have sought to improve revenue collection and identification of people without insurance coverage.

There are, however, some problems that impede full realization of system goals. The model seems to provide excessive power to labor unions, which take advantage of this to increase their privileges. Medical unions have very distinct advantages relative to other public sector employees. Also at present, the model does not provide sufficient incentives for improving productivity or quality of health care services, since providers can ignore them without penalty. Additionally, many consider the medical unions to be at fault for blocking initiatives to change the current payment system, to apply new policies for reducing absenteeism, and to implement medical audits.

The existing payment mechanism in hospitals allocates funds according to what happened in the past, and not by performance. Despite repeated recommendations to shift to payment-for-performance systems, this has not yet been done. Salaries rise without any link to efficiency or quality, and sometimes faster than inflation and other public sector wages. It would seem that pressure from labor unions is a factor obstructing implementation of any performance-based payment system.

Conflict of interest, only weakly considered in the existing regulations, may also be a problem. A former Congressional commission that investigated irregularities in the CCSS detected years ago that some members of the board and the executive president belonged to private firms in the field of health care. This situation affects CCSS costs when the board member or executive president promotes the purchase of medical appliances, drugs, and services from their favored firms, which can then charge higher prices. It also affects the provision of services when a board member or executive president blocks important decisions. For example, if the CCSS proposed to purchase medical equipment that would compete with existing private services, a board member with a conflict of interest might influence the board in rejecting the proposal.

In summary, the evidence shows that the system has a good regulatory basis for achieving the core objectives. However, the gap between expected and actual outcomes suggests that the CCSS experiences some organizational problems that become a barrier to achieving its objectives. For some problems, like decreasing contributory coverage and weak conflict of interest regulations, the existing governance structure seems to be inadequate because the board itself is the governing body in charge of reforming or implementing appropriate decisions. Similar situations can be observed regarding the implementation of new payment incentives and in salary structures, given the representation that medical doctors have on the board.

Are the existing regulations and supervisory functions encouraging insurers to identify and affiliate new members?

Several interviewees argued that the system has adequate legislation for promoting contributory coverage. Thus the problem is not the absence of regulations or incentives for being insured, given the significant gap between the cost of private services and the average premium paid by a worker. There are other factors (internal and external to the institution) affecting contributory coverage. Some interviewees felt that one of those factors was seen in guidelines from the Ministry of Finance to limit the number of affiliated persons to publicly subsidized programs (in order to control the deficit). This condition has the limitation that, even if poor households are not affiliated to public programs, they will still be treated if they show up at a facility, obviously at a cost to the system. Given that in those cases the CCSS bears the costs, waiting lists act a cost-containment mechanism for the CCSS.

In short, contributory coverage is not a problem of absence of legal tools. From the point of view of the CCSS, it seems that administrative barriers, a relative healthy financial situation (despite high levels of evasion), possible conflicts of interest, and weak evasion-control policies are some of the reasons working against an increase in contributory coverage. From the point of view of users, they have a weak incentive to affiliate (as voluntary insured) given the long waiting lists.

Does the current model between insurers and health care providers improve cost control and quality of services?

The management agreement tool, introduced a decade ago, was a step toward improved quality, coverage, and efficiency in health care services. In its original idea, the tool was an attempt to link payments to coverage and quality outcomes. Parallel to this measure, the board adopted others to control costs and enhance quality: centralizing drug procurement, drawing up a list of basic medicines, and establishing Services Controller Offices. Yet despite these efforts, costs per discharge and per consultation have increased.

Several explanations for the cost increases were offered by interviewees.

- First, the pressure exercised by doctors and nurses over wages was higher than any gains from reduced average length of stay and other efficiency-oriented measures. In a similar way, unexpected resolutions of the Constitutional Court affected drug spending and raised total system costs. These two situations reflect undermined board power.

- Second, there is a general idea that management agreements have not been used as part of a broader purchasing plan for improving health services but instead as a means to co-administer services. This is the result of an unclear distinction between the insurance and the delivery functions of the CCSS and the level of autonomy of the providers. It is difficult for decisionmaking to be efficient given the mix of interests between these two areas.

- Third, health services managers (hospital directors, for instance) are not fully accountable to the board because they are appointed for life. Thus, managers have no incentive to pursue cost-control measures as the board aims to do. This situation is evidenced by increasing rates of drugs used and laboratory examinations per patient.

- Fourth, lack of clinical protocols weakens the scope of management agreements because this creates a gap between the central level and providers. Current norms to improve quality of care and to reduce queues and waiting lists run counter to current regulations for setting appointments and referring patients. Users are still not the center of attention in the health system.

- Fifth, the absence of cost-effectiveness analysis for generic drugs limits the capacity of the CCSS board to produce better drug procurement plans or to negotiate better prices with drug providers.

- Sixth, financial relationships between providers and the central level of the CCSS are largely governed by ad hoc mechanisms instead of by formal decisionmaking processes.

Lessons for low-income countries

The case of Costa Rica shows that the construction of a solid MHI is a process that requires time, political support, and technical skills. Since the very beginning of the scheme, the system faced several challenges but adopting correct, timely decisions was fundamental to consolidating the system. The success of a system providing universal coverage with a clear focus on primary health care is supported by the outcomes: Costa Rica has among the best health indicators of all middle-income countries and better than many higher-income countries. At the same time, supporting factors like strong institutions, a democratic policymaking framework, and strong human capital have no doubt played a key role in the MHI success in Costa Rica.

Given the wide range of situations facing other countries, it seems difficult to ensure that adopting Costa Rica's practices will yield similar outcomes. For that reason, the following paragraphs extract lessons of the case study that may be useful for low-income nations, with the caveat that current conditions may significantly differ from those in Costa Rica in the 1940s.

The first challenge was the implementation of the MHI system itself, as described earlier. Despite fierce opposition to the original project, political negotiation and the attraction of key partners were relevant for the approval of the project. The country's president of the time focused on potential benefits to the whole population, including workers and employers, despite the relative costs that each party had to bear. *The first lesson of the Costa Rican experience is having a concrete, convincing country-vision of the need for an MHI system; political support for its implementation; and the courage to make the necessary compromises to implement the adopted program, despite political considerations.*

The case also shows that *inadequate controlling and accountability mechanisms combined with a high level of institutional autonomy can harm the system, its efficiency, and the capability of generating positive outcomes.* A strong institutional basis is required. Despite the existence of supervisory institutions, the recent scandals show that the absence of specific mechanisms of control and weak regulations regarding conflict of interest may create incentives to behave against institutional objectives.

Political involvement is not always bad. The executive president of the CCSS is appointed by the president of the republic for a four-year term. This is controversial. On the one hand, it threatens autonomy; on the other, it allows for improved coordination between the various health sector institutions. Perhaps the key factor in understanding the relative success of the model is the suitability of these appointments: practically all the executive presidents of the CCSS have been medical doctors with long experience in the health sector working for the institution. This situation sharply contrasts with the situation of other autonomous institutions where the executive president is not necessarily someone who knows the entity or has a background in the field.

Another lesson makes reference to the size of the institution: *big institutions are difficult to manage.* As a monopoly, the CCSS is the second largest institution in Costa Rica (after the Ministry of Health) with around 35,000 employees. This monolithic nature, where the roles of planner, purchaser, and provider are integrated into one entity, makes it difficult for both the board and the executive president to have control over every single area or department.

The model also shows *how difficult good governance is under an inflexible human resource system without adequate incentives for improving efficiency and quality.* One of the key bottlenecks prior to the reforms of the last decade or so related to poorly trained human resources, the absence of performance-based payment systems, and the inflexibility of the system with regard to contracting or sacking workers. Although the reform agenda proposed several changes to the existing human resource system, opposition from medical unions made their implementation impossible. The current system does, indeed, provide stability to workers (it avoids frequent changes in medical staff arising from changes in government), but it also generates pervasive motivation for acting against the main objectives of the CCSS.

Annex 3.1 Dimensions, features, and indicators of good governance in mandatory health insurance: Costa Rica

Dimension	Features	Indicators	Value	Explanation
Coherent decisionmaking structures	1. Responsibility for MHI objectives must correspond with decisionmaking power and capacity in each institution involved in the management of the system.	Yes/No Examples: Provisions for costs and resources of MHI regulators and MHI entities are made in legal texts. Responsibility, such as coverage for a prescribed benefits package by MHI entities, has to go hand in hand with the decisionmaking power on premium levels and/or provision of care. Regular reviews of the cost of coverage, appropriateness of premium levels, and methods of provision are established in legal texts or by the regulator. Review committees with wide stakeholder participation on coverage, premium levels, etc., are in place.	+	Constitutionally, the CCSS is an administrative autonomous institution, and most recent legislation confirms that, among all public entities, the CCSS may be is the most autonomous of all. The board of directors and the executive president have enough power to establish new regulatory conditions without the approval of external entities. Among other things, the board is entitled to: (a) manage the MHI system; (b) make investment plans; (c) establish internal and external regulations; and (d) approve the institutional budget. According to various professionals in this field, the CCSS board has such power that its regulations have the same effect as an act approved by Congress. In other words, the board is not tied by most of the regulations that affect other autonomous institutions. However, there is one major constraint on full autonomy: the executive president is designated by the country's president.

2. All MHI entities have routine risk assessment and management strategies in place.	Yes/No Examples: Clear regulations on MHI entities' continuous risk assessment and risk management are in place. Strategies are in place, i.e. MHI entities follow and analyze the evolution of expenditures and contributions. MHI entities have the capacity to manage risks, i.e. to take corrective action in order to ensure the financial sustainability of the system by modifying some of the parameters influencing it (contribution rate, composition of the benefits package, etc.).	+	Existing regulations grant full autonomy to the CCSS to administer the system. The CCSS is, thus, entitled to alter contribution rates, partially limit wage increments, manage reserves, and redefine the package of benefits and essential drugs. Despite this, the CCSS does not have a permanent program for analyzing and managing risk, although it closely tracks the evolution of revenues and expenditures. The institution has a special department of Actuarial Studies and Economic Planning, but risk assessment is more the exception than the rule.
3. The cost of regulating and administering MHI institutions is reasonable and appropriate.	Yes/No Examples: Maximum administration costs for MHI entities are set in legal texts or regulations. Administrative costs are monitored by the regulator. Provisions for covering the costs of the MHI regulator are stipulated in legal texts. Before new regulations are put in place, a cost-benefit assessment is conducted.	+	The existing legal framework defines in Article 16 (h) that the board of directors has responsibility for defining maximum administrative costs. Such costs are tracked by the Controller-General of the Republic through the internal auditor, who reports to the board if the limit is exceeded. The internal auditor is an employee who, in essence, works for the Controller-General, but he or she is paid by the CCSS. There is no evidence that cost-benefit analyses are carried out to evaluate the impact of new regulations.

(continues)

Dimension	Features	Indicators	Value	Explanation
Stakeholder participation	4. Stakeholders have effective representation in the governing bodies of MHI entities.	Yes/No Examples: Governing bodies of regulatory oversight and institutional governance (board of directors, oversight body) have representatives of government agencies, regulatory bodies, MHI entities, unions, employers' organizations, beneficiaries, providers, and independent experts. Representation is effective, i.e. different stakeholders' views are considered in decisionmaking.	++	The board of directors is a tripartite body with representatives from employees, employers, and government. Each group represents several parties, for example when medical doctors are representatives of workers. The range of key stakeholders is, therefore, relatively wide and diverse. Some experts feel that, despite the balance of power on the board, final users were always underrepresented, and were one of the major weaknesses of the model. The creation of community boards was an attempt to approach users to the decisionmaking process by incorporating citizens to the discussion of local health problems and by opening a channel to help providers implement better clinical and administrative processes.
Transparency and information	5. The objectives of MHI are formally and clearly defined.	Yes/No Examples: Objectives are stated in a high-level legal text (e.g. the Constitution or a law). Objectives are publicized and easily accessible to the public. Objectives are clearly defined and easily understandable. Objectives have remained substantially the same in the recent past.	++	Article 73 of the Constitution defines the CCSS as the institution in charge of administering the health insurance system. In addition, the Constitutive Law (Ley Constitutiva) of the CCSS, No. 17 (and subsequent amendments) and Law No. 7983 (of 2000) establishes the scope, objectives, structure, responsibilities, sanctions, methods of conflict resolution, and other issues regarding the organization and dynamics of the CCSS. The objectives of the health insurance system have remained unaltered since its creation in 1941, and the Constitutive Law has stayed largely the same since its promulgation in 1943. Changes have been made, but on average only once every 10 years. The Constitutive Law can be accessed at http://www.ccss.sa.cr/reglamentos/leycons0.htm. This link also includes amendments approved by Congress since 1943.

| 6. MHI relies upon an explicit and an appropriately designed institutional and legal framework. | ++ | Yes/No

Examples:

The main characteristics of the system are defined in legal texts (coverage, benefits package, financing, provision, regulatory oversight, and institutional governance).

The framework is appropriate given the country MHI context (i.e. it is not too restrictive, considers special local circumstances, and does not ignore important parts or players in the system).

The regulatory agency is independent or not.

The status and responsibilities of each MHI institution in the system are clearly defined and transparent. | Based on the Constitutive Law, the country has developed a wide range of legal texts, codes, and related regulatory papers. The main elements of the system are covered in a body of 10 *laws*, 7 regulations (*reglamentos*), and 2 codes, including one code of conduct for CCSS employees. The legal framework includes:

• The Code of Labor

• The Constitutive Law of 1943 and amendments

• The Act of Internal Control

• The Act on CCSS Hospital and Clinics Decentralization

• The Health Insurance Regulation, which covers financing, benefits packages, provisions, beneficiaries, and related issues on the organization of the system

• The Code of Ethics of CCSS employees

The general perception is that the MHI model works and has worked during the last 65 years. The existing model is the result of several decades of adaptation to new social and economic conditions, the result of a solid institutional framework that has wide acceptance among the population. The CCSS is the public institution with the highest level of approval among Costa Ricans. As it is now, the model presents several advantages: key actors are represented and directly involved in the system; no one is excluded from receiving health care services, even migrants; the package of benefits is generous (with just a few exceptions); and the whole population is covered by basic health services (though this does not mean that the system is problem free). |

(continues)

Dimension	Features	Indicators	Value	Explanation
				The different regulatory agencies (Controller-General, ministries of Health and Finance) are partially independent but their functions are well defined by the Constitution (as in the case of the Controller-General), the Constitutive Law of the Ministry of Health, and that ministry's different regulations. Partial independence means that the entities are independent in their functions, but all of them (except the Controller-General) are appointed by the president of Costa Rica, including the executive president of the CCSS. The Controller-General is appointed by Congress. One remarkable feature is that all the regulatory institutions are solid entities with at least 50 years of existence.
	7. Clear information, disclosure, and transparency rules are in place.	Yes/No Examples: Explicit disclosure regulations exist in the law or regulations of the law. Business activities, ownership, and financial positions are regularly disclosed (i.e. the rules are followed). MHI entities deliver to a beneficiary on demand a copy of its rules and the latest annual financial statements.	++	The legal framework establishes that the information of government institutions is "public" and must be available to the population. Some exceptions apply in those cases where reasons of national security prevail (the Constitutional Court has ruled on that issue). In the CCSS, examples of timely and appropriate disclosure of information can be found in its Web page, which has audited financial reports and minutes of board sessions (see Article 54 of the Constitutive Law). The CCSS has to report regular activities to the Ministry of Finance and the Controller-General. Annual reports with information on financial performance, investments, new projects, clinical indicators, and similar data are published and are available to the population in paper or electronic format. Audited financial statements are available online.

8. MHI entities have minimum requirements in regard to protecting the insured.	Yes/No Examples: Consumer protection regulations exist in law, including consumer information, and independent mechanisms for resolution of complaints, appeals, grievances, and disputes. The insured can obtain timely, complete, and relevant information on changes in benefits, premiums, length of coverage, etc. Consumer complaint mechanisms exist and are being used. Appeals and grievance mechanisms exist and are being used. Independent dispute resolution mechanisms exist and are being used.	++	Articles 54 to 56 of the Constitutive Law define conflict resolution mechanisms, and offer guidelines on information availability and the mechanisms for resolution of disputes, complaints, grievances, and appeals. Any complaint must be solved within 20 days of the start of the process. The CCSS has a special site (http://www.ccss.sa.cr/tramit01.html) where people can submit complaints using a template. Additionally, all hospitals must have a Service Comptroller's Office to evaluate users' complaints. Recently, several users have started using the Ombudsman's office or the Constitutional Court for their complaints instead of the institutional channels created by the CCSS, an indication that people do not fully trust the insurer to solve their problems.
9. Rules on compliance, enforcement and sanctions for MHI supervision are clearly defined.	Yes/No Examples: A comprehensive law and regulations for the MHI system exist. Rules on compliance and sanctions are defined in legal texts. Corrective actions are imposed, based on clear and objective criteria that are publicly disclosed. Adequate capacity for the execution of these functions is provided. Cases of rule violation and subsequent actions by the regulator are publicized.		Broadly speaking, the CCSS is regulated but not always supervised as expected, at least not by every entity entitled to do this. Despite the existence of clear indications that the Ministry of Health is the institution in charge of supervising CCSS activities, in practice supervision is weak or nonexistent. The CCSS is one of the few institutions exempted from the financial regulations established by the Ministry of Finance. Only in terms of employment is the institution forced to follow Ministry of Finance regulations. Any other type of regulation, either issued by the Ministry of Finance or by the executive power, do not apply to the CCSS. The CCSS presents its financial statements only to the Ministry of Finance. The CCSS has complete autonomy, established by its Constitutive Law and the Law on Workers' Protection, to manage its funds and reserves as required.

(continues)

Dimension	Features	Value	Indicators	Explanation
				Congress exercises "political supervision" but this does not involve any formal control over CCSS activities. Links between Congress and the CCSS are not formally defined and appear only in case of force majeure. On similar lines, the Ombudsman frequently monitors clinical and administrative activities of the CCSS (based on complaints lodged by people); however, the CCSS is not obliged to follow any recommendation from the Ombudsman.
				The Controller-General has the strongest supervisory power over the CCSS. It is entitled to approve or reject the budget of the CCSS and exerts significant power in the approval of investment projects. No project of the CCSS can begin without the formal approval of the Controller-General.
				Sections II and VI of the Constitutive Law refer to sanctions and conflict resolution mechanisms. Section II gives the reasons for removing a member of the board while Section VI establishes sanctions to those physical or legal bodies that do not comply with the legal framework. Other documents, like the Law on Internal Control, apply to all public agencies, including the CCSS. Despite the existence of explicit references to "invalid behavior," existing legislation suffers major weaknesses such as:
				(1) Some of the described situations are simply obsolete or not clearly specified. For instance, if a member of the board is legally accused but not formally convicted, should that person be removed from the post?
				(2) No clear and objective sanctions are defined. For example, although the legislation defines situations to remove a director, there are no sanctions or penalties associated with the original act, except removal itself.

Supervision and regulation	10. Financial management rules for MHI entities are clearly defined and enforced.	Yes/No Examples: Financial standards for MHI entities are defined in legal texts or regulations. Clear financial licensure/market-entry rules are defined (minimum capital requirements). Ongoing reserve and solvency requirements are defined. Regulations of assets and financial investments are defined.	(3) Most of the supervisory regulations apply in ex post situations, and do not work to prevent a problem. (4) In some cases where sanctions are clearly defined, the penalty is inadequate. For instance, for evaders, fines represent around US$350, irrespective of the size of the debt. (5) Even if the sanction is correctly specified, administrative problems and processes tend to complicate the work of the institutions. For example in the CCSS, the number of supervisors is quite small for monitoring more than 6,000 firms. The judicial process may take more than two years to shut down a company. (6) Publicized scandals are mostly the result of mass media investigations and not the outcome of institutionalized mechanisms to prevent and detect corruption. The Constitutive Law devotes several sections to defining guidelines on revenues (Section III), investments (Section V), and general financial rules (Section VIII); definition of entry rules is not necessary due to the monopolistic market structure in Costa Rica. Management of reserves is one of the board's responsibilities. However, only broad guidelines are given in legal texts for reserves and investments. The Constitutive Law simply mentions, for instance, that CCSS reserves (including pension reserves) must be invested in secure and profitable investments. The CCSS is not bound by externally defined financial limits, unlike all other autonomous institutions. Since 2000 the CCSS has been excluded from Ministry of Finance budgetary limits, with the result that all financial administration of the institution depends on decisions

(continues)

Dimension	Features	Indicators	Value	Explanation
		Audit (internal and external) rules are defined.		made by the board and the executive president. Financial management must follow the guidelines of the Controller-General, which frequently monitors the evolution of expenditures and their nature.
		Rules for financial standards are enforced.		Internal audits are part of the daily tasks of the Internal Auditing Department that every public institution must have. Although paid by the CCSS, the internal auditor is regarded as an employee of the Controller-General and the scope of his or her work is defined by the Controller-General's guidelines. External audits, especially financial audits, are requested at least once a year and their results are published on the Web. The CCSS has not implemented a program of medical audits to track quality of clinical services.
	11. The MHI system has structures for ongoing supervision and monitoring in place.	Yes/No Examples: Clear nonfinancial licensure/market entry rules are defined.	+	Due to its monopolistic condition of the CCSS, legislation has not defined rules regarding entry/exit conditions, product registration, or similar issues.
		Insurance product filing/registration is defined and regulated. Adequate on-site inspections and off-site monitoring are in place.		The CCSS has created specific departments for on-site and off-site inspections, such as the Procurement Department and the Medical Management Department. Additionally, the Law on Internal Control No. 8292 aims to standardize control practices and reporting of public funds management.
		Ongoing financial reporting rules are defined and provided information is accurate and timely. Clear market exit/dissolution rules are in place.		However, the capacity to inspect related activities effectively is often constrained by limited resources, by the weak scope of responsibilities defined by Law, and by the low priority that the CCSS accords to inspections. Financial information is provided to the public via Web sites, but both financial and clinical data are generally one year behind.

Consistency and stability	12. The main qualities of the MHI system are stable.	Yes/No	++	The Constitutive Law of the CCSS has been largely the same since its promulgation in 1943. Most of the main components of the MHI remain unaltered or changed only after several years of implementation. For instance, regulations on population coverage change, on average, every 10 years. The benefits package remains practically unaltered and most of the changes occur when the Constitutional Court forces the CCSS to include any special treatment as part of the package (AIDS antiretrovirals, for instance). The core legislation of the basic list of drugs dates from 1989 and is an example of the stability of the system.
		Examples:		
		Fundamental characteristics of the MHI system (e.g. benefits package, rules for affiliation, contribution requirements, basic protection rights for the insured, and basic institutional requirements for operators) are defined in law.		Stability is also evident at the management level. Since 1974 only two executive presidents did not complete their term, one because of death and the other due to a corruption scandal.
		The law has remained substantially the same in the recent past (i.e. independent of political elections or economic crises).		

++ = relevant to Costa Rica; + = relevant to Costa Rica to some extent; – = not relevant to Costa Rica.

Endnotes

1. For this book we have been selective, including only those features of the organizational structure that are most important to the discussion on important governance mechanisms.

2. Reforms during the 1990s resulted in a new model of care consisting of a comprehensive network of local health teams to provide primary care and act as gatekeepers for access to the health system.

Reference list and bibliography

Arias Valverde, Oscar. 2004. "La estructuración jurídica progresiva de la Seguridad Social en Costa Rica." In Guido Miranda Gutiérrez and Carlos Zamora Zamora, eds., *La Construcción de la Seguridad Social*. San José: Universidad Estatal a Distancia.

Asamblea Legislativa de Costa Rica. 2002. "Derechos y deberes de las personas usuarias de los servicios de salud públicos y privados." Law No. 8239, published in *La Gaceta* No. 75.

Asamblea Legislativa de Costa Rica: Comisión Permanente de Asuntos Sociales. 2004. "Ley para que los asegurados de la CCSS Costarricense de Seguro Social puedan escoger donde reciben el servicio." Dictamen afirmativo de Minoría. Expediente No. 17.713. December.

Asamblea Legislativa de Costa Rica: Informe de Mayoría. 2001. "Comisión Especial que proceda a: Analizar la calidad de servicios, compra de servicios privados, utilización de recursos de la CCSS para la enseñanza universitaria privada, medicamentos y pensiones." Expediente No. 13.980. April.

Asamblea Legislativa de Costa Rica. 1974. "Modificación a la integración de las juntas directivas y gerencias de instituciones autónomas." Law No. 5507, published in *La Gaceta* No. 87, 10 May.

———. 1998. "Ley de Desconcentración de los hospitales y las clínicas de la CCSS Costarricense de Seguro Social." Law No. 7852 of 30 November, published in *La Gaceta* No. 250, 24 December.

Avalos, Ángela. 2006. "Enfermos del corazón mueren esperando una cirugía." *La Nación*. 2 February.

CCSS (Caja Costarricense de Seguro Social). 1943. "Ley Constitutiva."

———. 1999. "Código de Ética."

———. 1997. "Reglamento del Seguro de Salud."

———. 2004. "El Sistema Nacional de Salud en Costa Rica: Generalidades." San José: Curso de Gestión Local de Salud para Técnicos del Primer Nivel de Atención. Primera Unidad Modular.

———. 2005. Gerencia División Administrativa, Dirección de Compra de Servicios de Salud. "Compromiso de Gestión Áreas de Salud 1 y 2" (desconcentradas).

———. 2005. Gerencia División Administrativa, Dirección de Compra de Servicios de Salud. "Compromiso de Gestión Hospital Calderón Guardia" (desconcentrado).

Comisión Investigadora de la CCSS. 2004. *Informe de Mayoría*. August.

———. 2004. *Informe de Minoría*. September.

"Ley General de la Administración Pública." 2006. 10th edition. San José: Editec Editores.

"Ley orgánica de la Contraloría General de la República." Internet revision, 1 May 2006. http://zebra.cgr.go.cr/ifs/files/public/documentos/normativa/leyorgan/ley_organica_cgr _2004.doc.

Esquivel, Máx, and Juany Guzmán. 1999. *El Trato Ciudadano en Costa Rica: Apuntes sobre la vivencia cotidiana de la Democracia.* UNDP (United Nations Development Programme)- Estado de la Nación. October.

Estado de la Nacion. 2005. *XI Informe del Estado de la Nacion.* San José: Litografía e Imprenta Guilá.

Fallas Santana, Carmen. 2004. *Élite, negocios y política en Costa Rica: 1849–1859.* 1st edition. Museo Histórico Cultural Juan Santamaría.

Garcia-Prado, Ariadna, and Mukesh Chawla. 2006. "The Impact of Hospital Management Reforms on Absenteeism in Costa Rica." *Health Policy and Planning* 21(1):91–100.

González, E. 2005. "Case study: Grand Corruption in Costa Rica." In Transparency International, *Global Corruption Report 2006.*

ILO (International Labour Organization), http://www.oit.or.cr/estad/td/si.php.

INEC (Instituto Nacional de Estadística y Censos). 2006. *Encuesta Nacional de Ingresos y Gastos de los Hogares 2004: Principales Resultados.* San José.

Lehoucq, F. 1997. *Lucha electoral y sistema político en Costa Rica 1948–1998.* San José: Editorial Porvenir.

Martínez, Juliana, and Carmelo Mesa-Lago. 2003. *Las Reformas Inconclusas: Pensiones y Salud en Costa Rica: Avances–Problemas–Recomendaciones.* San José: Fundación Friedrich Ebert.

Quirós Coronado, Roberto. 1990. *Autonomía, Gobierno y Tripartismo en la Seguridad Social.* 2nd edition. EDNASS-CCSS.

Ramirez, Olman. 2004. Arreglos de Convivencia de la Población Adulta Mayor. In Luis Rosero-Bixby, ed., *Costa Rica a la luz del censo del 2000.* San José: Centro Centroamericano de Población de la Universidad de Costa Rica.

Raventós, Ciska. 2005. "Más allá del escándalo: Bases políticas e institucionales de la corrupción en Costa Rica." In *Revista Centroamericana de Ciencias Sociales* 11(3). July.

Ron, A., B. Abel-Smith, and G. Tamburi. 1990. *Health Insurance in Developing Countries: The Social Security Approach.* Geneva: International Labour Organization.

Rosero-Bixby, Luis. 2004. "Acceso y disponibilidad de servicios de salud en Costa Rica 2000." In Luis Rosero-Bixby, ed., *Costa Rica a la luz del censo del 2000.* San José: Centro Centroamericano de Población de la Universidad de Costa Rica.

Transparency International. 2005. *Global Corruption Report 2006,* http://www.transparency. org/publications/gcr/download_gcr/download_gcr_2006/.

WHO (World Health Organization). 2004. "Reaching Universal Coverage via Social Health Insurance: Key Design Features in the Transition Period." Discussion Paper No. 2. Geneva.

Interviewees

Lic. Oscar Arias, former Secretary of the Board of the CCSS, 1973–1981. San José, February 2006.

Dr. Alvaro Salas, former Executive President of the CCSS, 1994–1998. San José, February 2006.

Lic. Guillermo López, Vice-Director of Actuarial Studies and Economic Planning of the Health Insurance. San José, February 2006.

Ing. René Escalante, Manager of the Administrative Division. San José, February 2006.

A legal expert in the field of health care organizations in the public sector. San José, March 2006.

4

Governing a single-payer mandatory health insurance system: The case of Estonia

Triin Habicht [1]

Editors' introduction

Mandatory health insurance was established in Estonia when the country gained its independence, and replaced the Soviet-era system of centralized health care management. The new system separated financing and provision, and decentralized financing into 22 regional health insurers. During the next decade, Estonia consolidated these insurers into a single national scheme, the Estonian Health Insurance Fund (EHIF). The EHIF is constituted as an independent legal body, governed by a supervisory board comprising representatives of government, employers, and beneficiaries. The EHIF has some autonomy, but most significant decisions—such as contribution rates, fee schedules for providers, and benefit definitions—are in the hands of the executive branch and Parliament. The EHIF has performed quite well in coverage (reaching 94 percent of the population), solvency, low administrative expenses (less than 2 percent of total spending), and transparency (cited as the best public agency for the contents of its annual report). These achievements, however, were made in a rapidly growing economy, with increasing revenues, clean government, and strong political support, so it is difficult to judge how much the EHIF's governance structure contributed to its good performance.

This case study suggests several lessons for governing mandatory health insurance:

- *Political involvement in the health insurer's governance is not necessarily inimical to good performance, although the quality of the country's political governance then becomes critical. The EHIF benefited from the emergence of a broad political consensus on an efficient single-payer system and a government internationally recognized for its exceptional integrity.*
- *Accountability is most effective for measured performance indicators. In Estonia, the supervisory board, the government, and the public pay considerable attention to the EHIF's financial solvency, administrative expenses, and waiting lists—all*

measured and reported regularly. Less can be said about performance in the quality of health care services, as the governing bodies do not even have much of this information.

- *Explicitly recognizing the impact of different decisionmaking bodies by creating separate financial reserve accounts is potentially useful. The EHIF has a financial reserve fund that the supervisory board can access to cover normal commercial risks and management problems associated with managing the EHIF. The additional reserve can be released only by the government and is meant to cover the costs of government decisions affecting EHIF finances (for example, changing contribution rates and setting fee schedules).*

- *Consolidation of health insurance entities can make operational performance more efficient, particularly for small populations. Estonia's decision to consolidate 22 regional insurers into a single fund covering the country's 1.3 million people appears to have substantially reduced administrative costs.*

- *That the insurer will be less efficient and less responsive if it does not face competition is a concern for single-payer systems. Estonia's limited experience with a single health insurance fund suggests that—with appropriate accountability mechanisms and in a favorable economic context—efficiency can be achieved without competition.*

- *Relations with health care providers can be just as difficult when financing and provision are separated as when they are integrated. Despite such separation, health care providers influence negotiations on fee schedules and conditions of payment. This influence has restricted the EHIF's ability to improve its bargaining power through selective contracting.*

Brief history and overview of the health insurance system

The history of mandatory health insurance in Estonia goes back to the beginning of the 20th century, when sickness funds were established by region or industry. These funds were abolished in 1940, when the Union of Soviet Socialist Republics occupied the country. During the Soviet era, the health care system was centrally planned and all citizens had free access to services. Quality and access were good, according to the standards set, except for the unavailability of innovative pharmaceuticals.

Estonia regained its independence in 1991 after 50 years of Soviet occupation. Health financing reform has shifted from an integrated state model to a decentralized social health insurance model, while protecting health funds through earmarked taxes and enhancing efficiency and responsiveness.

The structure of the health insurance fund has been altered several times since 1992, when the social health insurance system began with 22 regional noncompeting sickness funds. The successful implementation of health insurance was largely due to the commitment of political parties to the system and to political stability between 1993 and 1995. Support from the medical profession was also important. In the insurance system, doctors saw a chance to ensure sustainable funding for medical care in the new economic environment.

The first Health Insurance Act (1991) organized sickness funds through county or city governments, though statutes and rules of benefit calculations were approved by the national government. The Ministry of Social Affairs supervised the system, while the local county and city governments were responsible for approving the regional sickness fund management boards and hiring the board chairs. Attempts were made to decentralize other health care functions to the municipalities, but these failed—the 250 municipalities were too small and fragmented, and their staff lacked planning and administrative skills.

Based on early experience, the Central Sickness Fund was established in 1994 to strengthen central functions. After this change, regional sickness funds—reduced to 17 to economize resources—were directly subordinated to the Central Sickness Fund.

At the same time, the State Health Insurance Council was established with 15 members. Mainly advisory, it was responsible for approving the state health insurance budget and for developing price lists for health care services. Regional health insurance councils were also established for each sickness fund. Although their role was also advisory, they had a strong influence on contracting.

The sickness funds had been quasi-public since their establishment in 1992. After years of debate, special legislation in 2001 created the Estonian Health Insurance Fund (EHIF), a single national insurance fund established as a public independent entity with seven regional departments. This fundamental change clarified the roles of the central and regional departments. The EHIF's main responsibilities are to contract health care providers, pay for health care services, reimburse beneficiaries for pharmaceutical expenditures, and pay for temporary sick leave and maternity benefits.

Context
Demographic and epidemiological situation
At about 1.35 million, the population of Estonia has declined steadily since 1991, due mainly to emigration and natural reduction. The declining—and aging—population has serious consequences for health care due to the smaller tax base, since health expenditures are mainly financed through labor taxes to support noncontributing children and the elderly. An epidemiological transition, with an increasing burden from chronic illnesses, also puts pressure on health spending.

Economic situation and fiscal policy
The Estonian economy is one of the most liberal in the world. Radical reforms to restore a market economy started in 1987. Estonia's gross domestic product (GDP)

decreased rapidly between 1991 and 1994, but has grown by an average of 6 percent a year since 1995. By 2005 real GDP was US$16,005 in purchasing power parity terms, about two-thirds of the European Union (EU) average.

Corruption

Corruption is not serious in Estonia. According to the Transparency International Corruption Perceptions Index, Estonia is the least corrupt of all Central and Eastern European countries, with an index of 6.4 in 2005 (27th globally). Available information suggests that corruption is also rare in the health sector. A survey financed by the Organisation for Economic Co-operation and Development found that unofficial payments are rare and relatively small.

Politics and social partners

The implementation of health insurance succeeded largely because of the commitment of political parties to the system and to political stability between 1993 and 1995. Although the full political spectrum supports the health insurance system, right and right-center governments have taken only modest steps. The most important expansions of social protection occurred under social democratic governments.

Partnerships among government, employers, labor unions, and civil society organizations are poorly developed in Estonia. Dialogue is better developed at the national level, but missing virtually everywhere else. This weakness of "social partnership," as understood in Western Europe, is mainly the result of weak institutions for representing employers, workers, and other civil society groups.

Labor union membership is small, at about 14 percent of workers in 2002. Almost 100 percent at the end of the 1980s, it declined to 21 percent in 1996. It is somewhat higher in the public sector and among non-Estonians. The most prominent professional group in health care is the Estonian Medical Association (EMA), which represents about half of Estonian doctors. Reestablished in 1988, it is the main representative association for doctors involved in negotiations with employers or the Ministry of Social Affairs.

The EMA had a particularly prominent role during the first wave of health care reforms that established the health insurance system in the early 1990s. During the mid- and late 1990s the role of the EMA declined as that of the Ministry of Social Affairs came to prominence. Since 2003 doctors have again become active in politics. Several doctors, including the chair of the EMA, were elected to Parliament, leading to a new post in the Ministry of Social Affairs: Political Assistant Minister for Health.

Acting more like a labor union than an umbrella professional body, EMA is prominent in collective bargaining for doctors, and doctors' salaries have increased substantially. By 2004 doctors' average salary was almost twice the country average (1.6 times per capita GDP). The rising salaries have put additional pressure on the EHIF budget.

Representing about half of nurses, the Estonian Nurses' Union has increased its power. In 2002 it became the only organization to call a strike successfully, attempting to force the Estonian Hospital Association to enter negotiations for a minimum wage. The union has also been active in redefining professional standards and improving the training curriculum.

Hospitals formed the Estonian Hospital Association, and recently the Estonian Patient Representative Union emerged as the most prominent patient representative. These organizations have only a limited impact on EHIF decisions, though.

Governance of the Estonian health insurance system

Governance of the EHIF entails many different institutions and procedures. Its most critical dimensions are the legal status of the EHIF, status of its ownership, representation on its supervisory board, responsibilities of management, forms and scope of government supervision, financing, and reporting requirements.

Legal status

When the health insurance system was established, sickness funds operated as autonomous entities. After health care providers came under private law and other legislative changes occurred, the legal status of the Central Sickness Fund and the regional sickness funds became unclear, constraining further development of contractual arrangements with providers. After considering alternatives, Estonia chose to convert the sickness funds into independent public entities, which can enter into contractual arrangements without public service regulations applying to their employees.

The government chose to create a single fund rather than several regional funds because it seemed more efficient for Estonia's relatively small population. The minister of social affairs favored this alternative, and the new Health Insurance Fund Act was drafted in 1999 under his direction and approved by Parliament in 2001.

Ownership

The EHIF, as the owner of its assets, can use them according to the procedures in the Health Insurance Fund Act and the statutes of the EHIF (a body of government regulations). The state cannot use EHIF assets for other purposes. If the EHIF is dissolved, however, its remaining assets transfer to the state.

About 99 percent of EHIF revenues comes from state health insurance taxes, and a tiny proportion from premiums. Health insurance tax inflows have grown by more than 10 percent a year since 2000, triggered by a rise in wage taxes due to a favorable economic environment and more efficient collection of taxes by the Tax and Customs Board. This abundance has raised providers' expectations for yearly increases in budgets and prices, enabling them to avoid rationing.

The Health Insurance Fund Act makes the EHIF fully liable for its obligations, prohibiting it from declaring bankruptcy. There are two exceptions. First, if health insurance tax revenues are lower than budgeted, the state becomes responsible for

EHIF obligations. Second, if the government or minister of social affairs establishes prices or rates in a way that prevents the EHIF from meeting its contractual obligations or paying health insurance benefits, the state again becomes responsible. This bounded liability creates an opportunity for providers to gain extra financing. If they pressure health service prices upward, the state has to take over the EHIF's obligations if the budget is insufficient. This occurred in 2004, though larger than expected revenues meant that the state did not have to step in. But the incentive to put such pressure on the EHIF budget is clear.

Mechanisms of representation

The highest body of the EHIF is the 15-member supervisory board—five representatives from the state, five from employers, and five from beneficiaries (Figure 4.1). Three state representatives are ex officio board members: the minister of social affairs, the minister of finance, and the chair of the Parliamentary Committee of Social Affairs. The fourth state representative is a member of Parliament. An official of the Ministry of Social Affairs named by the government on the nomination of the minister of social affairs is the fifth.

The rest of the 10 members are named by the government, five from nominations by organizations representing beneficiaries and five from nominations by organizations representing employers. The list of representing organizations is designated by the government.

The term for ex officio board members lasts until they resign their positions. The term of Members of Parliament lasts until the term of Parliament ends or

FIGURE 4.1   Organizational structure of the Estonian Health Insurance Fund, 2006

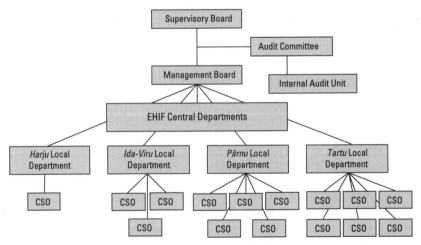

Note: CSO = county client service office; EHIF = Estonian Health Insurance Fund.

until their status as a member of Parliament ends or is suspended. The other members' term is three years, with a maximum of two consecutive terms.

The minister of social affairs is the ex officio chair of the supervisory board, organizing work, running meetings, and representing it. Board decisions usually require the approval of half or two-thirds of participating members, but the chair has the deciding vote for adopting the budget and setting limits for waiting times.

Members of the supervisory board are liable as a group for any damage caused to the EHIF by failure to perform their duties or by violations of Parliamentary acts and EHIF statutes. The EHIF insures members of the supervisory board against losses, with deductibles established by EHIF statutes (of approximately US$4,000 in 2006).

The supervisory board's primary responsibility is overseeing the management board. It (or its delegates) has the right to examine all necessary documents to audit the accuracy of accounting, existence of assets, and conformity with Parliamentary acts, EHIF statutes, and its own decisions.

Unless the supervisory board decides otherwise, the management board prepares the materials and drafts the decisions discussed by the supervisory board. At the request of the management board or its chair, the supervisory board may decide other issues related to the EHIF. All supervisory board decisions are public and published on the EHIF homepage (http://www.haigekassa.ee/haigekassa/otsused/).

Responsibilities of management

With three to seven members, the management board oversees EHIF operations. The management board prepares the three-year development plan, an annual action plan, and the budget for the approval of the supervisory board. Currently three members hold different responsibilities: one for the administration of health services and pharmaceutical benefits, another for financial issues and information systems, and the third (the chair) for legal issues, international agreements, and public relations. The chair is selected by the supervisory board through a transparent and competitive process.

The EHIF central departments are responsible for supervising regional departments and for the planning and control of finances. Regional responsibilities have decreased. They currently include regional population needs assessment, claims processing, contracting providers (within the central plan's parameters and with authority delegated by the management board), and the operation of small offices that provide client services in each county.

Forms and scope of government supervision

The EHIF was established by Parliament's 2001 Estonian Health Insurance Fund Act, which created the basis for the EHIF's functioning and set out its objectives, structures, bodies, assets, and obligations. More specific organizational details

---

BOX 4.1 *Sources of main regulations*

Establishment of system objectives and principles: Health Insurance Act (2002).
Contributions definition: Social Tax Act (2000).
Contributions rate: Social Tax Act.
Coverage (eligibility): Health Insurance Act.
Copayments: Principles and general regulations for upper limits are established in the Health Insurance Act. Actual copayments are defined in the List of Health Services (government regulation). Copayments for pharmaceuticals are defined in the Reference Prices of Pharmaceuticals and List of Reimbursed Pharmaceuticals (ministerial decree).
Benefits package: Basic principles are established in the Health Insurance Act. The actual benefits package is defined in the List of Health Services.

Provider payment methods: The List of Health Services and its application (Ministry of Social Affairs decree).
Prices (level of funding): Prices are defined in the List of Health Services. Price calculation methodology is defined in ministerial regulations.
Contracting: Basic principles (list of criteria for provider selection, terms, and necessary parts of contracts) are established in the Health Insurance Act. Application rules for provider selection criteria are defined by supervisory board decisions.
Budget: Basic principles are established in the Health Insurance Act. Line items are detailed in supervisory board decisions.
Waiting time limits: Supervisory board decisions.

(such as rules of procedure for board meetings) are defined in the EHIF statutes. These statutes give to the EHIF broad autonomy to contract with service providers, and maintain government supervision and participation. Important policy decisions about the health insurance system are for Parliament, the government, or the Ministry of Social Affairs (Box 4.1).

Government representatives have an important role, both through their regulatory authority and through the supervisory board. Most relevant legislation, including regulations on reimbursement, is drafted by the EHIF and forwarded to the Ministry of Social Affairs, after the approval of supervisory board.

The Ministry of Social Affairs (then called the Ministry of Health) had a weak role in health insurance at the system's establishment in 1991. Its importance grew with the creation of the Central Sickness Fund in 1994, but its authority remained largely formal—most decisions were made by the Central Sickness Fund. The Ministry of Social Affairs, however, became more active in regulating providers (with licensing, for example), sometimes bringing the ministry into conflict with the EHIF. The state owns strategic hospitals and the Ministry of Social Affairs represents the state on their boards—so it often protects provider interests. The increasing role of the ministry is partly due to providers becoming more active in politics (with the creation of an assistant minister for Health, for example). (Figure 4.2 and Table 4.1 present an overview of the health financing system.)

FIGURE 4.2   Overview of the Estonian health financing system

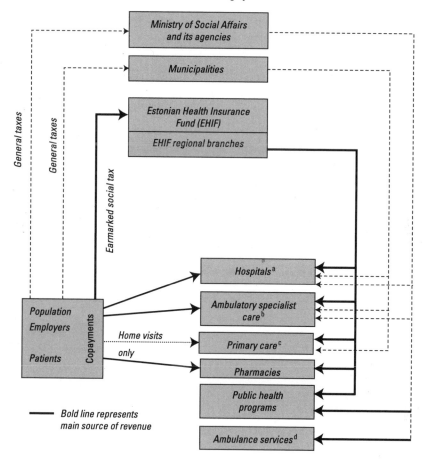

Source: Adapted by the authors from Jesse et al. 2004.

Notes: [a] Fee-for-service and daily rate and some per case payments; 50% of each case is reimbursed using diagnosis-related-group prices; close-ended case-volume contracts. [b] Fee-for-service; close-ended case-volume contracts. [c] Weighted capitation and fee-for-service and additional fixed payments. [d] General budget and fixed payment per provider unit.

Financing

The budget of the EHIF must balance revenues and expenditures each financial year, which is common fiscal policy in Estonia. Because the EHIF budget depends on the national budget, the former cannot be approved by the supervisory board until the latter budget is passed. Before the national budget is approved, monthly expenditures may be up to a twelfth of that of the preceding fiscal year.

TABLE 4.1 Influence on decisions made by the Estonian health financing system

Decisionmaking	Appointment of supervisory board	Appointment of management board	Financing	Services	Prices	Payment methods	Contracting	Reserves	Fund management
President	–	–	–	–	–	–	–	–	–
Parliament	–	–	++	+	+	+	–	+	–
Government	++	+	+	++	++	++	+	++	–
Ministry of Social Affairs	+	+	+	++	++	++	+	+	–
Ministry of Finance	–	–	++	–	–	–	–	+	–
Supervisory board	–	++	+	++	++	++	+	+	+
Management board	–	+	–	+	+	+	++	+	++
Providers	–	–	–	+	+	+	++	–	–

++: Strong influence; + moderate influence; – no influence.

The EHIF has three reserves to ensure solvency. The first, the cash reserve (liquidity portfolio), ensures that daily cash flows are managed smoothly. Administered by the State Fund, it consists of instruments such as local deposits and commercial paper.

The second reserve, the legal reserve, decreases risk from macroeconomic changes. Set at 6 percent of the EHIF's yearly budget, the legal reserve was created through the transfer of at least a fiftieth of the budget to the reserve every year since the EHIF's inception. The legal reserve requirement was 8 percent until 2004, but it was lowered to cover increased tariffs from the new health professionals' wage agreement. The legal reserve may be used only after a government order on the recommendation of the minister of social affairs, made after consultation with the supervisory board. The minister of finance ensures fund preservation, liquidity, and returns; funds are invested mostly in bonds of highly rated European issuers.

The third reserve, the risk reserve, minimizes risks arising from health insurance obligations. Set at 2 percent of the budget, the risk reserve can be used only after a decision of the supervisory board.

The EHIF is audited by the State Audit Office and an external, independent auditor. The State Audit Office audits public sector entities, which present their annual reports to it. It also conducts performance audits—thematic and usually covering several institutions—to see whether public sector resources are being used appropriately, and it gives feedback on how institutions can improve operations. Although some performance audits have covered the EHIF, proposing suggestions and publishing reports, their impact has not been significant.

The audit committee—a temporary supervisory board committee—also selects an external, independent auditor, excluding from consideration all employees of the EHIF and members of the supervisory and management boards. The external auditor examines the EHIF annual report, emphasizing financial issues over performance. An internal audit unit, under the authority of the audit committee, examines internal procedures and suggests ways to rationalize them.

Reporting requirements

The reporting requirements of the EHIF, set by the supervisory board, are as follows:

- The supervisory board presents the EHIF annual report to the government through the Ministry of Social Affairs.
- The management board presents an overview of the activities and economic situation of the EHIF to the supervisory board at least once every three months.

To increase transparency and improve performance, the EHIF adopted a new strategy in 2001 that uses a "balanced scorecard"—a planning and evaluation tool that links EHIF goals to specific activities, responsibilities, and budgets. Each year the supervisory board approves the strategy, with goals and priority initiatives for the current year and a plan for the next two years. The management board then discusses objectives with unit directors, dividing the yearly scorecards into two half-year scorecards to establish unit measurements and initiatives. The unit scorecards are then divided into individual scorecards for each staff member, whose wages are related to outcomes. These activity scorecards are linked to the accounting system, using an activity-based costing model.

The reporting system works from the bottom up. Each employee reports achievements. Unit directors evaluate the unit scorecards and report to the management board, which then reports to the supervisory board.

This approach has pushed staff to think more strategically, and encourages all to speak in a "common language." The quarterly and annual activity reports are made public, published on the EHIF Web page. The EHIF annual report has three times received the "Public Sector Accounting Flagship" award as the most transparent and best-content annual report in the Estonian public sector.

Performance of the Estonian health insurance system
Objectives
The objectives of the Estonian health insurance system were set by the 2002 Health Insurance Act: access to care and financial protection. The act also emphasized the importance of operating efficiently. The Estonian Health Insurance Fund Act charged EHIF with accomplishing these objectives with available resources. In addition to the objectives and principles defined in legislation, the 2005–07 EHIF Development Plan set five strategic objectives—access to care, financial protection, universal coverage, financial balance, and operational efficiency—measured by quantitative indicators.

Access to care
The most important objective is ensuring access to care with available resources, measured by beneficiaries' subjective assessments (through a yearly population survey conducted by the EHIF) and by objective measures (if beneficiaries have timely access to primary and specialist care). Limits for specialty-care waiting times are established by supervisory board decisions. Requirements for general practitioners are set in contracts. Quarterly access reports indicate that the EHIF has mostly succeeded, except in outpatient specialist care, where about 40 percent of beneficiaries wait longer than the set limits.

Measured since 2001 (with similar surveys conducted in the late 1990s), satisfaction with access (the share of respondents assessing access as good or rather good) has decreased from 56 percent in 2001 to 49 percent in 2005 (Figure 4.3). But satisfaction remains quite high.

Evaluation of access barriers is also conducted by examining the proportion of the population unable to get medical care when health problems occur. According

FIGURE 4.3 **Population satisfaction with access to care, 2001–05**

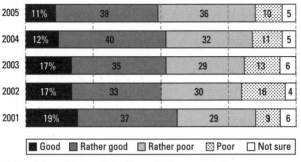

Source: Faktum. 2005. "Population satisfaction with health care." Tallinn, www.haigekassa.ee.

to the 2004 Income and Living Conditions Survey, 7 percent of the adult population did not get needed general practitioner care due to financial reasons (mostly the uninsured, who face out-of-pocket payments), long waiting times, and long distances. About 8 percent did not get needed specialist care and 15 percent did not get needed dental care. The access barriers are larger for lower socioeconomic groups and for those in rural areas.

The use of health care services is an alternative access measure. In the late 1980s the number of outpatient contacts per person was about 10, but the number of contacts fell sharply to 5 in 1992 (Figure 4.4). The number of contacts has since slowly increased to the EU average. Acute care hospital admissions follow similar patterns: high at the end of the 1980s, declining at the beginning of the 1990s, then converging to the EU average (17 admissions per 100 inhabitants).

Although the performance of the EHIF in access seems very good and the population's assessment of access is positive, the Estonian people still see long waiting times and other aspects of access as the health system's biggest problems. According to the EHIF population survey in 2005 about a third of the population named long waiting times as the biggest problem in health care.

Financial protection

Financial protection is a growing concern—out-of-pocket expenditures rose from 13.7 percent of total health expenditures in 1998 to 24.0 percent in 2004 (Figure 4.5). Estimates of informal payments are unavailable, but the absence of major complaints indicates that they are likely to be small.

Comparing out-of-pocket health expenditures with the household's ability to pay—health expenditures' share in the household budget after food needs are met—offers a better understanding of the financial burden of out-of-pocket payments. The share of households facing high health expenditures has risen, with 1.6 percent of households spending health more than 40 percent of their nonfood budgets on health care in 2002, compared with 0.3 percent in 1995 (Figure 4.6).

FIGURE 4.4   Outpatient contacts and acute care admissions, 1985–2003

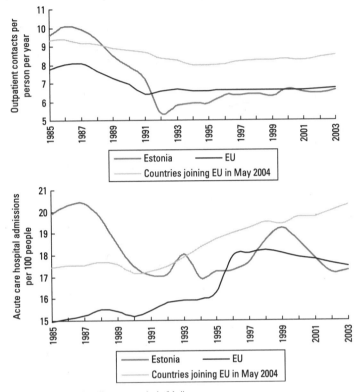

Source: Health for All Database, http://www.euro.who.int/hfadb.

FIGURE 4.5   Out-of-pocket payments for health care, 1998–2004

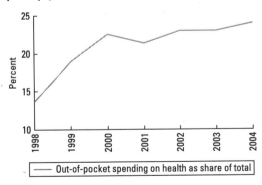

Source: Ministry of Social Affairs, www.sm.ee.

FIGURE 4.6 Share of households with high health payments, 1995, 2001, and 2002

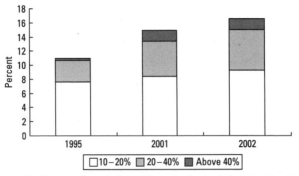

Source: T. Habicht et al. 2006. "Detecting Changes in Financial Protection: Creating Evidence for Policy in Estonia." *Health Policy and Planning* 21:421-431. November.

Increasing out-of-pocket payments raises concerns, though the public share of spending remains high. The financial impact of the recent increases in out-of-pocket payments on poor people has not yet been evaluated, but their situation has probably become worse. Those with chronic diseases are the most vulnerable, due to the high patient share of pharmaceutical costs—44 percent for prescription drugs in 2004.

Universal coverage

Although health insurance coverage in Estonia is mandatory, there are some population groups that remain uninsured as long-term unemployed. The EHIF covered 94.5 percent of the population in 2004. The percentage of uninsured decreased from 6.6 percent in 2004 to 5.5 percent in 2004, mainly through rising labor market participation and falling unemployment (from 13.8 percent to 9.9 percent over the same period). The 2002 Health Insurance Act revised eligibility criteria in ways unfavorable to some groups (spouses, for example). But large increases in the uninsured were not seen because the possibility of buying voluntary EHIF coverage (for those not eligible for free coverage) was introduced at the same time.

Children and pensioners are all covered, so the uninsured come from the working-age population. The uninsured are mostly men (6 percent of men are uninsured, as against 3 percent of women), ages 35 to 54. The uninsured tend to have less education and live in rural areas (Statistical Office of Estonia 2004).

Financial balance

The EHIF is legally required to balance yearly revenues and expenditures—a requirement fulfilled every year except in 1999, when economic crisis and reductions in health insurance revenues pushed expenditures above revenues (Figure 4.7). The deficit that year was covered by the fund's reserve and no extra allocations

FIGURE 4.7 Estonian Health Insurance Fund revenues and expenditures, 1992–2006

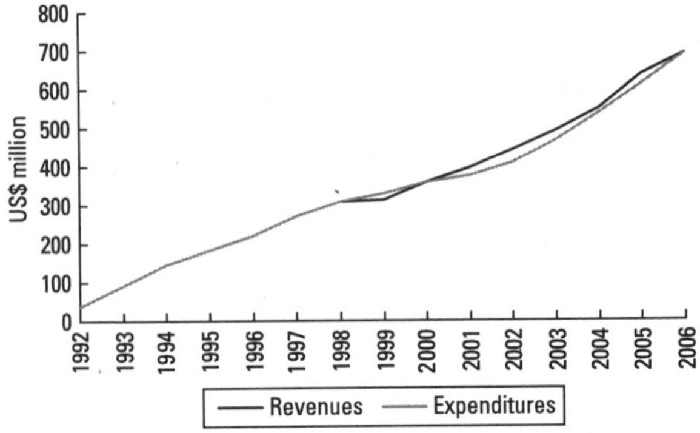

Source: Estonian Health Insurance Fund, www.haigekassa.ee.

Note: 2006 based on estimates.

from state budget were made. The EHIF's ability to adjust provider contract volumes to reflect diminished revenues has partly driven this stability, but rapidly increasing health insurance tax revenues have been more important.

Operational efficiency

Increasing operational efficiency has been the objective of the management board since the EHIF's establishment in 2001. Focusing on containing administrative costs—consistently less than 2 percent of the budget—the management board has improved governance practices (with the balanced scorecard, for example). Centralizing functions and closing regional offices raised operational efficiency.

Governance and performance

How do governance mechanisms affect performance? The following are some of the questions raised by the preceding discussion.

Does the supervisory board's independence help maintain financial solvency?

Changes in EHIF regulations require Parliamentary decisions and are not within the authority of the supervisory board. So even though the supervisory board is quite independent, its influence on financial solvency is limited to supervising management, encouraging operational efficiency, and using a small commercial risk fund. All other major financial parameters—revenues, prices for services, even the size of reserves—are outside its control, which could make it difficult to comply with the regulatory framework and government mandates that require the EHIF to remain financially solvent. The balance of interests on the supervisory board, however, may contribute to balancing the budget, with representatives accountable to political officials (ministers, for example) and to other important stakeholders (employers and beneficiaries). Even so, to date rapid economic growth has made financial solvency relatively painless. It remains to be seen whether the system can remain solvent if there is a significant and lengthy slow-down in revenue growth.

Does the negotiating process between EHIF and health care providers lower costs?

Two types of negotiation with providers affect health care service costs: price setting for individual services and contract negotiations. Price-setting negotiations control costs by setting unit service costs, but negotiations on service prices have been difficult—it is almost impossible for the EHIF to contest provider cost data, even if exaggeration is clear.

By limiting price increases, the fixed total budget is probably more important in containing service prices. If price changes are planned, their impact on budgets and access to care is calculated. This enables the management board to identify different solutions and assess their effects on access and the budget. Contract negotiations are based on the cost of treating cases and providers' expected service volume. Since the EHIF's budget, which depends almost entirely on tax revenues, cannot be exceeded, this creates a strict constraint to ensure that revenues cover expenditures. This constraint is important in limiting provider demands.

Does regular reporting contribute to ensuring access to care?

All levels of the EHIF are responsible for ensuring access to care. The supervisory board sets criteria for queues and waiting times. Every quarter the management board reports performance and access indicators to the supervisory board. Various measurement tools—number of people in queues, waiting time reporting, telephone surveys, and population surveys—include the whole organization in monitoring. The most important of these monitoring tools are queue lengths; waiting times; and the number of cases treated by region, specialty, and so on. Subjective assessments are also used, but have less impact on planning, budgeting, and contracting.

Access to care is arguably the most important objective of the management board's regular financial and performance reports, and the supervisory board often releases public announcements on access as well. Meeting access targets is also linked to the performance wages of the management board and central staff. Reporting requirements and performance feedback to managers and staff are the most important contributors to maintaining good access.

Do hard budget constraints create incentives to increase operational efficiency?

Hard budget constraints are a strong incentive for the EHIF to keep administrative costs down while increasing operational efficiency. The requirement that the EHIF report and explain administrative costs also plays a role. The EHIF's administrative costs are low, and it is unlikely that it could significantly lower them further. So limited revenues can be overcome only by improving efficiency.

Does regulation affect the financial protection of insured people?

Financial protection has not been the EHIF's main priority, perhaps because out-of-pocket payments were not a serious concern in the past. Primary care has no cost sharing (except for a small fee for home visits). Even so, overall budget constraints mean that ensuring access sometimes conflicts with providing financial protection. Nevertheless, within these constraints, the EHIF has provided substantial financial protection.

Summary

The governance structure of the Estonian health insurance system is well designed to balance EHIF obligations and resources. Even within a strict regulatory framework, the EHIF has the tools for strategic purchasing. But the history of Estonia's health insurance system is short—only 15 years overall and only 5 years under the current governance system. So it is hard to assess how much of the EHIF's good performance is linked to its governance mechanisms and how much to economic growth and broader national governance. Economic growth has raised EHIF revenues almost 20-fold during its 15-year history (in nominal terms), in line with GDP growth. Health expenditures' share of GDP, however, is moderate in Estonia relative to countries with similar incomes. Performance is good in coverage, financial protection, and access to care, suggesting that available resources are used efficiently. As the EHIF is responsible for most of the funds in the health system (about 66 percent of the total and 87 percent of public expenditures), it seems that its organization and governance structure contribute significantly to the good performance of the health insurance system.

Three aspects of the health insurance system merit emphasis. First, linking health insurance entitlement to labor market participation can create an incentive to reduce the informal labor market. As the economy develops over the long run, however, having only salary-linked contributions threatens the system's financial sustainability. Options to broaden the revenue base should therefore be considered. Second, even when dialogue with social actors is poorly developed, a tripartite governing body (through the supervisory board in Estonia) increases the accountability of politicians, providers, and EHIF managers. If done transparently, this mechanism supports the development of a sustainable health insurance system. Third, sound contracts between the EHIF and providers, stipulating clear responsibilities for both, are an important tool for improving performance in health care quality and accessibility. A participatory process can create clear expectations on both sides.

Annex 4.1 Dimensions, features, and indicators of good governance in mandatory health insurance: Estonia

Dimension	Features	Value	Indicators	Value	Explanation
Coherent decisionmaking structures	1. Responsibility for MHI objectives must correspond with decision-power and capacity in each institution involved in the management of the system.	Yes	The institution responsible for the financial sustainability of the system must be able to change at least one of the parameters on which it depends (e.g. conditions of affiliation, contribution rates, benefits package, ability to act a strategic purchaser, or tariffs).	++	The EHIF is fully liable for its obligations with all its assets, and its yearly revenues and expenditures have to be balanced. However, in two cases the state becomes responsible for EHIF obligations. First, if health insurance tax revenues are lower than in the state budget adopted. Second, if the minister of social affairs or the government establishes prices or rates of health insurance benefits in a way that prevents the EHIF from performing its contractual obligations or to pay health insurance benefits. This is important because most regulatory power for the health insurance system is at higher levels (Ministry of Social Affairs, government, Parliament) than the EHIF management or supervisory board, and so the EHIF cannot decide on contribution rates, affiliation conditions, tariffs, or benefits package independently. Still, the budget line items are decided by the EHIF supervisory board, which is a very important method for balancing revenues and expenditures. In addition, contract volumes with service providers can be modified if revenues are lower than expected.
			The institution in charge of the supervision of sickness funds has the capacity to fulfill its responsibilities (i.e. it has enough skilled staff, it has access to the necessary information, and legal texts give it the authority to fulfill its role vis-à-vis sickness funds).	+	The governing body of the EHIF is the supervisory board, which has (according to legislation and the statutes of the EHIF) the necessary tools to fulfill its supervisory role. However, the competences and motivation of supervisory board members have received little attention, which might have an adverse effect on decisionmaking.
	2. All MHI entities have routine risk assessment and management strategies in place.	Yes	Clear regulations on MHI entities' continuous risk assessment and risk management are in place.	++	The EHIF's financial situation is strictly monitored. The EHIF management board presents quarterly reports on the financial situation to the supervisory board. In addition, periodic forecasting is performed to compare short- and medium-term expenditures.

(continues)

Dimension	Features	Value	Indicators	Explanation
		++	Strategies are in place, i.e. MHI entities follow and analyze the evolution of expenditures and contributions.	Three alternatives can be considered if the EHIF's expenditures exceed revenues. First, cover expenditures by using reserves available. Second, reduce the contract volumes with health care service providers, as other health insurance benefits (sick-leave benefits, prescription drug benefits) are open responsibilities and there are no mechanisms for the EHIF to reduce these. Third, the state becomes responsible for those of the EHIF's obligations that exceed its revenues if the EHIF's budget deficit is a result of decisions made by the minister of social affairs, government, or Parliament.
		+	MHI entities have the capacity to manage risks.	Contracts with providers are capped cost and volume contracts, which are monitored quarterly. If service providers exceed the contract volume, the excess costs are their own responsibility. This is an most important tool for the EHIF to balance revenues and expenditures.
3. The cost of regulating and administering MHI institutions is reasonable and appropriate.	Yes			
		–	Maximum administration costs for MHI entities are set out in legal texts or regulations.	The EHIF's target has been to contain administrative costs, which have been constantly lower than 2 percent of the total budget.
		–	Administrative costs are monitored by the regulator.	There is no specific regulation on administrative costs, but there are targets in the EHIF's development plan to contain the increase of administrative costs.
		++	Provisions for covering the costs of the MHI regulator are stipulated in legal texts.	The supervisory board monitors the accomplishment of this objective.
		–	Before new regulations are put in place, a cost-benefit assessment is conducted.	Cost-benefit analysis of new regulations is not usual practice, but for any decision the impact on expenditures is estimated and taken into account for decisionmaking.

| Stakeholder participation | 4. Stakeholders have effective representation in the governing bodies of MHI entities. | Yes | Governing bodies of regulatory oversight and institutional governance. | ++ | The highest body of the EHIF is the tripartite supervisory board with 15 members—five each from the state, employers, and beneficiaries. Three state representatives are board members ex officio: the minister of social affairs, the minister of finance, and the chair of the Parliamentary Committee of Social Affairs. The fourth state representative is a member of Parliament, who is named by Parliament on the proposal of the Parliamentary Committee of Social Affairs. The fifth state representative is an official of the Ministry of Social Affairs named by the government on the proposal of the minister of social affairs. |
| | | | Representation is effective, i.e. different stakeholders' views are considered in decisionmaking. | + | The other 10 members are named by the government, five following proposals from beneficiaries' organizations and five following proposals from employers' organizations. The list of these organizations is drawn up by the government. For employers, all five members are nominated by the Estonian Employers' Confederation, the country's leading employers' organization. The beneficiaries' representatives are nominated by the Association of Estonian Trade Unions, the Estonian Professional Employees' Unions Association, a pensioners' association, the Chamber of Disabled People, and the Union for Child Welfare.

Even though these 10 supervisory board members are named by the government, they may be removed only on the suggestion of the organization that proposed them. |

(continues)

Dimension	Features		Indicators	Value	Explanation
			Stakeholders satisfaction with partnership with MHI entities.	+	Providers' representatives are not explicitly included in the EHIF supervisory board. However, they have an important role in decisionmaking as all questions on the benefits package and contract conditions are negotiated with providers' representatives (mainly with their associations). Partners' involvement is important to the EHIF and progress is measured by partners' satisfaction surveys, which are currently conducted annually. In 2006 general satisfaction with partnership with the EHIF was quite high—76 percent of contracting partners considered it very good or rather good.
Transparency and information	5. The objectives of MHI are formally and clearly defined.	Yes	Objectives are stated in a high-level legal text.	++	The objectives of the Estonian health insurance system are stated in several documents. The basic principles of the health insurance system are given in the Health Insurance Act (2002), which states that "Health insurance is based on the solidarity of and limited cost-sharing by insured persons and on the principle that services are provided according to the needs of insured persons, that treatment is equally available in all regions and that health insurance funds are used for their intended purpose."
			Objectives are publicized and easily accessible to the public.	++	In addition to objectives and principles given in legislation, the Development Plan of EHIF 2006–08 restates these goals in operational terms. It sets the mission statement of the EHIF: "The Estonian Health Insurance Fund is committed to building a sense of security in the insured for facing and solving health problems."
			Objectives are clearly defined and easily understandable.	+	Both documents are public and easily accessible (e.g. through the Internet). Monitoring the overall objectives is carried out by developing more specific strategic objectives and indicators.

Objectives are known and understood by the public.	+	The goal of MHI has been explicitly stated since 2002 (implicitly since the establishment of MHI in 1992). Thus it may be said that the goal has remained unchanged. However, there is no evidence that the wider public understands the EHIF's objectives (as this question has not been included in public surveys).
6. MHI relies upon an explicit and an appropriately designed institutional and legal framework.	Yes	
The main characteristics of the system are defined in legal texts.	++	Since 2002 the legal framework for MHI can be considered explicit as all the main characteristics of the system are described in the Health Insurance Fund Act (mainly institutional aspects and regulatory oversight) and the Health Insurance Act (rules for coverage, benefits package, purchasing). The current legal framework is balanced, and there have been only minor amendments.
The legal framework is appropriate given the country MHI context.	++	Current legislation of the MHI system is developed and enforced in parallel with reorganization of health service providers' legal environment at the beginning of this century. Changes were needed as the general legal environment had changed and the legal environment for health system actors had become unclear.
The status and responsibilities of each different MHI institutions in the system are clearly defined and transparent.	++	Under the Health Insurance Fund Act, EHIF's legal status (as a public independent legal body) and responsibilities are clearly defined and well balanced. Both the Health Insurance Act and the Health Insurance Fund Act state the decisionmaking rights of the EHIF management board, supervisory board, ministers of health and of finance, the government, and Parliament in terms of the main characteristics of the health insurance system. In addition, the areas of responsibility of the EHIF's central and regional departments are clearly stated by regulation, and important activities are covered.

Dimension		Features	Value	Indicators	Explanation
	7. Clear information, disclosure, and transparency rules are in place.	Yes	++	Decisionmaking process is covered with explicit rules.	EHIF decisionmaking levels and processes are defined in corresponding legal texts.
			++	Explicit disclosure regulations exist in the law or regulations of the law.	Most supervisory board decisions are made if more than one-half (or in some cases two-thirds) of participating members vote in favor of a motion, but there are two cases where the chair has the deciding vote—when adopting the EHIF budget and setting maximum limits to waiting times.
			++	Beneficiaries have access to the financial information.	All decisions and agreements that are made by the supervisory board are put on the EHIF Web page and are also available on request. Legislative decisions are also made public. These moves have increased transparency considerably. In addition, the EHIF has provided explanatory materials on legislation.
					EHIF financial performance is monitored quarterly by the supervisory board. In addition to financial information, quarterly reports include overviews of EHIF performance in terms of strategic objectives and annual action plans. All quarterly reports are put on the EHIF web page. The EHIF annual report is more detailed and audited by an external auditor. This report is also public, and gained the best public reporting award for four straight years.
					Certain procedures govern internal priority decisionmaking, which shares the responsibilities between different structures and provides a clear framework for day-to-day operations.
					EHIF beneficiaries can access regulations and financial statements (quarterly and annual reports) by the Internet. Those who have no such access can ask for a hard copy. Beneficiaries also have the right to get more detailed information on their own data in the EHIF database (such as treatment costs).

8. MHI entities have minimum requirements in regard to protecting the insured.	Yes		
	Consumer protection regulations exist in law.	+	Currently there is no separate patient protection legislation in Estonia, but this area is regulated by the Law of Obligations, which regulates all contractual relationships in the economy and between different parties.
	Awareness among the insured of their obligations, rights, and benefits.	+	Beneficiaries have the right to present complaints to the EHIF, but there is no good procedure. If no agreement is reached then all complaints against the EHIF are adjudicated by an administrative court according to general procedures. However, this is not common practice.
	The insured can obtain timely, complete, and relevant information changes in benefits or premium, changes in coverage length etc.	+	To provide consumers with additional tools before they register a complaint (or just to increase choice) the insurance system provides the possibility of a second opinion, where insurance covers consultation from another specialist (in the same medical area) if needed.
	Consumer complaint mechanisms exist and are being used.	+	According to satisfaction surveys of the insured (annual population-based surveys), beneficiaries' awareness of their rights and of changes in the health insurance system is rather limited.
	Appeals and grievance mechanisms exist and are being used.	+	
	Independent dispute resolution mechanisms exist and are being used.	+	
Supervision and regulation	9. Rules on compliance, enforcement and sanctions for MHI supervision are clearly defined.	Yes	
	Rules on compliance and sanctions are defined in legal texts.	+	Members of the supervisory board are jointly liable for any damage wrongfully caused to the EHIF if they violate the requirements of acts or statutes of the EHIF, or if they fail to perform their duties. In order to insure members of the supervisory board against such liability, the EHIF concludes a liability insurance contract. The same rule applies to the management board.
	Corrective actions are imposed, based on clear and objective criteria that are publicly disclosed.	–	

(continues)

Dimension	Features	Indicators	Value	Explanation
	10. Financial management rules for MHI entities are clearly defined and enforced.	Adequate capacity for the execution of these functions is provided.	++	As sanctions or corrective actions are not applied, it is difficult to comment on public discussions on them. At the same time, the structures exist to impose sanctions if needed.
		Cases of rule violation and subsequent actions by the regulator are publicized.	–	
Yes		Financial standards for MHI entities are defined in legal texts or regulations.	++	The EHIF strictly follows the rules of the Estonian General Accounting Act. This is monitored by the external auditor and the State Audit Office.
		Clear financial licensure/market-entry rules are defined (minimum capital requirements).	–	The EHIF has three types of reserves to ensure solvency. The first is the cash reserve (liquidity portfolio), which ensures that daily cash flows are managed smoothly. The second is the legal reserve, the aim of which is to reduce the risk of macroeconomic change harming the health insurance system. The legal reserve has to be at least 6 percent of the EHIF's yearly budget. The third is the risk reserve, which has the objective of minimizing the risks arising to the health insurance system from obligations assumed. The risk reserve has to be at least 2 percent of the EHIF's yearly budget and can be used following a decision of the EHIF supervisory board.
		Ongoing reserve and solvency requirements are defined.	++	
		Regulations of assets and financial investments are defined.	++	
		Audit (internal and external) rules are defined.	++	
		Rules for financial standards are enforced.	++	The EHIF is audited by the State Audit Office and the external auditor. The former is responsible for auditing public sector entities, which should present their reports annually. The EHIF is also audited by the external auditor who is appointed by the Audit Committee (a body under the EHIF supervisory board). The external auditor audits the EHIF annual report, focusing on financial issues rather than performance. An Internal Audit Unit is responsible mainly for auditing the work of the internal procedures of management and for making suggestions for rationalization.

	11. The MHI system has structures for ongoing supervision and monitoring in place.	Yes	Adequate on-site inspections and off-site monitoring are in place.	++	This entails financial and performance reporting as well as procedural reporting.
			Ongoing financial reporting rules are defined and provided information is accurate and timely.	++	To increase the transparency and to better link activities with the EHIF's objectives, a "balanced scorecard" strategy was introduced in 2001. The internal planning and reporting systems are currently in line with strategic objectives.
			Clear market exit/dissolution rules are in place.	++	The EHIF was established by a legislative act, which is a requirement for all public legal entities. It owns its assets and can use them according to the procedures of the Health Insurance Fund Act and statutes of the EHIF. The EHIF can be dissolved only by another legislative act, and its remaining assets would be transferred to the state.
			Clear nonfinancial licensure/market entry rules are defined.	–	
			Insurance product filing/registration is defined and regulated.	++	
Consistency and stability	12. There is stability of the main qualities of the MHI system.	Yes	The fundamental characteristics of the MHI system are defined in law and have remained same in the recent past.	++	The establishment of the health insurance system in 1992 was a radical change. The basic values and principles of the health insurance system have remained unchanged since then. There have been important changes in legislation, but these have been the result of the development of the system. For example, the contribution rate has remained at 13 percent, and only minor changes in entitlement rules have been made. Changes in political power have not had much influence on the important characteristics of the health insurance system.
			The law has remained substantially the same in the recent past.	+	

++ = relevant to Estonia; + = relevant to Estonia to some extent; – = not relevant to Estonia.

Endnote

1. The author gratefully acknowledges participants in a World Bank Seminar (May 23–24, 2006) for their valuable comments and William D. Savedoff for his crucial comments and suggestions. The author also thanks Dr. Peeter Laasik, Dr. Arvi Vask, Dr. Ivi Normet, Dr. Helvi Tarien, and Mr. Harri Taliga for their useful comments during interviews. Special thanks are due to Dr. Maris Jesse for sharing her ideas and materials and always finding time for discussions. Finally, the author is grateful to Dr. Jarno Habicht, whose support and comments have been important to this study. Responsibility for all inaccuracies and mistakes rests with the author.

Reference list

Faktum. 2005. Survey *Elanike rahulolu arstiabiga 2005* ("Population Satisfaction with Health Care"). Tallinn.

Habicht, J., K. Xu, A. Couffinhal, and J. Kutzin. 2006. "Detecting Changes in Financial Protection: Creating Evidence for Policy in Estonia." *Health Policy and Planning* 21:421–31.

Jesse, M., J. Habicht, A. Aaviksoo, A. Koppel, A. Irs, and S. Thomson. 2004. "Health Care Systems in Transition: Estonia." WHO Regional Office for Europe for the European Observatory on Health Systems and Policies, Copenhagen.

Statistical Office of Estonia. 2004. *Household Living Niveau 2003*. Tallinn. Special data query provided by Statistical Office. ·

5

Governing multiple health insurers in a corporatist setting: The case of the Netherlands

Hans Maarse

Editors' introduction

The mandatory health insurance system of the Netherlands evolved over more than a century and with very little government regulation. The sickness funds that emerged in the late 19th and early 20th century were nonprofit and nongovernmental organizations set up by unions and employers in urban areas and generally by physicians in rural areas. It was not until 1941, under the Nazi occupation, that significant legislation was enacted to regulate the country's sickness funds. This effectively made health insurance coverage mandatory for all individuals below a certain income level. As a consequence of lobbying by the medical profession, higher-income households were left out of the system and had to pay out of pocket or voluntarily seek other insurance arrangements.

Over time, government involvement has expanded in the form of special subsidized insurance schemes for the elderly or the poor, a scheme for universal catastrophic coverage, of risk-pooling arrangements across insurers, and of several commissions that supervised rates, payment schedules, and quality of care. Consequently by the 1990s, health insurers functioned more as administrators of a government-defined scheme than as entrepreneurs or risk managers.

In its latest reform, of 2006, the Netherlands eliminated the division of beneficiaries by income—allowing sickness funds and private insurers to compete with one another—and established regulations to establish a competitive health insurance market.

This case study suggests several lessons for governing mandatory health insurance:

- *Direct accountability of board members to shareholders, beneficiaries, or other actors does not appear to be a necessary condition for good governance when other mechanisms are in place. Although the supervisory boards of sickness funds are not directly accountable to anyone, some mechanisms appear to motivate appropriate behavior—transparency in the form of requiring public reports and audits; public pressure in the form of government pronouncements and press reports; and restricted decisionmaking powers through oversight by semi-public commissions.*

- *Governance mechanisms can engage representatives of different social groups in supervisory boards, but they can also be engaged in commissions that regulate health insurers. The prominent role of representative associations in health care regulatory commissions reflects a long-standing political tradition of shared responsibility for governance and provides checks in supervising highly autonomous health insurers.*

- *Governance mechanisms are embedded in a country's particular culture and politics. Thus, health insurers appear to perform well despite a number of potential obstacles because of a preference for seeking consensus, and an interest in reaching accommodations through collective bargaining.*

- *The existence of multiple competing health insurers does not guarantee improvements in efficiency if fundamental pricing and service decisions are imposed by the government. The Netherlands' recent health reform seeks to structure competition so that health insurers will suffer financially for poor management but not for insuring a disproportionately high-risk population.*

Introduction

The history of health insurance in the Netherlands dates back to the 19th century and is closely linked to the emergence of a medical profession and the advance of medicine, which led to a growing demand for health care.[1] In the cities, unions and employers took the lead in setting up sickness funds, and physicians in rural areas. By the beginning of the 20th century, some 10 percent of the population was affiliated with a sickness fund.

Sickness funds were originally the result of voluntary action by community groups without any involvement of the government. There were various attempts to introduce legislation on health insurance and sick leave, beginning in 1904, but all government proposals for a comprehensive approach stalled. Doctors were the best organized group and were strongly opposed. The National Medical Association was only willing to accept a public health insurance arrangement if (a) people covered by a sickness fund were free to choose their own doctor, (b) doctors possessed at least 50 percent of the seats in the sickness fund board, and (c) only people on low income could affiliate. As a result of the opposition from the National Medical Association, no integrated arrangement was ever adopted in the Netherlands, unlike other "Bismarckian" countries, like Germany and Belgium.

Because most sickness funds had contracted only a few doctors, which violated the principle of free doctor choice, doctors set up their own sickness funds with free doctor choice. These funds proved very successful and their market share soon exceeded that of the other funds.

One of the problems of the sickness funds was the very restricted package of health services covered (i.e. material scope). This led to the establishment of separate schemes for hospital care and nursing care in a sanatorium. Another problem was the limited personal scope of sickness funds, which was due to the low income ceiling applied at the behest of doctors. The effect of the limited scope was that persons with an income just above the ceiling could face great financial problems when sick. As a response to this problem, separate voluntary funds—the precursors of private insurance—began developing from about 1910 for people who could not enroll in a sickness fund. For decades, the division between social health insurance (sickness funds) and private health insurance was a basic characteristic of health insurance in the Netherlands.

Ironically, the first mandatory health insurance (MHI) law, the Sickness Fund Decree, was put through in 1941 by Germany when it occupied the Netherlands. Key elements of this arrangement were: (a) employers had to pay 50 percent of the income-dependent contributions; (b) a substantial extension of the health services covered (hospital care, nursing care in a sanatorium, and dental care were included); (c) the obligation of being affiliated with a sickness fund to be eligible for an income allowance when sick (which made affiliation with a sickness fund in effect mandatory); and (d) sickness funds had to apply for a state-issued license to operate as fund. As an immediate consequence of the Decree, only 291 of the 650 funds applied for a license, of which 204 applications were recognized. The number of insured grew from 45 percent in 1941 to 60 percent in 1943.

The Germans also took three other actions that would persist after the war. The first was a system of full risk pooling, which effectively transformed the sickness funds into fund administrators rather than risk managers. The second involved abolishing market competition by prohibiting members from switching their affiliation unless they moved to another region. Third, the Decree gave the national government a leading role, replacing what had been voluntary solidarity arrangements with a state-governed mandatory scheme.

After World War II, government efforts to introduce a single national scheme failed because of persistent conflicting interests and concerns over cost. It resulted in the passage of the Sickness Fund Act (Ziekenfondswet or ZFW) in 1964 which, in most respects, only codified the German Sickness Fund Decree.

In the postwar period, government efforts did expand coverage with specific schemes for those who would otherwise be excluded from the ZFW, such as the self-employed, disabled, and elderly. Private health insurance, which had started with commercial indemnity companies in the 1930s, also expanded. The sickness funds themselves entered this private market for health insurance by creating subsidiaries that proved quite successful.

The structure of mandatory health insurance in the Netherlands

Until 2006, insurance coverage in the health care system was divided by the kinds of health conditions that were covered and by enrollment categories (Figure 5.1). The Exceptional Medical Expenses Act (AWBZ) of 1968 provided universal coverage, primarily for long-term care. The ZFW covered acute, emergency, and elective care for 63 percent of the population, while another 35 percent of the population had these services covered by private health insurance. (The other 2 percent of the population had another type of insurance—military or prisoners' insurance—or no insurance.) Finally, complementary health insurance for services not covered in the other schemes was offered by private insurers and private subsidiaries of sickness funds.

The minister of health was responsible for assuring compliance with the relevant laws by institutions providing catastrophic and basic coverage (rows 1 and 2 above), but its responsibility for complementary health insurance (row 3) was restricted to assuring quality.

Public decisions regarding the scope of MHI include defining who is insured and what package is covered. Eligibility has gradually expanded or been added through special programs. Decisions regarding the package of services that are covered are the government's responsibility and subject to Parliamentary approval. The Health Care Insurance Board (College voor de Zorgverzekeringen or CVZ)— a semi-independent agency with both advisory and administrative tasks—advises the government on these decisions.

Risk solidarity is a cornerstone of the MHI system. Contributions are not adjusted for health risks and insurers must accept any applicant regardless of their likely cost. Risk solidarity differs explicitly from charging actuarial premiums, a practice that is commonly applied in private health insurance.

Another key element of MHI is income solidarity, which implies that contributions are related to ability-to-pay. Income solidarity is achieved by the arrangement that subscribers must pay a government-set percentage of their income as their contribution (though the introduction in 1989 of a flat-rate premium on top of the income-dependent contributions partially eroded this solidarity). In 2005

FIGURE 5.1   Three-compartment structure of health insurance before 2006

1	Exceptional Medical Expenses Act (AWBZ). Covered: mainly long-term care; and 100 percent of the population	
2	Sickness Fund Act (ZFW). Covered: acute, emergency, and elective care; and 63 percent of the population	Private health insurance.Covered 35 percent of the population
3	Complementary health insurance	

Note: The remaining 2 percent of the population in the second row had another type of insurance (military, prisoners) or no insurance at all.

TABLE 5.1 Composition of health care financing by source (percent)

Source of financing	1980	1990	2000	2002
Taxes	9	11	5	6
Exceptional Medical Expenses Scheme	37	33	37	38
Sickness Fund Scheme	23	31	37	36
Private health insurance	24	16	14	14
Out-of-pocket payments	7	9	7	6

Source: Ministry of Health.

Note: These figures may differ from those in other sources due to some specific accounting principles of the Ministry of Health.

the government set mandatory contributions at 8.2 percent, of which employers paid 6.75 percent and employees 1.45 percent. The maximum contribution was capped with an income ceiling. The 2005 mandatory contribution for the Exceptional Medical Expenses Scheme was an additional 13.45 percent.

A basic feature of the health care system is the absence of copayments, despite several failed attempts in the 1980s and 1990s to introduce them. However, copayments were common in private health insurance and in the Exceptional Medical Expenses Scheme.

Health care financing used to be mainly public: in 2002 public financing amounted to 80 percent.[2] Out-of-pocket payments play a limited role (Table 5.1).

Sickness funds

Under the Sickness Fund Act, sickness funds were the main insurers. Sickness funds are private agents, explicitly prohibited from seeking profits, and must be legally constituted as foundations or mutual societies.

Though private agents, sickness funds operate close to the government and are often viewed as semi-public. For a long period they operated as rule-driven bureaucratic task organizations in charge of the implementation of the Sickness Fund Scheme. This type of behavior began changing in the late 1990s when changes in the Sickness Fund Act required funds to set their own flat-rate premiums and permitted individuals to select their own sickness fund.

The total number of sickness funds has declined significantly through mergers, from 54 in 1980 to 21 in 2004; the number of new entrants is very low. The main reasons for merging were economics of scale, risk pooling, gaining a stronger market position and, in some cases, economies of scale.

Until the early 1990s health insurance legislation prohibited sickness funds from operating their own health care services. Therefore, the relationship between sickness funds and providers was shaped through contracts. Private health insurers followed this lead, although they were not forced to do so by law.

A direct consequence of health insurance legislation was that integrated systems such as health management organizations could not exist in the Netherlands. Furthermore, by prohibiting sickness funds from selectively contracting with providers, the law also blocked the creation of semi-integrated systems such as preferred provider networks. Recent revisions have softened these restrictions, allowing some health insurers to employ general practitioners or to purchase private practices, to own shares of newly established health service delivery organizations, or to selectively contract with individual providers. They have also been allowed to negotiate prices below an established maximum. However, negotiated tariffs in practice differed little from the maximum tariffs and selective contracting has been limited by consumer protests. The structure of local and regional markets also made selective contracting impractical.

Private health insurance

Private health insurance companies are legally constituted as nonprofit mutual societies or for-profit enterprises. In 2002 about 35 percent of the population had private health insurance, intended for those ineligible to enroll with a sickness fund and offering similar services. Most of these people were ineligible to enroll with sickness funds because their income exceeded the statutory limit. A slight majority of these people (55 percent) were enrolled through group contracts that were mostly employer-based. In addition to substitute health insurance, private health insurers also offered complementary health plans to cover health services that were not reimbursed by the Sickness Fund Scheme (including most forms of dental care) or supplementary health insurance to cover amenities (such as a private hospital room).

Private health insurance companies were more numerous than sickness funds and tended to be smaller. In 2003 there were 44 private insurers and 22 sickness funds.

Governance: System, insurers, and providers

Governance at the system level

Governance of the MHI system is highly centralized in the Netherlands, in part because the general public holds the national government politically responsible for almost anything that happens in health care. For example, in the late 1990s waiting lists became a hot political issue and the minister of health was put under great political pressure by doctors, provider organizations, insurers, the media and the general public to resolve the problem by increasing the nation's budget for health care. The national government continues to be held politically responsible, even after the 2006 reforms (see below) that eliminated the division between sickness funds and private insurance, modified the system for setting premiums, and reorganized various oversight bodies. What follows is a description of the system as it functioned prior to the 2006 reforms.

The minister of health is responsible for primary and secondary legislation regarding MHI, as well as establishing:

- Who was eligible for the ZFW
- Which health benefits were covered
- The level and composition of the contribution rate.

By contrast, it had little to do with regulating private health insurance.

The Ministry of Health has always been relatively small, with many basic administrative tasks being delegated to semi-independent bodies. In this regard, the governance of the system featured a high degree of functional decentralization—which, despite some changes, continues today.

The Ministry of Finance is another key player in national health care policymaking. As costs have risen, the importance of this ministry has increased in national health care policymaking, and remains strong.

Parliament (the second chamber) also plays several roles in health care policymaking. First, the government needs Parliamentary approval for all its legislative proposals and the annual budget for health care. Second, Parliament may take policy initiatives. A recent example is Parliament's proposal to reimburse costs for a treatment—the first in vitro fertilization treatment—that was previously not included in the insurance system's list of covered health care services.[3] Third, Parliament may discuss any government decision or issue. Since health care policies are very sensitive politically, Parliament frequently "bombards" the minister of health with requests for clarification or policy action. Many of these requests are media-driven or incident-led.

A number of independent regulatory bodies, which are not part of the government but operate closely with the Ministry of Health, are charged with essential administrative and supervisory tasks.

Prior to 2006, there were several such agencies. The first of these was the CVZ. Its most important governance tasks were: (a) giving advice to the minister of health on health insurance, in particular on contribution rates and health insurer budgets; (b) administering the system of risk pooling; (c) monitoring health insurance and reporting on bottlenecks in health insurance; (d) assessing the feasibility and efficiency of government plans; and (e) licensing health insurers.

The CVZ was created in the 1990s to take the place of the Sickness Fund Council, which was increasingly regarded as outdated and ineffective. It eschewed the interest-group representation of the Council for technical expertise and professional qualifications. It consisted of seven independent experts (with a maximum number of nine members) appointed by the minister of health for a four-year term (they could be reappointed twice).

The second agency was the Supervisory Board for Health Care Insurance (College Toezicht Zorgverzekeringen or CTZ), which was responsible for supervising implementation of the Sickness Fund Act and the Exceptional Medical Expenses Act. The CTZ did not supervise private health insurers.

The main task of the CTZ was to ensure that health insurers acted lawfully. Supervision was not only corrective when health insurers failed to carry out their statutory duties properly, but also preventive. Furthermore, the CTZ advised the minister of health on the feasibility of health legislation. As with the CVZ, the CTZ replaced another entity and was created with a board of five independent experts who were appointed for a four-year term by the minister of health. Again, each member could be reappointed twice.

Private health insurers were subject to supervision by a national agency that supervised all private insurance (Maarse et al. 2005).

Another agency dealing with administration was the Health Care Tariffs Board (College Tarieven Gezondheidszorg or CTG). The CTG was responsible for all tariff issues in health care, including hospital budgets. It was a semi-independent administrative body governed by a board of nine independent experts who were appointed by the minister of health for a four-year period, and who could be reappointed twice.

Another feature of the governance structure at the system level concerns the relation between the minister of health and the national associations of the major stakeholders. This relation has traditionally been characterized by frequent contact. For this reason there is some truth in viewing health care legislation as a negotiated agreement between the minister and the national associations. It is mostly the result of collective bargaining in a search for consensus. Not surprisingly, consensus-building often leads to incremental policymaking and slow progress, particularly when the associations have conflicting interests or when hard decisions have to be taken, for instance on expenditure cuts.

An interesting governance instrument is the so-called collective contract between the minister of health and national associations. A recent example is the contract with the associations of providers and insurers in which the minister agreed not to implement further expenditure cuts in long-term care in exchange for an obligation from the associations to increase their productivity by 1.25 percent a year. A few years ago the minister also signed a collective contract with various national associations of pharmaceutical companies in which he agreed to abstain from price interventions in exchange for voluntary price reductions. An important motive for the national associations to sign the contract was to avoid "unfriendly" price interventions by the minister. They negotiated "under the shadow of hierarchy."

From the viewpoint of the minister, collective contracts have several advantages. An agreement is always preferable to unilateral decisions. A contract will also add to the legitimacy and effectiveness of policy interventions and create an opportunity to make use of relevant information provided by the associations. But there are also some disadvantages. Accepting the terms of a contract by the association's members often depends on voluntary action and cannot be legally enforced. Therefore, the organizational strength of the association is critical. Furthermore, a collective contract requires willingness to compromise.

From the viewpoint of the associations, there are advantages and disadvantages as well. Collective contracting enables them to effectively articulate their interests and policy demands. They can directly influence policymaking. A potential danger is, however, that interest groups may be squeezed politically between the government and their members who demand a tough position or even radical action. Keeping internal control and cohesion may also be a difficult task. An interesting question is how collective policy contracting will develop in the future as market competition in health care advances under the 2006 reforms.

Governance at the insurer-provider level

Collective bargaining has always been a constituent element of health care governance in the Netherlands. Lijphart (1999) considers collective bargaining an essential element of what he terms the consensual type of democracy. Effective collective bargaining requires that at least three basic conditions be met: that both providers and insurers organize themselves in national associations of common interests; that the parties involved on each side are united in a single association; and that the association is cohesive. Generally, health care policymaking in the Netherlands has met these conditions, particularly since the 1980s.

A further distinction can be made between formal and informal bargaining. The Health Care Tariffs Law (Wet Tarieven Gezondheidszorg) enacted in 1982 provided a legal framework for bargaining over tariffs between the national associations of provider agents and health insurers. This law established formal rules for negotiating prices, and gave specific competencies to the CTG, the Ministry of Health, and the associations.

Nevertheless, the national associations meet in numerous informal settings where they exchange information, solve problems, and negotiate agreements. These informal arrangements reflect a deeply rooted propensity both to seek consensus and joint solutions, and to share responsibility.

Although collective bargaining has always been a prime characteristic of the relationship between provider agents and health insurers, since the early 1990s the trend has been toward more bilateral contracting. The ongoing extension of market competition will not only reinforce this trend, but also significantly alter the relationship between health insurers and provider agents by converting it into a commercial relationship.

Despite important differences with the sickness funds, private health insurers always participated in the machinery of collective contracting. They were also involved in negotiating volume agreements with hospitals. The main parties in these negotiations were the sickness fund with a dominant position in the region where the hospital was located, and the hospital. Private health insurers participated in the negotiations by means of a regional agent representing the interests of all private insurers. Thus, volume agreements were basically a contract between the hospital, the regionally dominant sickness fund, and the regional representative of private insurers.

Governance at the insurer level

Sickness funds in the Netherlands do not have shareholders: they are private nonprofit organizations (either a private foundation or a mutual society). Most private health insurers have no shareholders because they are organized as nonprofit mutuals. Only a few private insurers operate on a for-profit basis and have shareholders.

Although there is some variation, most sickness funds are managed by an executive board, consisting of two or three persons and presided over by a chief executive officer. The board, in turn, is controlled by a supervisory board. Control means that all strategic decisions of the executive board, including the annual budget estimate and financial account report, must be approved by the supervisory board. The supervisory board is also expected to function as a "sounding board" for the executive board. An important duty of the supervisory board is to appoint and remove members of the executive board.

There are no government regulations on the composition of the executive and supervisory boards. The members of the executive board are selected because of their professional and managerial competence; there is no duty to appoint a physician. The selection of the members of the supervisory board has become an important issue now that the financial and strategic accountability of sickness funds has significantly increased. A national commission published a report on health care governance, which set out several principles and rules on the composition and activities of the supervisory board, as well as on the relation between the supervisory and executive boards. These principles and rules were recently translated into a Code on Health Care Governance, which addresses professionalism, transparency, and accountability.

A weak element in the governance structure is that nobody controls the supervisory board. There are no shareholders. Therefore, supervisory boards are now requested to publish an annual report on their activities. When a supervisory board has seriously failed, its members can be held personally liable for the financial damage, but this is highly exceptional. Instead, one sees greater public control. For example, the minister of health recently openly criticized some boards for their approval of "excessive salaries" for executive board members. Media attention on the functioning of supervisory boards is also growing.

As far as internal structures are concerned, sickness funds are highly professional organizations. They must have well-developed internal audit systems. They must also select an independent external auditor. Before 2006, if the internal administrative structure did not meet professional standards, the CTZ could intervene. (The

CTZ's successor is now responsible for such oversight.) Each sickness fund has a medical adviser who may always be overruled by the fund's management.

Performance of mandatory health insurance
Role of contextual factors

Mandatory health insurance is embedded in the social system and many contextual factors influence its structure and performance. This section briefly analyzes four contexts: economic, political and administrative, demographic, and societal.

An MHI presupposes a well-structured *economy* because it is financed largely through payroll contributions and this requires that each subscriber's income must be known to the authorities. Systems that rely on such income-related contributions cannot properly function in economies with a large informal sector. The informal sector in the Netherlands is quite small.

As the economy has grown, the health insurance system has remained reasonably well financed. Nevertheless, the future is less certain. Policymakers have expressed concerns over the system's long-term financial sustainability. There are reports predicting that the fraction of health care expenditures in gross domestic product (now about 10 percent) may further grow to 18 percent or even higher, due to aging, new advances in medical technology, or other factors.

A second contextual factor is the *political and administrative* environment. The Netherlands has the capacity to manage this highly complex technical structure with a well-developed information system. Reforms involving greater financial accountability and risk-adjusted capitation payments increase the need for professional management that is neither subject to political influence nor driven by the self-interest of specific groups.

The structural incorporation of representative associations is a feature that also supports good governance for the system (Lijphart 1999). It rests on the concept—particularly prevalent in Christian democratic political thought—that responsibility for public policymaking and political power should not solely be concentrated in the state but should also be shared with representative associations. This governance model is assumed to increase the effectiveness and legitimacy of public policymaking. The prominent role of representative associations in health care governance reflects a long-standing political tradition in the Netherlands that is embedded in its political and administrative tradition.

The third contextual factor is *demography*. Because MHI is "pay-as-you-go," the working population pays the bulk of the costs. In the past, the Netherlands had a favorable dependency ratio (number of dependents to workers), but this is changing due to aging and to falling birth rates. The compound result is that a shrinking part of the population must pay for a rising number of elderly.

Another aspect of demographic change concerns the significant growth in immigrants. A large group of people living in the Netherlands have migrated from

Morocco, Netherlands Antilles, Surinam, and Turkey among other countries. The fraction of non-Western immigrant residents is now 10.4 percent of the population. This can create problems of communication between sickness funds and their members if the immigrants do not speak Dutch well. It also appears that immigrant residents tend to consume more health care than other residents.

The fourth contextual factor is the *attitude of the population* toward the system. The country has a long history of broad popular support for the Sickness Fund Scheme. For instance, Gevers et al. (2000) found that 77.7 percent of respondents to a Euro barometer survey agreed with the statement that "the government has to ensure that care is provided to all people residing legally here, irrespective of their income."

Cost control

Cost control has always been an important policy issue in health care policymaking in the Netherlands, but it became a top issue in the 1970s after the first oil crisis. Since then, the government has started many policy programs to limit health care expenditures through planning (including bed-reduction programs), fixed budgets, delisting, stricter eligibility criteria for health services and, to a lesser extent, cost sharing. Costs have, however, continued to rise. Largely in response to these rising costs, the government has adopted further reforms to introduce competition in health care, hoping that this would provide an additional check on rising costs.

Operational efficiency

The incentives for sickness funds to operate efficiently have always been weak. This was especially true before the 1990s because they were protected by full risk pooling. The structural absence of financial accountability encouraged the funds to play the "easy life game": why make trouble with providers if you have all your expenses reimbursed and you cannot benefit yourself from any financial gain? This situation began to change after risk-adjusted capitation payments were introduced in the 1990s.

One study (Douven and Schut 2006) suggests that these earlier reforms did not achieve their aims of encouraging greater operational efficiency by making sickness funds assume financial risk and face competition. Rather than market competition, the most important determinant of premiums was whether a fund had to build up sufficient financial reserves to obtain the required solvency margin. Another factor that influenced premiums was legislation stipulating that financial reserves may not exceed a certain amount (roughly 2.5 times the required minimum solvency margin). If a fund had more reserves, it was requested to pay back the surplus to the government. Therefore, sickness funds set their premiums to avoid such payments. This situation has radically changed with the 2006 reforms and sickness funds are more heavily influenced by a competitive market. Early indications show that funds have used their reserves for aggressive premium setting.

Administrative efficiency

Administrative costs made up a smaller share of costs in sickness funds than in private health insurance in 2003: 3.8 percent versus 10.4 percent.[4] This finding is consistent with observations in other countries. Various explanations are given, including that marketing costs for sickness funds are lower and they tend to have more members, allowing them to benefit from economies of scale.

Cost overruns

Fixed budgets have become a key instrument in cost control. The government defines ex ante budgets for the health care sector. Health insurers are involved in the procedure for setting these ex ante budgets for provider organizations by negotiating volume contracts. When costs overrun, the government usually takes measures to compensate for these overruns in later years. This is a political decision. The role of health insurers in correcting cost overruns by provider organizations is in most cases limited. However, this is changing as a consequence of greater market competition since the 2006 reforms. Monitoring actual production volume to see if it is in accordance with the volume contract is becoming an essential element of the relationship between provider and insurer.

Consumer choice

For a long time consumer choice in MHI was quite limited. Only a few regions had two or more sickness funds. This situation altered in 1992 when sickness funds were given the option to operate nationally like their private counterparts. Competition among the funds remained limited, generating limited consumer mobility (4–5 percent a year) during the time it was in effect.

Income distribution effects

Van Doorslaer and Wagstaff (1993) found that health care financing in the Netherlands is slightly regressive. At first sight, their finding may look strange, given the prominent role of solidarity arrangements. However, two factors contribute to this. First, about 35 percent of the population had private health insurance prior to 2006 and therefore did not contribute to the ZFW. Second, the existence of a statutory ceiling on contributions limited the amount paid by higher-income individuals.

Waiting lists

Health care in the Netherlands has always featured waiting lists, but they became a hot political issue in the late 1990s. The government came under increasing political pressure to take action. The media and a few court rulings played a prominent role in the process of agenda setting at that time, focusing on waiting lists in long-term care as well as in acute and elective care. The sickness funds could hardly be blamed for the "waiting list crisis" because they had little discretion to address it. Budget constraints, lack of powerful incentives to shorten waiting times, and organizational problems were the main causes of the crisis. Yet the sickness funds seized the opportunity offered by the waiting list crisis to strengthen their market profile, for instance by negotiating for the possibility of purchasing care in other countries (particularly Belgium).

Consumer satisfaction

A new development in health insurance is that consumers have Internet access to information on consumer satisfaction on insurers. Most insurers score between 7 and 8 on a scale from 1 to 10. Criteria are: personal treatment by the insurer; information; accessibility of client service; assistance to clients over the telephone; reimbursement issues; clarity of copayment arrangements; and complaints.

The new health insurance scheme

This section contains a brief overview of the key elements of the new health insurance legislation that came into effect in January 2006. The reforms are comprehensive, addressing issues that were perceived as highly problematic, such as the division between sickness funds and private health insurers and weak incentives for managing risk and for operating efficiently (Box 5.1).

Governance and the public purpose

The government presents the new health insurance scheme as an arrangement under private law in contrast with the former Sickness Fund Scheme, which was a scheme under public law. The relationship between insurer and subscriber is construed as a private one-year contractual relationship that the subscriber may renew each year but also terminate and replace with another relationship. Insurers for their part have the right to remove defaulters from the list of insured. Furthermore, insurers can set their own flat premium rates and may operate on a for-profit basis.

Nevertheless, the purpose of the new health insurance scheme is clearly public: to ensure that health insurance is accessible and affordable to the entire population. It contains many provisions to protect the "social good" and it is still fundamentally based upon the notion of solidarity (Maarse and Paulus 2003) because:

- Health insurers are forbidden to vary premiums with health risk and must accept each applicant. This provision is key to *risk* solidarity. But risk selection is only forbidden for the basic health plan, as the new legislation permits insurers to introduce risk-related premiums in complementary health plans. There is no legal obligation to accept each applicant either.

- To protect *income* solidarity, the government introduced an income-related allowance to make the purchase of a basic plan affordable to subscribers on low incomes, even if premiums rise sharply.

- The new scheme is mandatory for all legal residents and, therefore, puts an end to the traditional dividing line between social and private health insurance. One may argue that the new legislation implies greater solidarity than formerly because the previous scheme was limited to 63 percent of the population.

BOX 5.1 *Overview of the 2006 reforms*

The new health insurance legislation (Maarse and Bartholomée 2006) that came into effect in January 2006 puts an end to the traditional dividing line between sickness funds and private health insurers (Maarse and Okma 2004). A single health insurance scheme covers the entire population. Despite political resistance to reform and skepticism as to its effects, there has always been a broad consensus on the merits of a single scheme because it makes health insurance less complex and strengthens solidarity (Maarse and Paulus 2003).

A second key element concerns the extension of market competition in health insurance. Health insurers—which may operate on a for-profit basis—must compete on premiums, quality of care, and type of policy. With a few exceptions, all consumers have the right to choose their own insurer and type of policy (Maarse and ter Meulen 2006). In addition, they now have the right to switch to an alternative policy or another health insurer by the end of each calendar year. In order to guarantee consumer choice, insurers must accept each applicant. Health insurance legislation forbids any form of risk selection by denying access, charging a higher premium, or introducing exclusion waivers for preexisting medical disorders.

A third element regards premium setting. According to the new legislation, insurers must set a single flat premium rate for each type of health policy. According to government calculations, the premium rate of a standard policy was expected to average approximately €1,100 a year for each insured person. (In addition, all insured people must pay an income-related premium: 6 percent for the employed and 4.4 percent for the self-employed. The income level over which an

income-related premium must be paid is Ä30,000. The income-related premium is set by the government.) Insurers are forbidden to vary premium rates with age, gender, or specific health risks. Thus, a healthy 25-year-old man pays the same premium as a 75-year-old woman with chronic medical disorders if they purchase the same policy. However, legislation permits health insurers to develop a variety of policies with varying premium rates. The government pays the premium for children under 18. Subscribers on low incomes receive a government subsidy (a "health insurance subsidy") to maintain income solidarity and enable them to purchase a policy.

Market competition is expected to encourage health insurers to negotiate favorable contracts with health care providers in order to reinforce their position in the health insurance market. So as to reinforce their negotiating power, insurers are no longer obliged to contract with each provider. The new legislation allows them to sign contracts with only a limited number of "preferred providers," which include specific agreements on prices, waiting periods, and other themes.

A final element of the reforms introduces what the government terms "public constraints," by which the government seeks to ensure that, among other things, market competition improves the efficiency and quality of health care and does not erode access to it. Examples of public constraints are a ban on risk selection, an obligation to every citizen to purchase a basic policy, a centralized decision-making structure concerning the package of health services covered by the new health insurance scheme (the package is determined by the government), and a revised structure for supervision.

- The health services package of the scheme is fairly comprehensive and comparable to the package of the former Sickness Fund Scheme. The government, not insurers, decides upon the content of the package.
- The new health insurance scheme contains an extensive system of risk equalization to compensate health insurers for major differences in the risk profiles of their clients.

All these provisions to protect the social good contrast the new health insurance scheme with fully private systems, which tend to have a high degree of voluntary action, differentiated benefits packages, risk-related premiums, an absence of income-related premium rates, medical underwriting, and less state regulation (Colombo and Tapay 2004; Mossialos and Thomson 2004).

A hybrid system

The new MHI system can be best described as a scheme under private law with a public purpose. In other words, it is a hybrid, consisting of public and private elements. One could argue that this hybrid structure is not new because the former Sickness Fund Scheme also featured a public-private mix (Maarse and Okma 2004). Though this observation is correct, it misses an important point: the public-private mix of the new legislation differs in many respects from the public-private mix of the previous Sickness Fund Scheme. In particular, it allows for market and commercial (for-profit) elements in health insurance.

This hybrid structure may have important repercussions. One may predict (growing) tensions between the public and private elements. An analytical distinction can be made between tensions and coping strategies at the local level where health insurers and provider agents operate, and at the central level where the minister of health, Parliament, and other key national policymakers are involved.

In addition, traditionally sickness funds were bureaucratic, rule-driven task organizations charged with implementing statutory health insurance. They responded primarily to the state and not to the consumer. The introduction of market competition implies that they are transforming from such organizations into consumer-driven market-led organizations in which responding to consumers plays a primary role. More than ever, health insurers are hybrid agents that are expected to reconcile a bureaucratic orientation (the state as principal) with a market orientation (the consumer as principal). This hybrid structure will probably cause tensions because insurers as market agents will opt for strategies that may conflict with their role as agents for the public purpose. For instance, insurers will not negotiate a group contract with patient groups from whom they expect losses, even when underwriting those groups would be socially desirable.

New relationships

The new health insurance legislation aims at a reconstruction of the relationships between (a) the government and key market players (health insurers, providers) and (b) the market players among themselves. The introduction of market competition implies, in the view of the government, a fundamental change in the relationship between the government and insurers as well as providers, in which the market players have more room for playing their role as market agents, while the government restricts itself to defining the general framework for health care and its objectives.

Supervision

The introduction of market competition goes with a complete revision of the supervisory structure. Three generic supervisory agents currently regulate health insurers (and other private corporations): the Netherlands Competition Authority (Nederlandse Mededingingsautoriteit or NMa), the Netherlands Bank (De Nederlandse Bank), and the Financial Market Authority (Autoriteit Financiële Markten). There are also two health care-specific supervisory agents: the Health Care Inspectorate (Inspectie voor de Gezondheidszorg) and the Netherlands Health Care Authority (Nederlandse Zorgautoriteit or NZA).

The NMa supervises compliance with competition law. It must approve consolidations between insurers or provider organizations. Another of its supervisory tasks concerns compliance with the ban on cartels and the abuse of economic power. The activities of the NMa are closely related to EU regulations on market competition.

The Netherlands Bank is charged with the financial supervision of health insurers. It monitors whether a health insurer meets all license conditions, including solvency margin requirements. It also grants licenses to new entrants to the health insurance market.

The last generic supervisory agent is the Financial Market Authority. It is charged with supervising the market behavior of health insurers. Health insurers are forbidden—as are all providers of financial services—to spread misleading marketing information. The Law on Financial Services obliges them to inform their clients honestly and properly.

A traditional task of the Health Care Inspectorate is to supervise the quality of health care. A new task is to provide consumers with accurate and comparative information on the quality of health care of provider organizations such as hospitals or nursing homes. For that purpose the Inspectorate has started a project on health care performance indicators.

The NZA is a newly created agency in health care, and replaces both the CTG and the CTZ, which has ceased to operate as a separate organization and has been fully integrated into the NZA. The NZA has several tasks.

First, it must supervise the market behavior of health insurers and provider agents. With regard to health insurance, the NZA has responsibility to control whether health insurers act in accordance with the new legislation. Of particular importance in this respect are the insurer's obligation to contract health care of sufficiently high quality for its affiliates, the ban on risk selection by insurers, and the ban on premium differentiation by insurers.[5]

Another important duty of the NZA concerns the supervision of market behavior in health care purchasing. Here, it has the authority to impose obligations on agents with substantial market power as a policy intervention in order to ensure competition and compensate for market imperfections. For instance, the NZA can limit the maximum volume of care that a large health insurer can purchase in a geographic area if this will stop the insurer destroying market competition in that area by purchasing (almost) all provider capacity. In a similar way, the NZA is authorized to impose limits on health care providers with substantial market power in a particular geographic area. In short, it is the task of the NZA to create the conditions for market competition and to protect consumer rights.

The NZA is not, however, restricted to supervision. It is also charged with:

- Performing analyses of submarkets in health care.
- Advising the minister of health on which submarkets in health care can be opened for market competition. The NZA must assess whether the conditions for market competition are fulfilled.
- Regulating prices in submarkets not (yet) opened for market competition.
- Regulating the description of health care products.
- Giving consumers information about health insurers and health care providers to which they are entitled.

As can be seen, the NZA has a double-governance remit: it performs not only supervisory but also regulatory tasks, including market-making tasks. It remains to be seen if these two strands are fully compatible.

The new supervisory structure is quite complex. There are multiple supervisory agencies with sometimes overlapping roles. Protocols have therefore been signed to regulate the "administrative traffic" between these agencies and to avoid confronting health insurers and providers with conflicting demands and administrative burdens. Another point is the division of tasks and responsibilities between the minister of health and the NZA. A further concern is whether the NZA is able to perform its supervisory and administrative tasks properly. It has various legal instruments with which to intervene, but will intervention be timely to avoid "market accidents"? A final key issue involves finding a proper balance between strict supervision and giving sufficient flexibility to allow competition and innovation to flourish.

Information for consumers

An important condition for market competition is information. Consumers must have access to reliable and comparative information on health plans and the performance of health insurers to make an optimal choice on their health plan. Patients and clients must have adequate information on the performance of health care providers. Access to adequate and comparative information is problematic in health care. There is not only the problem of information asymmetry between provider agents and patients/clients, but also the problem of lack of transparency in the health insurance market.

In order to tackle this problem, the government has been spending much energy on informing the public. Web site information (www.kiesbeter.nl) plays a key role in this respect. There are also private providers of comparative information on performance in health care (see, for example, www.independer.nl). The information industry for health care in the Netherlands is rapidly growing.

Preliminary results

In their first six months, the 2006 reforms led to significant changes. First, almost 20 percent of the insured switched to another insurer (Vektis 2006), a percentage much higher than expected by all experts. Research suggests that consumers were sensitive to premium differences as well as to the expected performance of health insurers (Deloitte 2006). The flat-rate premiums charged by insurers were also lower than expected by the minister of health. However, some commentators are concerned that such low premiums are unsustainable and predict a 15–20 percent rise. Third, market competition has led to further consolidation: two major mergers were announced in the first half of 2006, each covering about 25 percent of the total market, although they both await NMa approval.

Some lessons

The Netherlands experience suggests the following:

- No single blueprint exists for MHI schemes. To a large extent, the specific shape of each system can even be viewed as a particular political compromise between diverging interests. Countries considering the introduction of MHI should avoid the temptation to copy what has been established elsewhere.
- From what has been seen in the Netherlands, it seems that countries implementing MHI should aim for a single scheme covering the entire population. The coexistence of MHI and private health insurance is a source of administrative problems. Specific schemes for selected groups also cause structural fragmentation in health insurance.
- An institutional split is necessary if countries want health insurers to negotiate with provider organizations. A disadvantage of legislating such a split is that it renders impossible arrangements that integrate health insurance and health care delivery.
- Public health insurance systems can involve private organizations. Netherlands sickness funds are private agents offering health insurance within a publicly mandated scheme. All hospitals and other provider institutions are private nonprofit agents.
- Effective collective bargaining between interest groups in health care policymaking may need a consensual type of democracy with notions of shared responsibility. It may also require strong representative associations that can speak for their members and that are capable of implementing contracts negotiated with the government.

Annex 5.1   Governance in mandatory health insurance

	Composition of board (CTG, CTZ, CVZ)	Nomination of board chair	Health care legislation	Level of financing	Package decisions	Regulations
Prime minister	–	–	+	+	–	–
Constitutional Court	–	–	–	–	–	–
Minister of health	++	++	++	++	++	++
Minister of finance	–	–	–	++	–	–
Parliament	–	–	++	+	++	+
CVZ	–	–	+	+	+	+
CTZ	–	–	–	–	–	+
CTG	–	–	–	–	–	+
Health insurers	–	–	–	+	+	–
Providers	–	–	–	–	–	–
Ombudsman	–	–	–	–	–	–

Note: CTG = Health Care Tariffs Board; CTZ = Supervisory Board for Health Care Insurance; CVZ = Health Care Insurance Board.

++ = strong influence; + = moderate influence; – = no influence.

Capital investments	Contracting	Procurement	Quality improvement	User protection	Salaries	Information
–	-	–	–	–	–	–
–	+	+	–	+	–	–
++	+	–	++	–	–	+
–	–	–	–	–	-	–
+	-	-	–	–	-	–
–	–	–	+	–	–	–
–	–	–	–	+	–	–
+	+	–	–	–	–	+
+	+	+	+	–	–	+
+	+	+	+	–	–	+
–	–	–	–	++	–	–

Annex 5.2 Dimensions, features, and indicators of good governance in mandatory health insurance: The Netherlands

Dimension	Features	Indicators	Value	Explanation
Coherent decisionmaking structures	1. Responsibility for MHI objectives must correspond with decisionmaking power and capacity in each institution involved in the management of the system.	Yes/No Examples: Provisions for the administration costs/resources of MHI regulators and MHI entities are made in legal texts.	++	Such provisions existed before the 2006 reforms (with a fixed budget for administrative costs). Under the present regulations they are no longer important, because health insurers have an economic interest in keeping their administrative costs as low as possible (due to market competition).
		Responsibility, like coverage for a prescribed benefits package by MHI entities, has to go hand in hand with the decisionmaking power for premium levels and/or provision of care.	++	Prior to 2006, the government was responsible for deciding coverage and premium levels. Under new legislation, the government has kept power to regulate the benefits package, but insurers can now set their own flat-rate premium. They also have some freedom as regards the benefits package. For example, they are permitted to offer a package with or without a deductible or a preferred provider network. This is all regulated in the new health insurance law.
		Regular reviews of the cost of coverage, appropriateness of premium levels, and ways of provision are established in legal texts or by the regulator.	–	No government regulations exist for this. However, health insurers will set up regular reviews to assess their market position.
		Review committees with wide stakeholder participation on coverage, premium level etc. are in place.	–	They are in place but there seems to be no regulation in this respect. Patient groups and other interested groups may set up their own reviews. Such reviews may also be organized by health insurers to keep in touch with their insured.

	Yes/No Example:		
2. All MHI entities have routine risk assessment and management strategies in place.	Clear regulations on MHI entities' continuous risk assessment and risk management are in place.	++	These have always been in place, but have gained further importance after the introduction of market competition in the 2006 reforms (which led to a large increase in the risks that health insurers incur).
	Strategies are in place, i.e. MHI entities follow and analyze the evolution of expenditures and contributions.	++	These have always been in place. The trend is that health insurers have gained a stronger interest in this type of analysis.
	MHI entities have the capacity to manage risks, i.e. to take corrective action in order to ensure the financial sustainability of the system by modifying some of the parameters influencing it (contribution rate, composition of the benefits package etc.).	++	
3. The cost of regulating and administering MHI institutions is reasonable and appropriate.	**Yes/No** Example: Maximum administration costs for MHI entities are set in legal texts or regulations.	+	This was the case before 2006 (with fixed administrative costs), but no longer because it is in the insurers' interests to keep these costs low.
	Administrative costs are monitored by the regulator.	+	This has always been the case.
	Provisions for covering the costs of the MHI regulator are stipulated in legal texts.	++	Increasing the efficiency of MHI is currently an important objective of the reforms. One tool is to reduce administrative costs. Therefore, assessment of administrative costs and benefits has become part of the legislative procedure.
	Before new regulations are put in place a cost-benefit assessment is conducted.	++	The government expects that market competition will cause a decrease in administrative costs but many have doubts on this. Some costs are likely to decline, but other costs will certainly grow rapidly.

(continues)

Dimension	Features	Indicators	Value	Explanation
Stakeholder participation	4. Stakeholders have effective representation in the governing bodies of MHI entities.	Yes/No Examples: Governing bodies of regulatory oversight and institutional governance (board of directors, oversight body) have representatives of government agencies, regulatory bodies, MHI entities, unions, employers' organizations, beneficiaries, providers and independent experts.	+	Before the 1990s, representatives of employers, unions, providers, and insurers had their representatives on the board of these bodies. Reforms of these bodies has ended this representative model. Currently, the board consists of independent experts, appointed by the minister of health. However, under the board there are usually various working groups active, in which stakeholders often have their own representatives.
		Representation is effective, i.e. different stakeholders' views are considered in decisionmaking.	++	In these working groups representation is effective. According to health care policymaking tradition in the Netherlands, the minister of health is expected, if not required, to negotiate bilaterally with interest groups on health care issues in order to build consensus. The Netherlands also has a long tradition of corporatist policymaking. In this model, interest groups are given a prominent role in both making and implementing policy.
Transparency and information	5. The objectives of MHI are formally and clearly defined.	Yes/No Examples: Objectives are stated in a high-level legal text (e.g. the Constitution or a law).	++	Objectives are stated in the Sickness Fund Law and the Exceptional Medical Expenses Law. However, both laws are framework laws providing the legal basis for many additional regulations on specific topics.
		Objectives are publicized and easily accessible to the public.	+	Objectives are publicized and/or clearly defined but are not so easily accessible to or understandable by the general public. This is due to the highly complex nature of the legislation, and the fact that it consists of numerous detailed regulations.
		Objectives are clearly defined and easily understandable.	+	Though many changes in the legislation have been made, the main objectives have remained substantially the same over the last few decades.

6. MHI relies upon an explicit and an appropriately designed institutional and legal framework.	Objectives have remained substantially the same in the recent past.	++	The legislation's objectives after the 2006 reforms are also formally and clearly defined. Risk solidarity as well as income solidarity remain the cornerstone of health insurance legislation.
	Yes/No		
	Examples:		
	The main characteristics of the system are defined in legal texts (coverage, benefits package, financing, provision, regulatory oversight, and institutional governance).	++	All elements of MHI are defined in legal texts. According to national law, all government programs or interventions must have a proper legal basis. This is the principle of legality (or the rule of law). Legislation provides the legal basis for specific regulations on coverage, benefits package, and so on.
	The framework is appropriate given the country MHI context (i.e. it is not too restrictive, considers special local circumstances and does not ignore important parts or players in the system).	+	The framework has been considered appropriate for a long period, though many saw the limited personal scope (the Sickness Fund Law covered only 63 percent of the population) as a significant weakness. Currently, the framework is no longer considered appropriate because it lacks powerful incentives for efficiency, innovation, and high-quality care. Health insurers should also be given more policy discretion to serve their insured, but within a set of strict regulations, termed "public constraints". This is a cornerstone of the ongoing reforms toward regulated market competition.
	The regulatory agency is independent or not.	++	The regulatory agencies (CTZ and CVZ) were granted independent status in 2001. The status of the regulatory body on health care tariffs (CTG) has always been semi-independent. It has frequently received instructions from the minister of health.
	The status and responsibilities of each different MHI institution in the system are clearly defined and transparent.	++	Generally yes, though there is always some debate on lack of a clear division of responsibilities and lack of transparency. The institutional and legal framework for MHI legislation underwent substantial reform in 2006 when the new Health Insurance Law came into effect.

(continues)

Dimension	Features	Indicators	Value	Explanation
7. Clear information, disclosure, and transparency rules are in place.		Yes/No		
		Examples:		
		Explicit disclosure regulations exist in the law or regulations of the law.	++	Until recently, this was not a big issue because sickness funds were not permitted to engage in business activities. A new disclosure arrangement is that each health insurer (or provider) must annually publish information on its chief executive's salary.
		Business activities, ownership, and financial positions are regularly disclosed (i.e. the rules are followed).	+	
		MHI entities deliver to a beneficiary on demand a copy of its rules and the latest annual financial statements.	+	This topic is now becoming extremely important. Because health insurers can develop various health plans, applicants are strongly recommended to ask for a copy of the rules in the plan. The problem is that these rules can only be properly understood by experts. There seems to be no obligation to deliver the latest annual financial statements. Probably, the insurer will send its annual report, which also includes some data on its financial position.
		The presence of a free press.	++	Not only formal agencies but also social agencies such as citizen groups and the press play a role here. Currently, their role is becoming far more important. For instance, the salaries of the chief executives in health insurance (health care) companies, and other public and semi-public policy sectors, are now reported.
		Information on performance (quality of care, costs, consumer satisfaction).	++	There are now many efforts to measure the performance of health insurers and provider organizations and to disclose information to the general public through the Internet.

8. MHI entities have minimum requirements in regard to protecting the insured.	Yes/No		
	Examples:		
Consumer protection regulations exist in law, including consumer information, and independent mechanisms for resolution of complaints, appeals, grievances, and disputes.		+	A weak form of consumer protection is the institution of the "Ombudsman". The insured have the formal right to appeal decisions of their sickness fund, but it is unlikely that they have used this right frequently. Note that consumer protection is also a fundamental argument for setting up an effective supervisory structure. The supervisory agent must ensure that sickness funds abide by MHI legislation and that their solvency is guaranteed.
The insured can obtain timely, complete and relevant information changes in benefits or premium, changes in coverage length etc.		+	This has never been a big issue in MHI legislation in the Netherlands. MHI was a low-interest good for most citizens. Changes in coverage length were not relevant because of the principle of lifetime cover. This was likely only an issue for those people who switched between MHI and private health insurance. Since the 2006 reforms, the need for timely, complete, and relevant information has become a key issue. The rights and duties of all parties (insurers, insured) are well defined in the new health insurance legislation.
Consumer complaint mechanisms exist and are being used.		++	Most likely not often used, though this may now be changing after the 2006 reforms.
Appeals and grievance mechanisms exist and are being used.		+	See above.
Independent dispute resolution mechanisms exist and are being used.		+	See above.

(continues)

Dimension	Features	Indicators	Value	Explanation
Supervision and regulation	9. Rules on compliance, enforcement and sanctions for MHI supervision are clearly defined.	Yes/No Examples: Rules on compliance and sanctions are defined in legal texts.	++	They are clearly defined, but there is always room for different interpretations.
		Corrective actions are imposed, based on clear and objective criteria that are publicly disclosed.	++	CTZ has imposed corrective actions (mainly financial).
		Adequate capacity for the execution of these functions is provided.	+	Regulatory bodies tend to complain on this issue.
		Cases of rule violation and subsequent actions by the regulator are publicized.	+	All regulatory agents publish annual reports with information on these issues.
	10. Financial management rules for MHI entities are clearly defined and enforced.	Yes/No Examples: Financial standards for MHI entities are defined in legal text or regulations.	+	For a long time financial standards were not important for the sickness funds because they had all their expenses reimbursed from the central fund, provided that they were legal, i.e. in accordance with MHI-legislation. This changed somewhat after the introduction of a fixed budget for administrative expenses. Under the 2006 reforms, financial standards gained importance. There are now regulations for solvency and minimum levels of financial reserves.
		Clear financial licensure/market-entry rules are defined (minimum capital requirements).	++	Not important in the past. The trend was consolidation of sickness funds.
		Ongoing reserve and solvency requirements are defined.	+	This is more important in the present legislation, although the trend will remain one of consolidation of health insurers.

Regulations of assets and financial investments are defined.	++	Solvency and reserves were not important in the past. They are now very important because of market competition.
Audit (internal and external) rules are defined.	+	This has always been important because sickness funds could make "excess revenues" (not the same as a profit).
Rules for financial standards are enforced.	++	These rules are essential in a system of regulated market competition.
11. The MHI system has structures for ongoing supervision and monitoring in place.	Yes/No Examples:	
Clear nonfinancial licensure/market entry rules are defined.	+	A weakness of the system was that there were no clear rules on the governance of sickness funds (and provider service organizations in general). This is still an institutional weakness. There is now a Health Care Governance Code, which is a product of self-regulation.
Insurance product filing/registration is defined and regulated.	++	Note that product filing/registration in MHI was a government task, and has remained so in the new legislation. Furthermore, there is general regulation product filing/registration in private insurance schemes.
Adequate on-site inspections and off-site monitoring are in place.	++	Regulatory agencies play an important role in this respect.
Ongoing financial reporting rules are defined and provided information is accurate and timely.	++	
Clear market exit/dissolution rules are in place.	++	

(continues)

Dimension	Features	Indicators	Value	Explanation
Consistency and stability	12. The main qualities of the MHI system are stable.	Yes/No Examples: The fundamental characteristics of the MHI system (e.g. benefits package, rules for affiliation, contribution requirements, basic protection rights for the insured and basic institutional requirements for operators) are defined in law.	++	Principle of legality (rule of law).
		The law has remained substantially the same in the recent past (i.e. independent of political elections or economic crises).	++	MHI legislation has remained substantially the same since its enactment in the 1960s. Of course, there have been many changes (e.g. extension of coverage with regard to people and the benefits package), but these did not substantially affect the basic structure of insurance. MHI has also been largely impervious to political changes and economic crises (although such crises always provoke a political debate on the need for more effective cost-control mechanisms in MHI). As spelled out elsewhere, substantial reforms were introduced in 2006. The former Sickness Fund Law has been replaced with the Health Insurance Act (2006).

++ = relevant to the Netherlands; + = relevant to the Netherlands to some extent; – = not relevant to the Netherlands.

Endnotes

1. For a history of health insurance in the Netherlands, see De Bruine and Schut (1990) and Schut (1995).
2. These figures are from the Ministry of Health and differ somewhat from Organisation for Economic Co-operation and Development data (of 62.4 percent in 2003) due to different accounting principles.
3. From 2007 under the ZFW, the insured are reimbursed for the costs of three in vitro fertilization treatments. At present, they are covered only for the second and third.
4. Under the AWBZ, administrative expenses accounted for 1.4 percent of total outlays.
5. The NZA is also in charge of supervising the AWBZ.

Reference list and bibliography

CVZ (College voor de Zorgverzekeringen). 2005. "Financiële positie Algemene Kas ZFW." Amstelveen, the Netherlands.

Colombo, F., and N. Tapay. 2004. "Private Health Insurance in OECD Countries: The Benefits and Costs for Individuals and Health Systems." OECD Health Working Papers No. 15. Paris.

De Bruine, M., and F. Schut. 1990. "Overheidsbeleid en ziektekostenverzekering." In J. Maarse and I. Mur-Veeman, eds., *Beleid en beheer in de gezondheidszorg*. Assen/Maastricht: Van Gorcum, pp. 114–149.

Deloitte. 2006. "Collectieve afhankelijkheid. Een onderzoek naar de mobiliteit in de verzekeringsmarkt." Amstelveen, the Netherlands.

Douven, R., and F. Schut. 2006. *Health Plan Pricing Behavior and Managed Competition.* The Hague: Centraal Planbureau.

Gevers, J., J. Gelissen, W. Arts, and R. Muffels. 2000. "Public Health Care in the Balance: Exploring Popular Support for Health Care Systems in the European Union." *International Journal of Social Welfare* 9(4):301–321.

Kuipers, S. 2004. *Cast in Concrete: The Institutional Dynamics of Belgian and Dutch Social Policy Reform.* Delft: Eburon

Lijphart, A. 1999. *Patterns of Democracy.* New Haven/London: Yale University Press.

Maarse, J., and A. Paulus. 2003. "Has Solidarity Survived? A Comparative Analysis of the Effect of Social Health Insurance Reform in Four European Countries." *Journal of Health Politics, Policy and Law* 28(4):585–614.

Maarse, J., and K. Okma. 2004. "The Privatisation Paradox in Dutch Health Care." In J. Maarse, ed., *The Privatisation of European Health Care: A Comparative Perspective in Eight Countries.* Maarssen: Elsevier Gezondheidszorg, pp. 97–116.

Maarse, J., A. Paulus, and G. Kuiper. 2005. "Supervision in Social Health Insurance: A Four-country Study." *Health Policy* 71(3):333–346.

Maarse, J., and Y. Bartholomée. 2006. "Health Insurance Reform in the Netherlands." *Eurohealth* 12(2).

Maarse, J., and R. ter Meulen. 2006. "Consumer Choice in Dutch Health Insurance after Reform." *Health Care Analysis* 14(1).

Mossialos, E., and S. Thomson. 2004. "Voluntary Health Insurance in the European Union." Brussels: European Observatory on Health Care Systems.

Palm, W. 2002. "Voluntary Health Insurance and EU Directives: Between Solidarity and the Market." In M. McKee, E. Mossialos, and R. Baeten, eds. *The Impact of EU Law on Health Care Systems.* Brussels: P.I.E. Peter Lang, pp. 195–234.

Saltman, R., R. Busse, and J. Figueras, eds. 2004. *Social Health Insurance Systems in Western Europe.* Maidenhead and New York City: The Open University Press.

Schut, F. 1995. *Competition in the Dutch Health Care Sector.* Ridderkerk: Ridderprint.

Van Doorslaer, E., and A. Wagstaff. 1993. *Equity in the Finance and Delivery of Health Care: An International Perspective.* Oxford: Oxford University Press.

Vektis. 2005. *Zorgmonitor.* Driebergen-Zeist.

6

Governing a hybrid mandatory health insurance system: The case of Chile

Ricardo Bitrán, Rodrigo Muñoz, Liliana Escobar, and Claudio Farah [1]

Editors' introduction

Chile has had a long-standing commitment to public health and initiated mandatory health insurance for formal sector workers in 1924. In a major health reform in the early 1980s, it created a single national public insurer, the National Health Insurance Fund (Fondo Nacional de Salud or FONASA), and allowed individuals to choose between FONASA and private health insurance funds called ISAPREs (instituciones de salud provisional). The private health insurance market was largely unregulated for its first 10 years, expanded fairly rapidly to reach about one-quarter of the population, but presented high administrative costs and widely varying benefits packages. In the 1990s Chilean governments gave FONASA greater financial and political support and introduced a more coherent regulatory structure for the ISAPREs. In 2004 a single regulatory office was created, to supervise both FONASA and the ISAPREs.

The country has two different forms of health insurer governance—one for FONASA, which is directly accountable to the government, and one for the ISAPREs, which are directly accountable to their shareholders but which also must abide by the government's regulations. Since FONASA covers almost 80 percent of the population, it has a substantial impact on prices, benefits, and market conditions.

This case study suggests several lessons for governing mandatory health insurance:

- *A public health insurer can perform well with direct accountability to the government. Chile demonstrates how a well-functioning government, with checks and balances provided by different ministries and an independent external auditor, appears capable of improving coverage and quality of services for beneficiaries primarily through a single payer.*
- *In systems with multiple insurers, common regulations and a single regulatory agency can facilitate equal treatment of beneficiaries, protect consumers, reduce risk selection, and increase transparency.*

- *It is possible for governments to introduce significant regulations for private health insurers. Chile's health insurers were largely unregulated for a decade. Subsequently, regulations were introduced to address client grievances, financial solvency, pricing, and benefits. These regulations restructured the health insurance market, forcing private health insurers to compete more on premiums and quality rather than using strategies such as risk selection or tailored insurance contracts.*

- *A well-regulated competitive health insurance market may not be viable. In response to the changing regulatory environment, the number of ISAPREs has declined significantly and the share of beneficiaries choosing these private health insurers has also declined. It remains to be seen whether private insurers in Chile will continue to operate for a small niche (less than 20 percent of the population) or whether they will disappear altogether for lack of financial viability.*

- *Transparency requires a variety of reporting mechanisms when multiple forms of health insurance are available. In Chile, FONASA reports annually to Congress, on a regular basis to the Controller-General's Office, and more recently also to the Superintendancy of Health (Superintendencia de Salud or SIS). Private health insurers are required to report key financial, operational, and performance indicators to the national health insurance regulatory office, and remain subject to the normal reporting requirements for private firms.*

- *A public health insurance agency can compete quite effectively with private health insurers if it is run well.*

Framework for analyzing governance and performance

This chapter seeks to analyze the relationship between the *governance* and the *performance* of Chile's mandatory health insurance (MHI) system. In its broader definition, governance encompasses "all of the relevant factors that influence the behavior of an organization" (Savedoff 2005). For MHI, these relevant factors can be classified into three categories (Figure 6.1):

- **Design.** How MHI is designed influences the kinds of governance forces that will be in place, and the consequences that these forces will have on health insurers' performance.

- **Accountability.** Health insurers are typically responsible for their actions and performance, and must be prepared to explain them to others. Generally, they are accountable to regulatory agencies, government and/or Congress, the legal system, beneficiaries, owners, government controllers-general, health care providers, payers (if different from the actual beneficiaries), and creditors.

- **Other Forces.** The behavior and performance of health insurers may also be affected by other forces that may (or may not) be a consequence of the MHI

FIGURE 6.1   Governance forces in mandatory health insurance: The general case

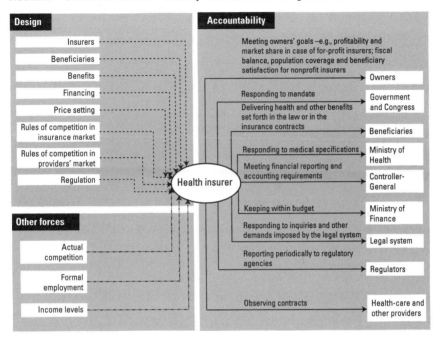

Source: Authors.

system's design. They include competition from other insurers and economic factors, such as the formal sector employment rate and income levels.

A key measure of performance within an MHI system is the degree to which insurers facilitate beneficiaries' access to a set of health care services, cover part or all the cost of those services, financially protect beneficiaries against catastrophically high health expenses, and keep beneficiaries satisfied overall with the insurance service provided (Figure 6.2). Policymakers and regulators generally have additional concerns, expecting insurers to remain financially solvent and sustainable, to achieve certain levels of population coverage, and to ensure that the health services covered respond to some minimum quality standards.

Drawing a causal link between governance and performance is naturally difficult given the multitude of factors simultaneously influencing insurers' performance. Furthermore, performance is influenced by variables not under a health insurer's control. These other factors include elements of the system's design, as well as external or exogenous influences shown as "other forces" in Figure 2.2. The analysis and conclusions that follow must be interpreted in light of this inherent complexity.

FIGURE 6.2   Influence of governance on health insurers' performance

Governance forces

Design	Accountability	Other forces

Health insurer

Remaining solvent and financially sustainable	Reaching population coverage objectives	Preserving standards of quality of health services	Facilitating beneficiaries' access to health services	Covering part of the cost of services	Financially protecting beneficiaries against catastrophic health expenses	Keeping beneficiaries satisfied overall with service

Health insurers' performance

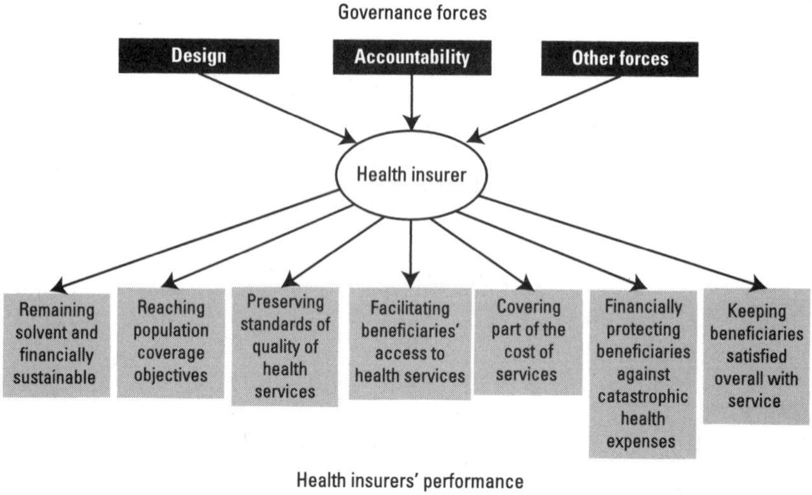

Source: Authors.

Governance

Overview of the mandatory health insurance system

Chile's MHI system has multiple competing insurers. It is supervised by the Superintendancy of Health (Superintendencia de Salud or SIS), which has authority over both public and private health insurers. Its main regulatory functions address beneficiary protection, financial solvency of ISAPREs, and compliance by both the National Health Insurance Fund (Fondo Nacional de Salud or FONASA) and health insurance funds (*instituciones de salud previsional* or ISAPREs) with the provision of benefits required by law. Before 2005 there was no such thing as a basic benefits package required of FONASA or ISAPREs, although the latter could not provide less financial coverage than the former. Starting in 2005 a new set of laws collectively known as "explicit health guarantees" (*garantías explícitas de salud* or GES) required all health insurers—public and private—to progressively expand coverage until they now include treatment for 56 legally defined health problems.

Chile's MHI system is also characterized by a split between financing and provision. By law, neither public nor private insurers can be vertically integrated with health care providers. In the public sector, FONASA acts solely as a financing agent, and provision is left in the hands of the Ministry of Health. In the private sector, ISAPREs are prohibited from direct provision of health care services.

This split has given beneficiaries a wider choice of provider alternatives. FONASA beneficiaries may choose to seek care from any provider, public or private, as long as it is registered with FONASA. If the provider is public (called

Modalidad de Atención Institucional or MAI), service is free or there is a nominal copayment. If the provider is private (Modalidad de Libre Elección or MLE), copayments are larger. ISAPRE beneficiaries have similar choices, but almost always seek care in the private sector.

Despite the split, FONASA is constrained by law to purchase the majority of the health services it covers from public hospitals and health centers, although it also provides a modest subsidy to its beneficiaries willing to buy private health care. Public health care providers must by law sell the majority of their services to FONASA, while being subject to tight limits on the kinds and volumes of services they may sell to private patients and to ISAPRE beneficiaries.

By law, all formal sector employees, retired workers with a pension, and independent workers with a retirement fund must enroll with a health insurer by making a monthly contribution equal to 7 percent of their income or pension. In return, they choose whether to be insured by FONASA or by a particular ISAPRE. Other individuals may enroll as well, including independent workers without a retirement fund, who may voluntarily enroll with FONASA or an ISAPRE conditional on their 7 percent contribution; and legally certified indigent citizens and legally unemployed workers, who are entitled to free coverage by FONASA. ISAPRE members can purchase additional benefits, such as lower copayments and more services, by making a monthly contribution above the required 7 percent contribution, and many do so.

FONASA, the single public insurer and by far the system's largest, with a market share of 79.5 percent at the end of 2003, came into existence in 1981, replacing the country's national health service (Figure 6.3). A decree issued by the Ministry of Health in 1981 authorized the private sector to offer health insurance through private corporations (the ISAPREs). Five of these entities were founded at the end of 1981. The number of ISAPREs grew steadily until it reached a peak of 35 in the first half of the 1990s. By the end of 2005 however, only 15 ISAPREs were still

FIGURE 6.3   Main design reforms in Chile's mandatory health insurance system, 1980–2005

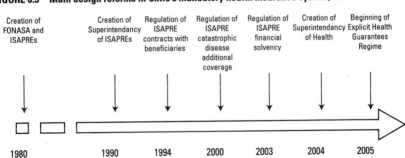

Source: Authors.

operating (Figure 6.4). From 1981 until the creation of the Superintendancy of ISAPREs in 1990, ISAPREs were largely unregulated. Today ISAPREs, like FONASA, are regulated by the SIS.

As the number of ISAPREs has fallen, market concentration has also increased. In 1990 the three largest ISAPREs captured 43 percent of the total ISAPRE market; by the end of 2005, that share had grown to just over two-thirds. There are two basic kinds of ISAPREs, open and closed. Open ISAPREs compete with each other for beneficiaries from the general population and most are for-profit entities. In 2005 open ISAPREs covered almost 95 percent of all individuals affiliated with ISAPREs. Closed ISAPREs, covering the remaining 5 percent, belonged to large companies in mining, oil, steel, and other industries, admitting as beneficiaries only employees and their dependents.

Governance through design

Discretion over who to insure. Individual insurers have different degrees of discretion over who to enroll. FONASA cannot deny coverage to anybody who applies if they are a legal citizen, and it has no discretion over premiums, which are established by law. ISAPREs, in contrast, are subject to fewer rules about enrollment. When ISAPREs were created in 1981, enrollment was scarcely regulated, and these private insurers used their discretionary powers to enroll or deny enrollment to applicants and to terminate contracts unilaterally. ISAPREs were also allowed to set their premiums, thus enabling them to charge higher premiums to higher-risk applicants or to refuse admission altogether. Recent regulations have limited these powers.

Discretion over what to cover. Before 2005 FONASA did not provide an explicit or detailed definition of its medical benefits. Whereas in principle all medical services made available by modern medicine were in FONASA's implicit set of benefits, in practice availability of care varied from service to service as a function of supply and demand. Queues were used to "ration" utilization by FONASA beneficiaries for the more scarce and expensive services. In contrast, the law has always required ISAPREs to explicitly define covered medical benefits through a formal contract to be signed between the ISAPRE and its member.

By law, health insurers must provide financial coverage for medical care and must fully or partly replace the member's income while that person is away from work during illness or on maternity leave. Both FONASA and ISAPREs cover all or part of the price of ambulatory and hospital services. At FONASA, this coverage drops as income rises. At ISAPREs though, coverage typically rises with income, because richer beneficiaries enroll in plans with higher financial coverage, thus making lower copayments when obtaining medical care. The legally mandated income replacement benefit during illness has an income limit of US$2,000

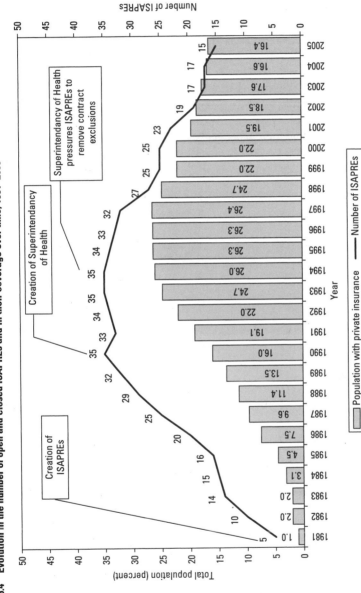

FIGURE 6.4 Evolution in the number of open and closed ISAPREs and in their coverage over time, 1981–2005

Source: Authors from Superintendancy of Health reports.

per month. Income replacement during maternity leave is financed by the government, and is also subject to the monthly limit of US$2,000.

The lack of a common set of benefits for FONASA and ISAPREs before 2005 meant that beneficiaries were often misinformed about their rights. It also limited competition among ISAPREs and between FONASA and the ISAPREs. Further, ISAPREs offered several thousand medical plans to potential clients, making comparison of plans of a single ISAPRE difficult and of different ISAPREs impractical. This led to limited transparency and competition. In response starting in 2005, the GES reform mandated that all health insurers cover 56 specific medical conditions, thus defining, for the first time, a floor of uniform benefits across all insurers in the system, both public and private.

Sources of funds. The Chilean MHI system relies on three major sources of funding: mandatory contributions, voluntary contributions, and government subsidies. The mandatory monthly contribution is a percentage of workers' gross salary: in 1980–84, it was 4 percent. In 1984 a world economic crisis and the military government's macroeconomic stabilization policy led it to increase this contribution to 7 percent. This had some impact on the profile of beneficiaries in ISAPREs, in the sense that the larger contribution established incentives for the ISAPREs to attract middle-income workers. The number of ISAPREs and ISAPRE beneficiaries then rose steeply (Figure 6.4 above). Another characteristic of MHI contributions is that they are capped at US$140 per month—equivalent to 2.3 percent of Chilean per capita gross domestic product (GDP) of around US$6,000. This cap was introduced because, otherwise, contributors with high salaries would be paying much more than the actuarially fair price of insurance benefit, and ISAPREs would be making excessive profits from mandatory contributions. The ceiling also deters high-income workers from evading or eluding contributions, or from avoiding formal labor.

Voluntary contributions are allowed in ISAPREs, but not in FONASA. In FONASA, such contributions make no sense, because plans are predefined and do not offer additional coverage as an option. ISAPREs, on the contrary, can offer additional coverage for beneficiaries who want it.

Government subsidies are the last major source of financing for the MHI system. Thirty-five percent of the cost of MHI benefits is financed by contributions from ISAPRE beneficiaries and 24 percent from FONASA beneficiaries. The remaining 41 percent is financed almost entirely by subsidies from general revenues, and is key to the system's sustainability.[2, 3] Therefore, setting FONASA's annual public budget appropriately is one of the most important government decisions influencing MHI system financing.

In 2003 Congress approved an additional source of funds, levying a 1 percentage point value-added tax increase (from 18 percent to 19 percent) to finance the newly created GES regime and the Chile Solidario Program (a cash and in-kind subsidy program targeted at families in extreme poverty).

FONASA's budget process and price setting. Because FONASA manages a majority of the health insurance system's funds and covers most of the population, the process for setting its budget is critical to governing the system. The process to define FONASA's annual budget starts with an estimation of the resources needed to cover the costs of all FONASA benefits, in order to determine the financing gaps between needed resources and contributions collected. The financing gap is calculated by FONASA and the Ministry of Health, and their main inputs are the prices set for providers and the expected utilization of services by FONASA beneficiaries. The exact roles of FONASA and the Ministry of Health in calculating the financing gap are not defined explicitly. Until recently FONASA took little part, and acted merely as a fund administrator. Today it is responsible for costing and setting prices at the secondary and tertiary care levels, while the Ministry of Health remains responsible for calculating the expected utilization of services and costing and setting prices at the primary care level. The final budget is set by the Ministry of Finance with inputs from the Ministry of Health and FONASA.

The prices of secondary and tertiary care services are set by FONASA through a combination of cost studies and inflation adjustments. Every year FONASA experts pick a subset of the services they need to set prices for, and carry out cost studies for them. Since carrying out annual cost studies for all the services for which FONASA pays would be impractical, the services not chosen for a cost study are adjusted by an average inflation index defined by FONASA experts.

In most cases, the relationship between FONASA and public and private providers is monopsonistic. FONASA defines a unique price list for public providers—the MAI price list—and three alternative price lists for private providers—the MLE price levels. Public providers contribute inputs to FONASA cost studies, but FONASA sets the MAI price list unilaterally. With private providers, the situation is similar in most cases, because FONASA is the largest customer in the health insurance market and is a reliable payer. In a few cases, providers have complained about the low prices, leading FONASA to request specific cost studies. In most of these cases, the studies have shown that the prices were appropriate, and providers desisted from their complaints. In the cases where studies showed that costs were underestimated, FONASA increased prices accordingly. For services with few providers, FONASA usually carries out informal discussion before setting the price, and there is no evidence of major conflicts. On the contrary, the number of providers working with FONASA is increasing.

Governance through accountability

Accountability in Chile's MHI system differs significantly from that in other Latin American countries such as Costa Rica, Ecuador, or Peru, where insurers are owned by contributors to the system (employers and workers) or include representatives of contributors on their governing bodies. In Chile, FONASA is directly accountable to the government while most ISAPREs are directly accountable to shareholders.

FONASA is an autonomous public institution with no board of directors and consequently lacks representation of contributors, patients, or providers in a direct governing function. Instead, it is directly accountable to the executive branch of government. By contrast, ISAPREs are private companies with the sole purpose of offering contribution-based health insurance to the population. ISAPREs are generally owned by shareholders that rarely include contributors, whether they are beneficiaries or employers.

Accountability of FONASA. FONASA is an autonomous public institution, but is accountable to many different actors. FONASA's director (there is only one) and staff report to the president of the republic, Congress, the Ministry of Finance, the Ministry of Health, the Controller-General's Office (Contraloría General de la República de Chile), the SIS, the law courts, health care providers, and beneficiaries (Figure 6.5). It also has its own internal accountability mechanisms.

Chile's president has sole authority to appoint or remove FONASA's director, so the appointment generally coincides with each government's term. This feature ensures that FONASA's policies are aligned with the government's policies. Since the president has direct control over FONASA, and over the Ministry of Finance and the Ministry of Health, it is unlikely that disputes will occur between these bodies or that FONASA will make any decision against the interests of the two ministries.

Congress also holds FONASA accountable through review of its Management Report (Balances de Gestión Integral). Like other public sector agencies, FONASA has been required to submit this report annually since 1998. The Management Report is a public document presenting quantitative indicators of the institution's management performance. Indicators are evaluated on the basis of goals set forth the year before through management improvement plans. The Management Report includes FONASA's statement of sources and uses of funds, financial management results, and degree of achievement of commitments.

The Ministry of Finance sets guidelines for and approves FONASA's Management Report and management improvement plans through its Public Budget Office (Dirección de Presupuestos or DIPRES). DIPRES defines performance indicators and sets goals for FONASA's fiscal year.

In the past, the Ministry of Health and the Secretary of the Presidency (Ministerio Secretaría General de la Presidencia or SEGPRES) also set goals for FONASA; however, this led to inconsistencies among its various goals. The government, aware of this conflict, handed exclusive responsibility to DIPRES. In addition to setting goals, DIPRES can offer incentives to encourage better performance. If goals are reached, DIPRES—and only DIPRES—can grant bonuses to FONASA's directors and staff up to 18 percent of their annual salary. If goals are not reached, bonuses are cut. The Ministry of Finance can also partially restrict monthly budgets to FONASA if it fails to comply with budget law regulations.

FIGURE 6.5   FONASA accountability mechanisms

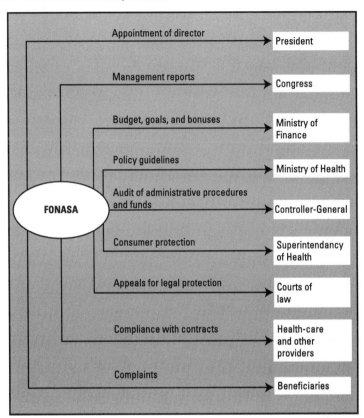

Source: Authors.

The Ministry of Health is the official channel through which the national president supervises FONASA. Even if FONASA is formally autonomous, it is effectively subordinate to the Ministry of Health. FONASA's director could legally make decisions that contravene those of the ministry, but it does not do so because that would implicitly go against the president, since he has delegated authority to the minister of health.

The Controller-General's Office is the highest public institution constitutionally responsible for controlling the finances and accounting procedures of public institutions. In this capacity, it is responsible for examining and evaluating FONASA's financial and accounting reports. The Office ensures that any regulations promulgated by FONASA are within the law. It can indict FONASA's directors or otherwise recommend disciplinary measures against them when obtaining evidence of misconduct.

The Controller-General's Office has substantial authority and independence. Although the president and Congress appoint the director of this Office, he or she cannot be removed unless indicted on constitutional grounds. The Office has its own monitoring bureau located inside FONASA's premises, which facilitates its oversight. If it detects any irregularities, the Office can request that FONASA or the Ministry of Health initiate an internal investigation. It can also initiate its own investigation if it finds large-scale anomalies. In sum, the Office is in charge of monitoring FONASA's administrative processes and accounts, while the Ministry of Health and the Ministry of Finance are in charge of monitoring its macro and micro technical performance, respectively.

The SIS is the successor to the agency that began regulating ISAPREs in 1990. In 2005 the SIS was given authority to regulate not only the ISAPREs but also FONASA. It is responsible for assuring that the rights of FONASA beneficiaries are safeguarded; it monitors FONASA's compliance with the GES; and it can call for the Ministry of Health to investigate and, if necessary, sanction FONASA's directors and staff. Specifically, the SIS monitors:

- Calculation of reimbursements and copayments
- Authorization of health loans for beneficiaries
- Compliance with GES
- Formal arbitration of disputes between FONASA and its beneficiaries
- Beneficiary satisfaction through opinion surveys.

Beneficiaries can hold FONASA accountable through three channels: direct complaints to FONASA, complaints through the SIS, and appeals for legal protection through a court of law. Beneficiaries generally use these channels in the order given, which alleviates the burden on the legal system. Formally, FONASA has 14 user committees—participatory bodies of patient associations and beneficiaries—which act as advisers to the director. Although they have no power to impose or vote on decisions, they have prompted some initiatives, such as the Mobile FONASA program in 1997 (an outreach program for remote locations with no FONASA office).

FONASA's internal organization consists of a director and a group of subordinate departments. Most decisions are made in three committees: the Executive Committee consisting of the director and the department chiefs; the Extended Executive Committee consisting of the director, the department chiefs, and regional directors; and a committee consisting of the director, the department chiefs, the regional directors, and the subdepartment chiefs. There is no voting in these committees, and the director has the final say. Even so, each department exercises a varying amount of influence over each of the decisions in their area of competence.

An important area of competence is that of the Management and Processes Control Subdepartment (part of the Strategic Planning Department). The Extended

Executive Committee defines an annual plan with goals and performance indicators. This annual plan, which includes DIPRES' management improvement plan as one of its components, is later handed to this subdepartment for follow-up. The subdepartment is empowered to request data and reports from FONASA staff, and has access to all internal FONASA documents. It reports its monitoring activities to the Extended Executive Committee.

Accountability of ISAPREs. ISAPREs are private firms created with the sole purpose of offering health insurance to the general population (open ISAPREs) or of managing health benefits for the workers of large firms and their dependents (closed ISAPREs). They are accountable to several entities including their owners, the SIS, the Internal Revenue Service (Servicio de Impuestos Internos), the National Economic Prosecutor's Office (Fiscalía Nacional Económica), the ISAPRE Association (see below), the courts, health care providers, and beneficiaries (Figure 6.6).

FIGURE 6.6   Accountability mechanisms for ISAPREs

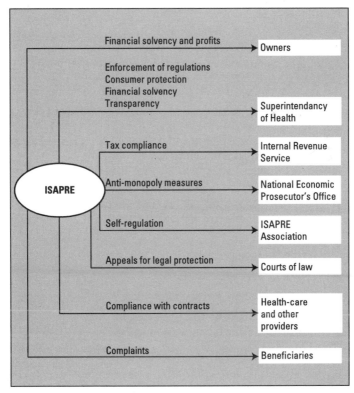

Source: Authors.

As private corporations, ISAPREs are directly accountable to their owners, but the forms of ownership vary. Closed ISAPREs are nonprofit organizations, and their owners are large public or private companies. Open ISAPREs may be corporations, joint-stock companies, international consortiums, and for-profit or nonprofit companies.

The selection process for boards of directors and chief executive officers in ISAPREs is not regulated. Therefore, the owners determine how they are chosen. In open ISAPREs, the board is elected by shareholders and nominates the chief executive officer. Since shareholders' generally want to maximize profit, directors are usually chosen for their professional skills.

The SIS assumed responsibility for regulating ISAPREs from its predecessor agency. With regard to ISAPREs, the SIS is legally responsible for:

- Authorizing the creation of new ISAPREs
- Applying the laws and regulations of ISAPREs
- Specifying the guidelines and standards for the application of regulations and reporting procedures
- Arbitrating conflicts between ISAPREs and beneficiaries
- Monitoring ISAPREs' financial solvency.

The number of accountability mechanisms in the hands of the SIS has increased over time. At present, it is also entitled to inspect all operations, goods, books of account, files, and documents from ISAPREs; request clarifications from ISAPRE administrators regarding the above information; access ISAPREs' financial balances at any time; and define which information should always be available at an ISAPRE's central office.

The bankruptcy of ISAPRE Vida Plena in 2003 triggered a set of measures to protect beneficiaries. Today, if an ISAPRE files for bankruptcy, the SIS will assign its beneficiaries to other ISAPREs in the market and compel them to enroll these beneficiaries under conditions similar to those they had in their previous ISAPRE.

The SIS has also established three standards to monitor and assess the financial solvency of ISAPREs:

- **Capital:** ISAPREs must maintain a capital ratio (capital/total liabilities) greater than or equal to 0.3.
- **Liquidity:** ISAPREs must maintain a liquidity ratio (liquid assets/current liabilities) greater than or equal to 0.8.
- **Guarantee:** ISAPREs must maintain a guarantee equivalent to their obligations with beneficiaries and providers.

Generally, solvency indicators of ISAPREs have improved since the establishment of these standards.

In order to mitigate the problems of asymmetry of information and risk selection, the SIS has taken the following steps:

- Publishing ISAPRE rankings
- Standardizing risk selection factors, based only on age and sex, and with minimum and maximum factors
- Obliging ISAPREs to present plans with a standardized table showing the benefits for key reference health interventions
- Prohibiting the exclusion of certain expensive diseases from ISAPRE plans
- Prohibiting ISAPREs from terminating contracts unilaterally.

As corporations, open ISAPREs are accountable to a number of agencies that regulate or supervise private commerce. Like any private company, they have to report and pay taxes to the Internal Revenue Service. Also, the National Economic Prosecutor's Office is charged with protecting free competition in Chilean markets, and it monitors ISAPREs with regard to price setting, collusion, and market concentration. That Office has the power to conduct investigations into ISAPREs.

ISAPREs have also initiated efforts at self-regulation. They created the ISAPRE Association to negotiate more effectively with government regulators, and they (or the Association) subsequently implemented two important self-regulatory actions. In 1993 and 1994, in response to government pressure, the ISAPRE Association announced that ISAPREs would no longer exclude certain high-cost diseases from their plans. In 2000, in order to improve their public image, ISAPREs agreed collectively to offer additional high-expense coverage for their plans—the Catastrophic Disease Additional Coverage initiative (Cobertura Adicional para Enfermedades Catastróficas or CAEC).

ISAPREs are accountable to the courts of law, health care providers, and beneficiaries in ways that are similar to FONASA. One difference is that beneficiaries are rarely represented on the boards of directors (which are similar to FONASA's user committees). Only in closed ISAPREs—where workers and beneficiaries are the same—do unions (often) have some kind of representation vis-à-vis the ISAPREs' upper management.

Governance through competition

The MHI system was designed to have multiple insurers, FONASA and ISAPREs, on the assumption that competition between them would encourage more efficient administration, better prices, and higher-quality service. The Chilean case shows that many—not all—of these expected benefits have been realized, but that there are some risks attached. The trade-off between benefits and risks is in great part determined by the level of regulation in the MHI market.

These expected benefits have not fully materialized for a variety of reasons. First, people on low incomes or with high health risks do not have a real alternative to FONASA because the private plans are too expensive. Second, for those who can afford private health insurance, once they have developed an expensive health condition they lose mobility and can no longer change insurers. Third, competition is less effective than it might otherwise be because individuals find it difficult to understand and compare insurance products. Fourth, health prevention activities are underemphasized, since an ISAPRE cannot be sure that it will see the returns of its investment in prevention, because subscribers with better health can change ISAPREs more easily.

Still, competition has contributed to some of the system's successes. For example, in 1998 after FONASA started a catastrophic insurance plan, the ISAPREs started losing members, hence their decision in 2000 to offer additional high-expense coverage. ISAPREs have also made efforts to contain administrative costs to finance more sales and marketing activities, and have negotiated large-scale purchases with providers for lower prices, which helped keep costs down. In addition, competition has spurred both FONASA and ISAPREs to automate processes that improve administrative efficiency and simplify reimbursement for their members.

Performance
Context affecting performance
The performance of the MHI system is affected by many factors besides its governance structure. A strong economy and low levels of corruption in government both play a role.

Over the last two decades, Chilean's real income has increased relatively steadily, and between 1983 and 2005, the unemployment rate fell by half from 18 percent to 9 percent. Growing incomes and a relatively strong formal labor market have facilitated enrollment in the MHI system and administration of payroll contributions. They have also generated resources that finance health insurance directly through premiums and indirectly through the general revenues that subsidize FONASA.

Governance and accountability are closely related to corruption and transparency. Depending on a given country's level of corruption, certain MHI design and accountability mechanisms will be more appropriate than others, and Chile has a strong rule of law and low corruption: in 2005 it was ranked 21 out of 159 countries and areas on Transparency International's Corruption Perceptions Index, with a score of 7.3.

Health insurance coverage and equity
In 1990 nearly two-thirds of Chileans were enrolled with FONASA, one in seven was covered by an ISAPRE, and only one in 10 either lacked MHI coverage, or was covered by the military health system. This high level of coverage reflects, in large part, the country's high level of formal employment (of about 60 percent).

Unlike many other Latin American countries, the population not covered by health insurance in Chile is not concentrated among the poor. Rather, the proportion of the population lacking coverage is about 10 percent of each income decile. Nevertheless, income does affect the choice of insurer. Almost 90 percent of the poorest decile are enrolled with FONASA, while less than 30 percent of those in the highest decile choose it. FONASA's benefits are progressive, because beneficiaries in the lower income groups get a greater share of their health care costs reimbursed than FONASA beneficiaries in higher income groups. This is possible because of the public subsidies that FONASA receives, and because of its risk-pooling structure, which cross-subsidizes contributions from wealthier to poorer members.

ISAPREs do not receive public subsidies, and, function as private companies selling a private good. Since ISAPREs are in competition with each other and with FONASA, they do not cross-subsidize poorer members as this would put them at a competitive disadvantage. Therefore, when ISAPREs sell health insurance plans to individual beneficiaries, they offer benefits reflecting the premium that the worker can afford and his or her health risk.[4] Competition between FONASA and ISAPREs, and among ISAPREs, results in an insured population that is segregated by income and health risk. Since FONASA's benefits are progressive and the ISAPREs' are in proportion to income, people that cannot afford to pay high premiums or that have large health risks opt for FONASA.

Costs

Provider cost escalation is an important problem in Chile. Per capita health expenditure in FONASA and the ISAPREs increased persistently in the 1990s. In FONASA, costs almost tripled in 10 years, with a constant inflation factor. In ISAPREs, costs increased only 50 percent, though the inflation factor is rising quickly. In fact, until 1996 FONASA's inflation was higher than ISAPREs, but this reversed in 1997. It may be an indication that FONASA was using its price-setting powers to constrain cost inflation.

Consequences of competition

Although intended for other purposes, many regulations from the Superintendancy of ISAPREs have affected competition between insurers, both positively and negatively. Some of its first regulations aimed to reduce risk selection by ISAPREs. The Superintendancy of ISAPREs imposed risk-factor tables based on age and sex, restricted the common practice of many ISAPRE of excluding benefits that could lead to high expenses, and regulated prices of insurance plans. These regulations have resulted in more homogeneous plans between ISAPREs in terms of prices and benefits. Thus they have forced ISAPREs to compete on other factors, namely administrative efficiency and quality of insurance and health services.

Other regulations aimed to reduce asymmetries of information between ISAPREs and beneficiaries, in an attempt to ensure greater transparency and to promote better consumer awareness of products in the market. The Superintendancy of ISAPREs created a ranking of ISAPREs based on indicators such as payment performance (in relation to both beneficiaries and providers), quality of care, work subsidies, complaints, and share of the local market. It also forced ISAPREs to make benefits more explicit using standard format contracts that showed reimbursement rates for key reference services. This made the plans more comparable, and ISAPREs had to struggle for comparative advantage, ultimately to the advantage of beneficiaries.

Finally, the market regulations were followed by an increase in market concentration, since they made the ISAPRE business less attractive, and only the most efficient and larger companies decided—or were able—to stay in the business.

One of the principles behind the vertical split of insurance and provision functions is to allow better competition in the provider market. In spite of its vertical split, there are some rules that regulate competition for MHI beneficiaries between public and private providers. To prevent inequities and abuses, public facilities are only allowed to sell to FONASA beneficiaries, except for 10 percent of their bed capacity, which can be used for patients who pay out of pocket, are enrolled with an ISAPRE, or are affiliated with FONASA but choose the MLE option.

Conversely, FONASA must buy services from public facilities, except for beneficiaries who choose the MLE option or are covered through GES or other special programs. Private facilities that wish to sell to FONASA beneficiaries, through MLE, are also required to comply with certain requirements, particularly with regard to certification by the Ministry of Health and to prices set by FONASA.

Beneficiary satisfaction

A beneficiary satisfaction survey (Adimark 2004) shows that beneficiaries consider good health care to be the main positive aspect of FONASA, but that long waiting lists are its worst aspect. Fifty-six percent of beneficiaries consider that FONASA improved during the 3 previous years. The number of complaints made directly to FONASA is generally low. In 2003, 515 complaints were received and, of these, 92 percent were registered as solved

Beneficiary satisfaction surveys contracted by the SIS (Adimark 2004) showed that 59 percent of beneficiaries of both FONASA and ISAPREs had insufficient information on how to use their insurance. Ninety-four percent of them agreed that ISAPREs should be regulated by government. One of the two main problems with the ISAPREs identified by beneficiaries was risk selection; the second was low financial coverage. Conversely, beneficiaries mentioned fast and good-quality health care as the most positive aspect of ISAPREs.

Does governance affect performance? FONASA's revival

It is often argued that public health insurance institutions must be autonomous from government in order to be governed properly and to perform well. Although this argument may hold in many contexts, it does not appear to apply to Chile. While many observers in the 1980s expected private health insurers to supplant FONASA, recent years have shown FONASA to be a strong and growing competitor.

When the system was created in 1980, all beneficiaries from the old system were automatically enrolled in FONASA (about 85 percent of the population). In 1981 ISAPREs were formed and began to enroll beneficiaries, some new to the system and others who had left FONASA. Until 1997, ISAPREs grew rapidly, enrolling beneficiaries at higher rates than FONASA, and from 1989 to 1994 FONASA faced net enrollment losses (Figure 6.7).

In 1995 FONASA stopped losing beneficiaries and began a period of significant expansion. At the same time, enrollment rates for ISAPREs began stalling and then fell, suggesting that people were migrating from ISAPREs to FONASA. Today, the relative enrollment levels seem to have stabilized.

There are several possible causes for the reemergence of FONASA in the mid-1990s, most of which can be attributed to government policies that improved performance of FONASA and strengthened regulation of ISAPREs.

First, a clear indication of the priority given to improving FONASA in the 1990s was the substantial increase in government expenditure on health. Before 1990, governments were less concerned with social conditions and, consequently, the Ministry of Health and FONASA invested relatively little, and the public sector did not perform as well as subsequently. However, when democracy returned, governments increased social spending. During the first six years of democratic

FIGURE 6.7   Number of beneficiaries enrolling each year in FONASA and ISAPREs, 1982–2005

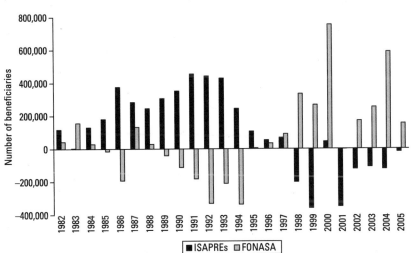

Source: Authors from FONASA and Superintendancy of Health.

government (1990–95), per capita government health expenditure rose by 60 percent. This money, used on capital investments, primary care, and special insurance programs, appears to have been spent well because utilization of health services and FONASA enrollment subsequently increased.

Second, FONASA implemented a series of special benefit programs in the 1990s: Catastrophic Insurance; a Health Care Opportunity Program; an Elderly Program; and Diagnosis-Linked Payment (Pago Asociado a Diagnóstico or PAD). These programs sought to increase the value of benefits in terms of financial coverage (Catastrophic Insurance), waiting times (Health Care Opportunity Program), and access to health care (Elderly Program). PAD was a payment mechanism designed to improve provider productivity, although it also reduced the variability of treatment prices to beneficiaries.

Third, regulations introduced or strengthened in the last 15 years have limited the ability of ISAPREs to make profits by cancelling coverage for members who fall ill, selectively accepting members, confusing potential clients over what is included in plans, or excluding high-cost illnesses from their packages. Regulations have also been tightened to assure financial solvency by requiring firms to maintain meet standards for capitalization and liquidity. As a result of these regulations, ISAPREs had to compete with FONASA on a more equal footing and raise their premiums to cover increasing claims.

Finally, FONASA's reemergence may also be related to other factors. For example, health costs could be rising faster in the private sector than in the public sector, or the media and other social communication channels might have altered public perceptions of the public and private insurers in favor of FONASA. Nevertheless, the evidence generally points to government policy as a significant contributor to FONASA's improved performance. The fact that FONASA itself is directly accountable to the government leads to the conclusion that good governance of all public institutions is a primary contributor to FONASA's good performance.

Conclusions

Chile's MHI system has many lessons to offer for the governance of both public and private insurance schemes. However, most lessons should be applied carefully, because the lessons may apply only in similar contexts. Some system design features that are critical to the Chilean context are: effective competition between one public and multiple private insurers; most public insurance beneficiaries using public health care and private insurance beneficiaries using private health care; and the vertical split between insurers and providers. Important economic factors are: high formal employment (about 60 percent); reasonable income (per capita GDP of around US$6,000); limited corruption (a Transparency International Corruption Perceptions Index of 7.3 in 2005); and strong social investment (public health expenditure of 3 percent of GDP).

As policymakers have gathered experience about FONASA and ISAPREs, governance arrangements have become better at improving the performance of MHI. In the case of ISAPREs, such arrangements have been evolving toward more regulations, affecting accountability and competition. Problems tackled with these regulations include risk selection, insurer financial sustainability, and lack of transparency and consumer information. These regulations have also reduced ISAPREs' share of the market by forcing them to raise their premiums and reducing their attractiveness to clients.

In the case of FONASA, governance arrangements have changed little, but policymakers have learned how to use them better. The system has benefited from the collaborative work between the Ministry of Health and FONASA. Both institutions' policies are aligned, in great part because FONASA is functionally dependent on the ministry, and both respond directly to the president of the republic. Even though FONASA is still subject to many rules and is accountable to other actors, there is little room for the intervention of these other actors (such as beneficiaries and providers) in decisionmaking. This arrangement can have positive results, provided that health sector government policy is sound and that the necessary financing is available.

Annex 6.1 Dimensions, features, and indicators of good governance in mandatory health insurance: Chile

Dimension	Features	Indicators	Public Yes or No	Private	Explanation
Coherent decisionmaking structures	1. Responsibility for MHI objectives must correspond with decisionmaking power and capacity in each institution involved in the management of the system.	The institution responsible for the financial sustainability of the system must be able to change at least one of the parameters on which it depends (e.g. conditions of affiliation, contribution rate, benefits package, ability to act a strategic purchaser, or tariffs).	Yes	Yes	FONASA and ISAPRES: Yes, the institution responsible for the financial sustainability of the system—the government—can control some of its parameters, for example, restricting the scope of the explicit health guarantees (*garantías explicitas de salud* or GES) basic benefits package. Some other parameters are less flexible, such as the conditions of affiliation and contribution rates. FONASA: On the public insurer's side, the government can change other parameters to control financial sustainability: (a) it is practically a monopsonic purchaser of health services, defining tariffs for public and private providers; (b) it controls the amount of financing coming from general government taxation.
		The institution in charge of the supervision of sickness funds has the capacity to fulfill its responsibilities (i.e. it has enough skilled staff, it has access to the necessary information, and legal texts give it the authority to fulfill its role vis-à-vis sickness funds).	No		FONASA: Recently, the Superintendancy of Health (SIS) has been granted some tools to supervise the public insurer, although they are seldom put into use, because it assumes that the public insurer achieves all its functions and respects all regulations. The tools are the following: • Calculation of reimbursements and copayments • Authorization of health loans for beneficiaries • Supervising; ensuring compliance with GES • Formal arbitration between FONASA and its beneficiaries • Beneficiary satisfaction through opinion surveys

2. All MHI entities have routine risk assessment and management strategies in place.	Clear regulations on MHI entities' continuous risk assessment and risk management are in place.	Yes	ISAPREs: The SIS has several tools to supervise private sickness funds: • Authorize the creation of new ISAPREs. • Apply the laws and regulations of ISAPREs. • Specify guidelines and standards for the application of regulations and reporting procedures. • Arbitrate between ISAPREs and beneficiaries. • Monitor ISAPREs' financial solvency. • Inspect all operations, goods, accounting books, files, and documents from ISAPREs. • Request clarifications from ISAPREs administrators regarding the above information. • Access ISAPREs' financial balances at any time. • Define which information should always be available at the ISAPREs' central office. In spite all the tools available to the SIS, it does not have all the resources needed to carry out its responsibilities. FONASA: Yes, the Ministry of Finance has clear procedures to supervise and set goals for FONASA's management and improvement.	Yes
	Strategies are in place, i.e. MHI entities follow and analyze the evolution of xpenditures and contributions.	Yes	ISAPREs: Yes, the SIS has established three standards to monitor and assess the financial solvency of ISAPREs. FONASA: Yes, the public MHI entity follows and analyzes the evolution of revenues and expenditures through annual performance reports. ISAPREs: Yes, ISAPREs analyze the evolution of revenues and expenditures. On the one hand, they have natural market incentives to do so. On the other, they are required to provide monthly financial reports to the SIS within income and expense statements.	Yes

(continues)

Dimension	Features	Indicators	Public Yes or No	Private Yes or No	Explanation
		MHI entities have the capacity to manage risks, i.e. to take corrective action in order to ensure the financial sustainability of the system by modifying some of the parameters influencing it (contribution rate, composition of the benefits package etc.).	Yes	No	FONASA: Yes, FONASA can manage risks by eventually reducing the amount of additional benefits (those not included in the basic package). ISAPREs: No, the ISAPREs are less and less able to adjust their parameters, as recent legislation restricts changes to premiums or benefits coverage.
3. The cost of regulating and administering MHI institutions is reasonable and appropriate.		Maximum administration costs for MHI entities are set in legal texts or regulations.	No	No	FONASA and ISAPREs: Maximum administration costs for MHI entities are not addressed in legal texts or regulations.
		Administrative costs are monitored by the regulator.	No	Yes	FONASA: No, there is no oversight of the public insurer's expenditures, i.e. in order to evaluate its efficiency. ISAPREs: Yes, the private insurers are audited, and they must report the percentage of total expenditures applied to administrative costs, as a way of evaluating their efficiency.
		Provisions for covering the costs of the MHI regulator are stipulated in legal texts.	Yes	Yes	FONASA and ISAPREs: Yes, as the Budget Law defines the funds allocated to each state entity.
		Before new regulations are put in place a cost-benefit assessment is conducted.	No	No	FONASA and ISAPREs: It is difficult to give a definitive answer. Few data are available, but a priori one assumes that such assessments are not usually conducted. Changes to these entities typically take place as a result of political initiatives rather than for technical reasons. However, FONASA does evaluate its spending capacity before making changes (increases) to its benefits package.

Stakeholder participation	4. Stakeholders have effective representation in the governing bodies of MHI entities.	Governing bodies of regulatory oversight and institutional governance (board of directors, oversight body) have representatives of government agencies, regulatory bodies, MHI entities, unions, employers' organizations, beneficiaries, providers and independent experts.	No	FONASA: No, FONASA's regulatory institution does not have representatives of all stakeholders. FONASA's regulatory institution is the government, acting through the Ministry of Health, and to a lesser extent, through the SIS. It has no representatives from unions, employers, beneficiaries, or providers. In spite of the existence of 14 user committees inside FONASA (participatory bodies of patient associations and beneficiaries, acting as advisers to FONASA's director), beneficiaries are not fully represented, because these committees have no power to impose, or vote on, decisions. ISAPREs: No, the SIS has no representatives from unions, employers, beneficiaries, or providers. Within ISAPREs, board structures are not regulated, and are left to the institutions.
		Representation is effective, i.e. different stakeholders' views are considered in decisionmaking.	No	FONASA and ISAPREs: In practical terms this indicator does not apply, because representation of different stakeholders is nonexistent. Anecdotally, the SIS rarely uses its governing powers over FONASA.
Transparency and information	5. The objectives of MHI are formally and clearly defined.	Objectives are stated in a high level legal text (e.g. the Constitution or a law).	Yes	FONASA and ISAPREs: Yes, the Constitution declares a "right to health care" and establishes the basis for access to health care, the role of the state, the mixed insurance market, and the freedom to choose one's own insurance plan. There are also laws that regulate both insurance systems: Law No. 18.469 regulates FONASA and Law No. 18.933 regulates the ISAPREs. FONASA: The law explicitly provides for the right to health care. ISAPREs: The law stipulates that the role of private insurers is strictly to pay for the care provided to its beneficiaries.

(continues)

Dimension	Features	Indicators	Public Yes or No	Private Yes or No	Explanation
		Objectives are publicized and easily accessible to the public.	Yes	Yes	FONASA and ISAPRES: Yes, the text of laws relating to MHI can be found on the Web page of the Ministry of Health and the SIS. Also, according to Chilean law, individuals are responsible for being aware of all laws, even if each law is not widely or clearly publicized.
		Objectives are clearly defined and easily understandable. *Comment: This indicator is subjective, in the sense that some people may consider the objectives easily understandable and some may not. Maybe the best indicator to qualify something as easily understandable is to measure if the population actually understands. If the population does not understand, it is difficult to qualify something as easily understandable. The following indicator is therefore suggested: Percent of beneficiaries who understand the objectives of SHI, and specifically, their rights.*	No	No	FONASA and ISAPRES: In Chile, objectives are clearly defined on paper, and apart from beneficiaries, most stakeholders understand them. However, an SIS opinion survey (Adimark 2004) showed that just over 20 percent of beneficiaries feel that they have enough information, 60 percent feel that they have little information, and the remaining 20 percent feel that they have none. The differences between FONASA and ISAPREs are small.

	Objectives have remained substantially the same in the recent past. *Comment: This indicator can be positive or negative, depending on the state of the objectives as initially defined; therefore, an indicator that measures progress in achieving the internationally recognized objectives regarding good practices for SHI is suggested.*	Yes	Yes	FONASA and ISAPREs: Yes, the basic objectives have remained the same over the recent past. A few changes have occurred, mainly in terms of expanding the rights and benefits of the insured. The current system was established in 1981, and lawmakers have sought to improve it over time. In 2004 a reform process was initiated, including new laws and new rights that apply to all beneficiaries, regardless of the insurance system.
6. MHI relies upon an explicit and an appropriately designed institutional and legal framework.	The main characteristics of the system are defined in legal texts.	Yes	Yes	*Mandates* FONASA and ISAPREs: The basic mandate is that health insurance is obligatory for all employees. *Coverage and benefits package* FONASA: The law regulating FONASA defines the coverage, benefits, and financing of the system. ISAPREs: Within the private system, the coverage provided depends on the plan; it is not defined by law. FONASA and ISAPREs: The GES (or AUGE plan) was introduced in 2005. This law defines a basic package of coverage for certain health problems and preventive health services for all citizens.

(continues)

Dimension	Features	Indicators	Public Yes or No	Private Yes or No	Explanation
					Financing FONASA: Beneficiaries of this system must contribute 7 percent of their salaries or pensions. The state provides funding for indigent beneficiaries' care as well as for health promotion and preventive health services for the entire population (including public goods such as epidemiological studies, vaccination drives). ISAPREs: Beneficiaries of this system contribute 7 percent of their salaries for basic coverage, or they may opt to make larger payments in exchange for greater coverage. *Provision* FONASA and ISAPREs: Health promotion and preventive health services are available to the public in health facilities run by the Ministry of Health. FONASA beneficiaries may use these public facilities for their health care as well, or they can opt to use certain private providers (except for indigent citizens). ISAPREs beneficiaries must use private providers for their health care, except in an emergency.
	The framework is appropriate given the country MHI context (i.e. it is not too restrictive, considers special local circumstances, and does not ignore important parts or players in the system).		N/A	N/A	

Comment: This indicator is very broad, as it attempts to measure several variables of the system that do not necessarily behave in the same way. Therefore, dividing this indicator into three indicators is suggested: (a) the legal framework is restrictive; (b) the legal framework is adequate given the local context; and (c) key players and beneficiaries participate in establishing the framework.

The legal framework is restrictive.	No	Yes	FONASA: There are no normative restrictions. ISAPREs: The legal framework imposes important restrictions and safeguards the rights of private sector beneficiaries.
The legal framework is adequate given the local context.	Yes	Yes	FONASA and ISAPREs: The system has adjusted to demographic changes, changes in the disease burden, and changes in national income.
Key players and beneficiaries participate in establishing the framework.	No	No	FONASA and ISAPREs: Key players, particularly beneficiaries, have no role in the insurers' decisions.
The regulatory agency exists.	Yes	Yes	FONASA and ISAPREs: There was no such agency for many years. The Superintendancy of ISAPREs was created in 1990. A regulatory agency for all insurers, the SIS, was created in 2004 (operational from 2005).

(continues)

Dimension	Features	Indicators	Public Yes or No	Private Yes or No	Explanation
		The regulatory agency is independent.	No	Yes	FONASA: No, the regulatory agency is not independent, because it is subordinate to the state and its highest official (the director) is subordinate to the president of the republic. The Ministry of Health selects the director after examining various candidates. The selection process is regulated by norms set forth by the Public Office, which oversees public health sector posts. The agency cannot be considered completely independent as the state can remove officials at its discretion. ISAPREs: Yes, the state regulatory agency is independent from these private sector insurers.
		The status and responsibilities of each different MHI institution in the system are clearly defined and transparent.	Yes	Yes	FONASA and ISAPRES: Yes, the law that created the SIS defines the functions of each institution within the system, as noted above.
7. Clear information, disclosure, and transparency rules are in place.		Explicit disclosure regulations exist in the law or regulations of the law.	No	Yes	There are explicit disclosure regulations within SHI, which vary according to the insurer and the variable. FONASA: No regular information is reported to the SIS, as there are no regulations for this. The difference between the two systems in terms of information available is evident in looking at the SIS Web page. No current information is available for FONASA (to date information is available only through 2003). ISAPREs: Must regularly report monthly financial information to the SIS.

Business activities, ownership, and financial positions are regularly disclosed (i.e. the rules are followed).	No	Yes	FONASA: No, because it is a state-run insurance entity. ISAPREs: Yes, most of these companies are corporations, and as such must report to the Securities and Insurance Commission. They must also report to the specific regulatory agency (SIS) that oversees their area. The new ISAPREs law (2005) provides basic financial regulations for private insurers.
MHI entities deliver to a beneficiary on demand a copy of its rules and the latest annual financial statements.	No	Yes	ISAPREs: The private insurers must provide their beneficiaries with information regarding changes in rules (especially in terms of benefits and new legal developments). This right is provided for by law and overseen by the regulatory agency. The insurers do not have to provide financial reports. However, the SIS Web page provides a periodic financial report from all private insurers. The insurers are not required to provide beneficiaries with regular financial statements.
Consumer protection regulations exist in law, including consumer information, and independent mechanisms for resolution of complaints, appeals, grievances, and disputes.	Yes	Yes	FONASA and ISAPREs: There are global consumer-protection guarantees, with more extensive guarantees for beneficiaries of private insurers. Beneficiaries of private insurers have the right to information about the complaint, appeal, grievance, and dispute resolution processes.
8. MHI entities have minimum requirements in regard to protecting the insured. The insured can obtain timely, complete and relevant information regarding changes in benefits or premium, changes in coverage length etc.	No	Yes	FONASA: There are no explicit regulations for the public insurer on this matter, as any change takes place as part of a legislative process. ISAPREs: Yes, insurers must provide this information within a defined time frame. This regulation tends to limit the number of changes to premiums and benefits.

(continues)

Dimension	Features	Indicators	Public Yes or No	Private Yes or No	Explanation
		Consumer complaint mechanisms exist and are being used.			
		Comment: It is suggested that this indicator be divided into two indicators: (a) consumer complaint mechanisms exist; and (b) consumer complaint mechanisms are being used.			
		Consumer complaint mechanisms exist.	Yes	Yes	FONASA and ISAPRES: Yes, although there are systems in place for consumer complaints in both systems, there is only a culture of exercising the right to consumer complaints within the private system.
		Consumer complaint mechanisms are being used.	No	Yes	FONASA: There are no data available regarding the rate of consumer complains in this system. ISAPRES: The regulatory agency periodically publishes data regarding the nature and rates of complaints for each of the private insurers, usually in the form of a ranked list.
		Appeals and grievance mechanisms exist and are being used.			

Comment: It is suggested that this indicator be divided into two indicators: (a) appeals and grievance mechanisms exist; and (b) appeals and grievance mechanisms are being used.		
Appeals and grievance mechanisms exist.	Yes	FONASA and ISAPREs: Yes, both systems provide a mechanism for filing appeals and grievances.
Appeals and grievance mechanisms are being used.	No	FONASA: No data are available.
		ISAPREs: Yes, appeals from private beneficiaries are being handled by the SIS. Recently, the regulatory agency implemented a mediation system with the goal of minimizing judicial disputes among beneficiaries, providers, and insurers.
Independent dispute resolution mechanisms exist and are being used.		
Comment: It is suggested that this indicator be divided into two indicators: (a) independent dispute resolution mechanisms exist; and (b) independent dispute resolution mechanisms are being used.		
Independent dispute resolution mechanisms exist.	Yes	FONASA and ISAPREs: Both systems provide a mechanism for independent dispute resolution.

(continues)

Dimension	Features	Indicators	Public Yes or No	Private	Explanation
		Independent dispute resolution mechanisms are being used.	No	Yes	FONASA: In practice, the mechanism is not used. ISAPREs: A few controversial cases between beneficiaries and private insurers have been resolved in justice tribunals.
Supervision and regulation	9. Rules on compliance, enforcement and sanctions for MHI supervision are clearly defined.	Rules on compliance and sanctions are defined in legal texts.	No	Yes	FONASA: The health authority does not decide how to sanction the public insurer if this entity fails to meet its obligations. ISAPREs: The health authority has established a mechanism for sanctioning private insurers.
		Corrective actions are imposed, based on clear and objective criteria that are publicly disclosed.	No	Yes	FONASA: There is no information regarding corrective actions imposed on FONASA. ISAPREs: The new laws provide the SIS with monetary sanctions that may be imposed on private insurers. However, the law does not link specific transgressions with certain sanctions. The SIS Web site publishes the sanctions imposed on private insurers, as well as the cause of the sanction and the fine.
		Adequate capacity for the execution of these functions is provided.	No	Yes	FONASA: The SIS has the right to audit FONASA's activities, but not to directly impose sanctions. Sanctions take the form of legislative investigations against the institution involved. ISAPREs: Specific regulations govern the oversight and imposition of sanctions against ISAPREs.

Cases of rule violation and subsequent actions by the regulator are publicized.	No	Yes	FONASA: No rule violations have been documented in the case of FONASA. ISAPREs: SIS publishes the sanctions imposed against ISAPREs on its Web page and in other media.
10. Financial management rules for MHI entities are clearly defined and enforced.			
Financial standards for MHI entities are defined in legal text or regulations.	Yes	Yes	FONASA: There is a Budget Law that applies to all public entities, including FONASA. ISAPREs: Yes, the Short Law of ISAPREs (2004) defines minimum financial conditions for these companies as well as an evaluation process to be carried out by SIS.
Clear financial licensure/ market-entry rules are defined (minimum capital requirements).	N/A	Yes	FONASA: This does not apply because the public insurer is a unique entity. ISAPREs: Yes, the law establishes entry rules (minimum capital of US$200,000 and a guarantee of US$80,000).
Ongoing reserve and solvency requirements are defined.	No	Yes	FONASA: No restrictions apply. ISAPREs: The SIS established three standards to monitor and assess financial solvency. ISAPREs must maintain: capital equal to or greater than 0.3 times their total liabilities; a liquidity ratio (liquid assets/current liabilities) equal to or greater than 0.8; and a guarantee equivalent to their obligations with beneficiaries and providers.
Regulations of assets and financial investments are defined.	Yes	Yes	FONASA: The public insurer, as with any other state entity, is not permitted to use its funds for speculation. ISAPREs: The private insurers may invest in the stock market as long as they adhere to the relevant financial regulations. The only specific regulations involve investing in health care companies.

(continues)

Dimension	Features	Indicators	Public Yes or No	Private Yes or No	Explanation
		Audit (internal and external) rules are defined.	Yes		FONASA: Yes, the Controller-General's Office is in charge of external audits of FONASA, using the same rules defined for any government body. Internal audits are carried out by the Management and Processes Control Subdepartment of FONASA, which is empowered to request data and reports from FONASA staff, and has access to all internal FONASA documents. This subdepartment reports on its monitoring activities back to FONASA's Extended Executive Committee.
				Yes	ISAPREs: ISAPREs are required to have an external auditing system.
		Rules for financial standards are enforced.	Yes		FONASA: Financial standards are supervised by the Controller-General and the Ministry of the Interior. There have been no documented rule violations.
				Yes	ISAPREs: The private insurers are audited periodically. There have been no documented rule violations to date.
11. The MHI system has structures for ongoing supervision and monitoring in place.		Clear nonfinancial licensure/market entry rules are defined.	N/A		FONASA: Does not apply, because the public insurer is unique.
				Yes	ISAPREs: Yes, nonfinancial entry rules are defined. For example, the director of an ISAPRE may not have legal ties or a work history with any institution that has been sanctioned by any superintendence. Additionally, ISAPREs may not own any health care company.

Insurance product filing/registration is defined and regulated.	Yes	Yes	FONASA and ISAPRES: Filing is regulated.
Adequate on-site inspections and off-site monitoring are in place.	No	Yes	FONASA: No, because the SIS does not carry out effectively its supervisory role over FONASA. ISAPRES: Yes, the SIS regularly audits various aspects of the ISAPREs' functions (financial, contractual, reporting, bonuses, compliance with the GES, and preventive health care goals).
Ongoing financial reporting rules are defined and provided information is accurate and timely.	Yes	Yes	FONASA: Yes, because like any other public institution, FONASA reports finances to the government every fiscal year. ISAPRES: Yes, because ISAPREs are also required to submit financial statements, and lack of accuracy and timeliness is punished with fines.
Clear market exit/dissolution rules are in place.	N/A	Yes	FONASA: Does not apply, because as a large government entity with critical social and legal mandates, FONASA cannot go bankrupt. ISAPRES: Yes, because recently the SIS defined rules protecting beneficiaries from ISAPRE bankruptcies. Beneficiaries are assigned to other ISAPREs under similar insurance plan conditions.

(continues)

Dimension	Features	Indicators	Public Yes or No	Private Yes or No	Explanation
Consistency and stability	12. The main qualities of the MHI system are stable.	The fundamental characteristics of the MHI system (e.g. benefits package, rules for affiliation, contribution requirements, basic protection rights for the insured, and basic institutional requirements for operators) are defined in law.	Yes	Yes	FONASA and ISAPREs: The Constitution states that insurance is mandatory for all employees and that individuals may choose the system by which they will be insured (public or private). Other legal documents define the premium for basic insurance coverage at 7 percent of the individual's salary (up to a ceiling). The GES (or AUGE plan) defines a basic benefits package covering 40 health problems (to date) for all beneficiaries of the public and private systems. FONASA: The law defines the characteristics of beneficiaries, the network of providers to be used (state facilities), coverage, etc. ISAPREs: The law defines a minimum basic package to be provided by the private companies (ISAPREs).
		The law has remained substantially the same in the recent past (i.e. independent of political elections or economic crises).	Yes	Yes	FONASA and ISAPREs: The laws have been modified as a result of legislation; however, the law has remained basically the same over time, and changes have been oriented to benefit consumers.

Endnotes

1. The authors wish to thank the following people: Rafael Caviedes, Gonzalo Simón, Hernán Doren, Carlos Kubik, and René Merino (ISAPREs); Alejandro Ferreiro, Manuel Inostroza, Ulises Nancuante, and Héctor Sánchez (Superintendancy of Health); Rony Lenz, Erika Díaz, César Oyarzo, and José Miguel Sánchez (FONASA); Ferrnando Muñoz and Antonio Infante (Ministry of Health); Marcelo Tockman (Ministry of Finance); and William Savedoff and Pablo Gottret (World Bank).

2. Only MHI benefits financed by insurers are included in this analysis. Copayments are excluded.

3. Government subsidies are not portable in Chile, and only reach the poorer half of FONASA beneficiaries.

4. However, when ISAPREs sell collective plans, some pooling occurs between workers in the same plan but with different income levels, and lower-income individuals can access more benefits than with an individual plan.

Reference list and bibliography

Adimark. 2004. "Estudio de Opinión Pública sobre el Sistema de Salud Chileno, para Superintendencia de Isapres."

Aedo, C. 2004. "Las reformas en la salud en Chile." Centro de Estudios Públicos, Santiago de Chile.

Baytelman, Y., K. Cowan, and J. de Gregorio. 1999. "Política económico-social y bienestar: El caso de Chile." Universidad de Chile, Santiago de Chile.

Bitrán, R., U. Giedion, and P. Gomez. 2004. "Métodos de pago para el Plan AUGE y para las demás atenciones financiadas por el sistema público de salud en Chile." Ministry of Health, Santiago de Chile.

Bitrán, R., and F.X. Almarza. 1997. "Las instituciones de salud previsional (ISAPREs) en Chile." Economic Commission for Latin America and the Caribbean.

Boletín Estadístico, 2002–2003. FONASA. Santiago de Chile.

Boletín Estadístico, 2004. SIS. Santiago de Chile.

Bossert, T., and A. González-Rossetti. 2000. "Enhancing the Political Feasibility of Health Reform: A Comparative Analysis of Chile, Colombia and Mexico." *Latin American and Caribbean Regional Health Sector Reform Initiative Report 36*. June.

Bustos, R. 1999. "La reforma de la salud en América Latina: ¿Qué camino seguir? (La experiencia chilena)." Colegio Médico de Chile, Santiago de Chile.

Economic Commission for Latin America and the Caribbean. *Chile: Proyecciones y estimaciones de población 1950–2050*. Santiago de Chile.

Figueroa, L., and V. Lazen. 2001. "Propuestas de políticas de salud privada en Chile." Universidad de Chile, Santiago de Chile.

Fisher, D., and P. Serra. 1997. "Análisis económico del sistema de seguros de salud en Chile." Universidad de Chile, Santiago de Chile.

FONASA (National Health Insurance Fund). 2005. "Balance de Gestión Integral." Santiago de Chile.

ILO (International Labour Organization). 2002. *Towards Decent Work: Social Protection in Health for All Workers and their Families.* Geneva.

———. 2005. "Can Low Income Countries Afford Basic Social Protection? First Results of a Modelling Exercise." ILO Background Note.

———. *Panorama Laboral 2005: América Latina y el Caribe.* Lima.

Law No. 18.469, "Regula el ejercicio del derecho constitucional a la protección de la salud y crea un régimen de prestaciones de salud." Published in *Diario Oficial,* 23 November 1985.

Law No. 18.933, "Ley larga de ISAPREs." Published in *Diario Oficial,* 9 March 1990.

Law No. 19.937, "De autoridad sanitaria." Published in *Diario Oficial,* 24 February 2004.

Law No. 19.966, "Régimen general de garantías en salud." Published in *Diario Oficial,* 3 September 2004.

MIDEPLAN (Ministerio de Planificación y Cooperación). 1999. *Situación de la salud en Chile, 1998.*

———. 2001. *Situación de la salud en Chile, 2000.*

MINSAL (Ministry of Health)-FONASA. 2002. "Programa de Mejoramiento de la Gestión." Santiago de Chile.

MINSAL. *Indicadores Básicos de Salud 2005.* 2005. Santiago de Chile.

Rámirez, A. 2002. "Reforma del estado y modernización de la gestión pública. Lecciones y aprendizajes de la experiencia chilena." Barcelona, Spain.

Rodríguez J., and M. Tokman. 2000. "Resultados y rendimiento del gasto en el sector público de salud en Chile 1990-1999." Economic Commission for Latin America and the Caribbean.

Sanchez, H. "Características e implicancias de la reducción de afiliados en el sistema de ISAPREs, período 1997–2002." *Salud y Futuro* 3(24).

Savedoff, W. 2005. "Mandatory Health Insurance in Developing Countries: Overview, Framework and Research Program," report submitted to World Bank by Social Insight, Portland, ME, April 27.

SIS (Superintendancy of Health). 2006. "Monitoreo y Seguimiento de la Reforma: Determinación de Línea Basal de Equidad en el Financiamiento y Protección Financiera." Departamento de Estudios y Desarrollo.

Temas Públicos. 2000. Santiago de Chile: Libertad y Desarrollo.

Titelman, D. 2000. "Reformas al sistema de saluden Chile: Desafíos pendientes." Economic Commission for Latin America and the Caribbean.

World Bank. 2000. *Chile Health Insurance Issues.*

The following Web sites were also consulted

Controller-General's Office (Contraloría General de la República de Chile), www.contraloria.cl.

Public Budget Office (Dirección de Presupuestos, DIPRES), www.dipres.cl.

National Economic Prosecutor's Office (Fiscalía Nacional Económica, FNE), www.fne.cl.

National Health Insurance Fund (Fondo Nacional de Salud, FONASA), www.fonasa.cl.

International Labour Organization (ILO), www.ilo.org.

National Statistics Institute (Instituto Nacional de Estadísticas, INE), www.ine.cl.

ISAPRE Association, www.isapres.cl.

Ministry of Health (Ministerio de Salud, MINSAL), www.minsal.cl.

Secretary of the Presidency (Ministerio Secretaría General de la Presidencia, SEGPRES), www.segpres.cl.

Internal Revenue Service (Servicio de Impuestos Internos, SII), www.sii.cl.

Superintendancy of Health (Superintendencia de Salud, SIS), www.sisp.cl.

7

Conclusions: Lessons from governance trends for developing countries

William D. Savedoff

Introduction

An early question in this book was: "Which forms of governance encourage the best performance by mandatory health insurers?" However, as the cases in this book have demonstrated, the effectiveness of particular governance mechanisms will vary in relation to a number of contextual factors—such as the presence of competition, the organization of civil society, relationships between insurance funds and health care providers, the effectiveness of political processes, and enforcement of laws. This suggests that the search for better governance mechanisms has to pay significant attention to how well the proposed mechanisms "fit" the structure of the health insurance system and its context.

Writing the general rules for good governance is fairly simple: align incentives and make information available and transparent. However, following these rules is not so simple. It requires making choices within each of the five governance dimensions presented earlier—coherent decisionmaking structures; stakeholder participation; transparency and information; supervision and regulation; and consistency and stability—and ensuring that those choices are both consistent with one another and appropriate to the system's context.

Two factors, in particular, appear critical to the design and functioning of mechanisms within the five governance dimensions: the number of insurers and the relationship between insurers and providers. First, in countries with multiple and competing insurers, external oversight mechanisms can pay less attention to efficiency and management, and focus more on consumer protection, inclusiveness, and preserving competition through anti-trust actions. By contrast, countries with a single health insurer need external oversight mechanisms that make the insurer accountable for integrity, quality, and productivity.

Second, the relationship between insurers and providers influences the impact of different governance mechanisms. In some countries, this relationship is openly antagonistic, while in others, it is more collaborative. The presence of providers' representatives on the decisionmaking bodies of health insurers or regulatory agencies will have different implications under these varied scenarios. In addition, where providers are direct employees of insurers, the character of negotiations and oversight needs to confront issues that arise in civil service codes or labor legislation, while countries where providers are independent of insurers need governance mechanisms that promote transparent and productive negotiations over prices and payment mechanisms.

The highly varied structures of governance presented in these cases demonstrate that particular structural elements do not, by themselves, explain health insurance fund performance; nevertheless, the patterns of reform efforts have converged noticeably in particular ways from which lessons can be extracted because these convergent trends represent solutions to common problems faced by different countries. In this regard, they represent policy choices that merit serious consideration by low-income countries that are designing their own insurance governance structures. But the evidence only goes so far, and the chapter concludes by discussing three unanswered questions that mark every effort at reforming governance mechanisms, in particular: How can countries assure solvency and balanced budgets? How can countries assure financial protection for the population? And how can countries promote efficiency and raise productivity?

Caveats for applying lessons in low-income countries

Before discussing the lessons from these four case studies, it is important to note a number of qualifications. First, the cases presented here are all relatively successful and a larger number of cases, including some failures, would be needed to draw truly rigorous conclusions. Second, the mandatory health insurance (MHI) funds in these cases were all established in countries with much higher income levels and degrees of economic formalization than is the case in today's low-income countries. In addition, these cases represent countries that are all economically and politically stable, with relatively effective governments, low corruption, and skilled workforces. With these caveats, these cases can be useful to low-income countries (Box 7.1).

Lessons

Coherent decisionmaking structures

The four case studies show that many different allocations of decisionmaking powers can function well, but responsibility for making decisions has to be matched with appropriate authority, resources, and managerial discretion.

Frequently, the main governance problem for MHI institutions resides in this balance between making these institutions accountable to governments and protecting against undue interference from those same governments. Indeed, given the political sensitivity of health insurance, governments are often tempted to

---

BOX 7.1 *Applicability of case studies to low-income countries*

The four case studies can be of use to low-income countries in three ways.

First, they provide a catalog of governance mechanisms that *can* work and, therefore, provide ideas to be assessed for their applicability to a new context.

Second, in those cases where they demon-strate convergence on similar solutions, they suggest particular choices that should be given strong consideration.

Third, they show how countries had to struggle with particular problems that a country beginning to establish a system might be able to avoid.

---

intervene in a wide range of financial and managerial decisions, sometimes even overstepping the bounds established by law, because they know that important interest groups and citizens alike will hold them accountable if things go wrong.

Managing this tendency for undue interference is likely to work better when the respective responsibilities of the government and the insurance schemes are distinct and clear; when independent authorities (such as the courts) can effectively enforce that division of responsibilities; and when each actor has authority and discretion over those decisions for which it is held accountable. For example, it is impossible for an insurance fund to be held accountable for its financial performance if another entity (perhaps the government) sets premiums, eligibility criteria for enrollment, and the package of covered health services.

On this last point, one way to improve the match between authority and responsibility is to insist that decisions made for political reasons are paid for out of a separate fund. Estonia, by creating two separate financial reserves—one fund, under the managerial control of the supervisory board to manage commercial risks, and another controlled by the government to respond to political decisions—has made this division of authority and responsibility quite explicit. In Chile and the Netherlands, private insurers have a much wider scope for decisionmaking (and face the consequent risk of bankruptcy), with the responsibility of structuring competition left in the hands of public regulatory agencies.

Countries that are creating or reforming MHI can use these experiences to see how roles and responsibilities are divided and assess which allocation of decision-making powers is likely to function best for them. If revenues are set and controlled by the government, then health insurers can only be held accountable for how they spend their money. If the government also retains the right to set health care benefits, then the insurers can only be held accountable for the efficiency with which they administer and pay funds. Following this line of reasoning can assist countries in allocating decisionmaking authority to be consistent with resources and responsibilities.

With regard to specific institutional arrangements, the four case studies demonstrate that mandatory health insurers can function reasonably well as parts of the executive branch (as in Chile), as autonomous public institutions (as in Estonia and Costa Rica), and as nonprofit private entities (as in the Netherlands). If a country has a well-functioning public sector, direct public administration might be the best option. Where the public sector is less effective, autonomous public institutions could be considered; however, special attention will be needed to assure accountability, avoid capture by special interests, and ensure effective tools for managing personnel. In countries where private nonprofit firms function well, this option should be considered. However, again, the accountability structures and attention to avoiding capture become more critical. Finding examples of well-functioning institutions within a country will give important clues to which form of ownership and legal status is likely to serve best.

Stakeholder participation

When MHI was adopted in Western European countries, it was associated with political and economic patterns of industrialization—particularly the rising importance of negotiations between large businesses and unions. The resulting governance structure of many social insurance funds therefore involved representatives from business, labor, and frequently government. This pattern was expected to provide appropriate checks and balances by bringing relevant stakeholders to the table. Over the course of the last century, however, the relationship between unions and employers changed politically, economically, and socially. Furthermore, in many countries with MHI outside Western Europe, associations of formal employees and employers do not play the same political roles nor do they necessarily represent large shares of the population or economy.

Consequently, governance models with representatives from economic interest groups have undergone significant shifts in countries with long experience of social insurance, and have taken on different forms where they are more recently adopted. Today, rather than by the interests of specific economic groups, representation is increasingly shaped by the desire to incorporate a wider range of social actors, increase transparency, and involve professionals with technical expertise. Nevertheless, to the extent that these mechanisms for representation continue to rely on organized groups, they are criticized for leaving out the interests of beneficiaries; by incorporating unions and employers, they are criticized for creating a bias toward constraining costs over providing service; and when representatives are relatively uninterested in health care, they are criticized for allowing medical professionals to capture the decisionmaking apparatus.

Of the four case studies, Costa Rica and Estonia are the two that explicitly select the members of supervisory boards to represent particular social groups or interests, such as business, labor, government, and beneficiaries. This approach is sometimes also followed in regulatory boards or negotiating committees. For example, Costa Rica's CCSS has created committees that provide social input to the management of health facilities and that comprise seven members, including delegates chosen by employers and civil society organizations. This approach—electing board members to represent different interest groups—does not appear to have made a substantial difference in the priority given to different measures of performance since, in both cases, boards have reportedly given priority to financial matters with significantly less attention to health care quality and productivity. Nor does the approach protect against conflicts of interest since both countries have experienced such problems.

In the Netherlands, the composition of sickness fund boards and of the independent agencies that supervise them has changed considerably. For example, the Sickness Fund Council, which supervised the country's sickness funds from 1949 until 1999, included representatives from national associations of employers, employees, health care providers, and the sickness funds themselves. It was increasingly viewed as incapable of making hard choices or serving as an adequate and timely forum for decisionmaking. Therefore, when it was replaced by the Health Care Insurance Board, the board of the new entity was created with seven independent experts appointed by the minister of health for a four-year term (with the possibility of being reappointed twice). Rather than representing particular organized groups, appointees to the boards of sickness funds and the independent agencies that supervise them are expected to be chosen more for their professional integrity and technical qualifications than as representatives of economic groups.

In Chile, FONASA operates without a board of directors and has no formal representation of business or labor groups at all. However, since FONASA is part of the government, it is influenced by normal political processes. The president, minister of health, minister of finance, and other executive branch officials make policy and decisions that govern FONASA in relation to the interplay of debates in Congress and society at large. To some extent, this may be more appropriate to modern democracies that have eschewed "corporatist" models of politics.

An important factor that conditions the performance of these different representational structures is the wider relationship between major actors. In the Netherlands, negotiations between business and labor are characterized by strong efforts to reach consensus without government involvement; in France, such negotiations are more combative, paralyzing the decisionmaking process and requiring frequent intervention by the government. Therefore, choices regarding the composition of boards and defining the roles of major actors have to take these broader social and political factors into consideration, if they are to ensure effective decisionmaking that is in the best interest of the population.

Countries that are creating autonomous public institutions or nonprofit insurers would do well to consider the supervisory board's mandate and what combination of qualifications and interests would best serve its goals. In some cases, taking nominations from a wide range of civil society organizations might ensure that the board represents not only the interests of taxpayers and formal sector employees and employers, but also the interests of health care service users, informal workers, and people who are not economically active. In other cases, countries may find it preferable to rely on the independence, integrity, and experience of technical experts.

Transparency and information

A critical aspect of governance is assuring the flow of useful information about performance to authorities who can do something about it. Mandatory health insurers need internal management information systems to be able to properly manage their own affairs—this includes information on cash flow, liabilities and assets, clients, revenues and expenditures, and personnel. Ultimately, management should be able to link process information to performance measures. For example, Estonia's "balanced scorecard" and Costa Rica's "management contracts" are both aimed at improving this link.

In addition to information required for management, all the health insurers studied here had internal audit units—departments with the responsibility to ensure that management information was being reported properly, to identify malfeasance when it occurs, and to assess performance. Such internal audit units generally report to the highest level of management. In the case of public insurance funds, like the EHIF and the CCSS, the internal audit units work closely with the national controller-general's office, giving them a degree of independence from the fund's management.

External auditing is also required by all the countries that were studied here. In most cases, supervisory boards engage a private accounting firm to conduct the external audit. This is true of public insurance funds, like those in Estonia and Costa Rica. It is also the case for nonprofit or commercial insurers, such as ISAPREs in Chile and the sickness funds and voluntary funds in the Netherlands. In this latter case, it has become standard practice to hire independent auditing firms and to rotate them every few years to avoid the development of relationships that jeopardize the auditing firm's independence.

In addition to management information and auditing, health insurers can be required to issue a number of reports and to make performance information available to the public. Annual reports to legislative bodies are required in Costa Rica and Estonia. Public annual reports are required of nonprofit and commercial insurers in Chile and the Netherlands. Increasingly, insurers are required to report performance measures that relate to nonfinancial aspects of performance. The EHIF is required to report on a series of indicators related to five different strategic areas: access to care, quality of care, efficiency in administering benefits, awareness among beneficiaries of their rights and responsibilities, and quality of corporate governance. In Costa Rica, too, reporting requirements now go beyond financial status to include indicators of operational efficiency, quality of services provided by health care facilities, and proper handling of data. New statutes passed in 2005 in Chile are explicitly defining conditions for health care access, waiting times, quality, and reimbursements that are to be monitored on a regular basis through reporting to the country's Superintendancy of Health.

To be effective, required reports and audits are designed to collect information that is useful to someone and that can be acted upon. Operational information is designed to give managers data for daily decisions, while performance measures might be designed for use by consumer advocates or legislators. Collecting too much information can be costly and can obscure data that are really important. Collecting too little information can hamper efforts to hold insurers accountable. In addition, reporting information to a variety of actors—managers, board members, government agencies, consumer groups—increases the chances that malfeasance or poor performance will be detected and acted upon.

Supervision and regulation

Supervision and regulation of insurers must be consistent with the structure of the health insurance system, but a number of lessons seem to be robust for almost all contexts. These include the benefits of unifying supervision, controlling conflicts of interest, monitoring financial status, assuring the quality of health care provision, and providing consumer-grievance procedures.

Unifying supervision. The unification of insurance fund supervision bears emphasis because it has such far-reaching implications and is so consistently pursued across widely varying contexts. In the Netherlands and Chile, multiple insurers were historically regulated differently. In the Netherlands, government oversight was generally lax due to difficulties of agreeing on legislation, and the sickness funds were largely self-regulated. Private funds weren't regulated at all until the 1960s, and then, under legislation that was general to all insurers, not just health insurance. Dissatisfaction with the differential treatment led to gradual unification of regulation. With the latest reform (2006) in the Netherlands, the sickness funds and private funds are now under a single regulator.

Chile's public insurer, FONASA, and the ISAPREs were created in the early 1980s and treated quite differently. FONASA was supervised directly by the government, while the ISAPREs were initially unregulated. A regulatory authority for the ISAPREs was established in the early 1990s and gradually increased its scope of action and authority. However, Chileans were concerned that the regulations being put in place to improve the quality of care financed by ISAPREs were not adequately addressed in FONASA. In 2004 Chile formally created a new regulatory authority, the Superintendancy of Health, with responsibility for supervising both the private and public insurers, as well as public and private health care providers.

These countries collectively chose to unify the supervisory institutions in order to ensure that individuals are treated similarly and fairly across different insurance funds. Whether a fund is private or public, individuals who are affiliated with that insurance fund still want assurances that the fund will remain solvent, that their benefits package is adequate, that they have opportunities to pursue grievances, and that they are not unfairly discriminated against. Though differences in ownership and governance may alter the tools available to supervisory agencies, countries that are establishing new supervisory institutions should strongly consider unifying supervision from the start so as to avoid the problems experienced by Chile and the Netherlands.

Conflicts of interest. In all the cases discussed here, conflicts of interest were a matter of concern, but one that is still imperfectly addressed. Countries that are creating or reforming MHI should use such an opportunity as a way to introduce measures to address such conflicts as soon as possible.

The most direct way of avoiding conflicts of interest is to exclude people from supervisory positions—in boards, management, or regulatory agencies—if they have financial or personal interests that can be affected by the decisions of these bodies. In many countries and cases, people who are qualified to serve will at least have some potential conflicts of interest, or conflicts of interest will arise around particular issues or decisions. For such cases, transparency is a critical tool for improving decisions and limiting damage. Governance codes should explicitly state the conditions that require board members and managers to recuse themselves from decisions; establish formal independent mechanisms for investigating conflicts of interest; and create transparent processes for determining appropriate sanctions or actions when conflicts are revealed. Board members and managers should also be required to report information on even *potential* conflicts of interest, and publicly disclose, for example, relevant financial holdings, contracts with pharmaceutical companies or equipment manufacturers, professional partnerships, and gifts or benefits they receive from interested parties. By requiring public disclosure of potential conflicts of interest, it is possible to bring social pressure to bear and keep boards and managers honest. Furthermore, when board members or managers hide information that should be public, an explicit threshold is crossed that can serve as an objective reason for removal.

Codes of corporate governance can also be used to promote greater integrity and better performance of MHI, especially in those cases with multiple funds. Codes of corporate governance address much more than conflicts of interest, but this is an important part of their content. Such codes are not binding, but experience has shown that making an explicit statement of appropriate corporate behavior can establish new social norms as well as become standards for enforcement of contracts and regulations.[1]

Financial supervision. Health insurers are, fundamentally, financial institutions and unless they operate according to sound financial principles, they cannot remain solvent or function well. Fortunately, the principles of sound financial management are well known and appropriate forms of financial supervision have been established in a wide range of countries and contexts.

In countries with many insurers, financial supervision must establish the basic conditions for assuring solvency. This generally includes setting minimum capital requirements for entering the market and requiring insurers to maintain minimum reserves to cover normal risks, purchase secondary insurance to cover unusual risks, and invest in financial instruments with acceptable levels of risk. In addition to these conditions, financial supervision may require that insurers demonstrate that they have adequate internal controls, subject themselves to external auditing, and provide timely financial reports to regulatory authorities.

In countries with a single insurer, the form of financial supervision is different, but still necessary. An adequate capital base, sufficient reserves, and investments in appropriate financial instruments are still required, but as a single insurer, commercial risk from competition is no longer an issue. Rather, ways to manage political risks become more important. Furthermore, reporting requirements can be tailored to the single insurance fund and a chain of internal and external auditing can be developed to assure timely identification of financial problems.

Health care quality supervision. Unlike other financial institutions, health insurers make commitments to pay for a service whose quality is not easily monitored or guaranteed. For health insurance to be effective, beneficiaries must be able to reach health care providers in a timely fashion. Furthermore, those health care providers need to be able to correctly diagnose an illness or injury and treat it appropriately—which requires medications, equipment, and staff to be available when needed.

In the case of integrated provision, such as the CCSS in Costa Rica, the insurer has direct managerial control over health care providers and assuring good quality health care is equivalent to good management. Holding an integrated provider accountable for the quality of health care is both easier—because the fund cannot evade its responsibilities—and more difficult—because the internally contracted providers are often resistant to outside pressures.

In cases where insurance is separate from provision, control of health care quality has at least two dimensions. The first dimension involves direct supervision of health care providers. This kind of supervision may include licensing requirements for medical care providers and facilities, ongoing accreditation requirements, reporting on quality indicators, being subject to malpractice suits, following professional association guidelines, or even explicit payments for demonstrated progress on quality of care.

The second dimension involves supervision of health insurers, requiring them to demonstrate that they can fulfill their contractual obligations by having negotiated contracts or established payment mechanisms with an adequate number of health care providers in the geographic regions that they serve. The challenge for health care quality supervision faced by all countries is to move beyond requirements associated with static qualifications or quantity of *inputs* to directly measuring the quality of care that has been provided. For example, medical professionals and facilities can be monitored for providing adequate health care, such as appropriate follow-up care to people with diabetes or cardiovascular diseases, or full vaccinations for children, as a condition for renewed licensing or eligibility for reimbursement by insurers.[2]

Consumer protection. In addition to financial supervision and health care quality supervision, countries have implemented a number of measures to strengthen direct accountability to patients and their families. A key element of this strategy is to ensure that patients and families understand their insurance coverage and responsibilities, that insurers provide good service other than medical care (including timeliness and accuracy of payments), and that patients and families have ways to pursue their grievances when all else fails.

Consumer protection generally requires both direct formal measures and the active involvement of independent and nongovernmental groups. Direct formal measures can include requirements that insurers establish grievance procedures and subject themselves, ultimately, to reviews in court. Other direct measures include standardization of how information in contracts is presented to assist consumers in comparing plans or to better understand their benefits and premiums. All four countries have made efforts to standardize information available to the public about benefits included in their health plans. Indirect measures can involve encouraging the formation of consumer protection associations; hosting conferences in which consumer groups, insurers, and health care providers can exchange information; and soliciting inputs from consumers when monitoring insurers' performance.

Consistency and stability

For most low-income countries, MHI is relatively new and without historical experience, and it can be difficult to establish the system's reputation for consistency and stability. In this regard, new systems often must rely on the credibility of associated institutions—for a public entity, the government's own practices; for a private entity, the reputation of the private sector and public regulators in other sectors. Establishing an open and respected process for changing rules and abiding by them in the early years of a new system also helps establish a reputation for consistency and stability.

All four countries score high in consistency and stability, but often for different reasons. In many ways, the stability of the Costa Rican and Netherlands health insurance systems was, until recently, a consequence of political deadlock. For Costa Rica, the autonomy of the CCSS, established by law and supported by the Constitution, was another factor contributing to its remarkable stability. A third contributing factor, though less amenable to policy decisions, is unwavering popular support for the health insurance system in both countries.

Chile and Estonia have also exhibited consistency and stability, in part as a consequence of broad popular support. Nevertheless, these countries have been able to make important adjustments to the systems without jeopardizing basic confidence in how they are governed. This achievement is due to relatively open political processes for debating and effecting changes. In Chile, even when private insurers may dislike new regulatory constraints, they are given some voice and warning before changes take place.

The lesson for low-income countries that emerges from these experiences is that when the government has strong credibility, public decision structures for health insurers, written into legislation or even the Constitution, may be the best way of establishing a consistent and stable system. If the government lacks such credibility, autonomous structures, protected by constitutional provisions or anchored in the private sector, may work better.

Another lesson is that stability can be achieved in a variety of circumstances. When political debates demonstrate broad agreement and support for the health insurance system, legislation and regulatory actions can articulate and implement that consensus. But even in cases where the system is the object of fierce political debate, stability can be achieved by maintaining the deadlock (assuming of course that the current structure is adequate and important changes are not needed).

Clear rules that are judiciously and reliably enforced are the best way for a country to assure consistency and stability for its MHI system. Given that circumstances will change over time, clear procedures for modifying those rules are also needed—preferably tailored to the degree of flexibility required. For example, the specific thresholds set under financial solvency requirements might be adjustable by a regulatory agency without substantial difficulty, but the premise that insurers will be subject to financial solvency and reporting requirements should probably be strongly protected from erosion.

Contextual factors

Competition. Whether a country has multiple funds or only one has a significant impact on the choices within the foregoing dimensions of governance. The case studies show convergence toward consolidating insurance funds, even in those countries whose systems include multiple competing insurers. The regulatory framework for systems with multiple insurers is also significantly different from that for systems with a single insurer.

One of the most striking trends in the experiences reviewed here is a marked decline in the number of health insurers, in both public and private sectors, through consolidation. Estonia's experience with MHI began with 22 regional funds in 1992, but the country almost immediately started to consolidate them into larger entities until the reform of 2001, which established the EHIF as the single national insurance fund. The Netherlands had some 600 sickness funds in 1941. Legislative requirements imposed by the Germans during World War II reduced that number to 204 by 1943. This trend continued in subsequent decades so that in 1986 there were only 48 sickness funds and 75 private insurers (i.e. voluntary funds), and by 1994 there were only 26 sickness funds and 50 private insurers. By 2004 only 21 sickness funds and 44 private insurers remained active. In Chile, the number of ISAPREs peaked at 26 in 1997 and subsequently declined to 15 in 2005. Costa Rica is the only country that began with relatively few insurance funds, consolidated them in the 1940s, and has stuck by its single payer system. Costa Rica never had to go through further processes of unifying insurance funds because whenever coverage was extended to a new population group, the responsibility for administering insurance was given to the CCSS. The most recent consolidation in Costa Rica occurred in 1993, when all public service provision was integrated into the CCSS (previously the Ministry of Health had its own network of services). This consolidation and unification of insurance funds is not specific to the cases analyzed in this book. Similar processes can be found in Colombia, the Republic of Korea, Taiwan (China), and Tunisia.

Consolidation in the private sector often results from efforts to exploit scale economies in administration, to spread fixed costs of marketing over a larger number of clients, and to assist in reducing the volatility of health expenditures by pooling a larger group of individuals and their associated health risks. Regulations also influence the survival and consolidation of private insurers. In both Chile and the Netherlands, a variety of regulations increased the costs of business or constrained entrepreneurial strategies in ways that encouraged consolidation. Some of those regulations set minimum capital and solvency requirements to avoid bankruptcies, and established standardized benefits packages and constraints on the insurers' ability to cancel policies in order to protect consumers. These factors account for some of the consolidation among ISAPREs in Chile and the voluntary funds in the Netherlands. An additional impetus to consolidation in Chile was created by competition from FONASA, which apparently increased its market share in recent years by improving the quality of its services.

Consolidation in the public sector is also motivated by efforts to increase administrative efficiency and take advantage of scale economies, as appears to have been the case in Estonia. But in most countries, the primary driving force in the public sector for consolidation appears to be improving equity. In MHI systems with multiple insurers, large differences can emerge between spending levels, equity of access, and quality of care. To address this, many countries establish complex risk-equalization mechanisms that transfer funds from schemes with wealthier and healthier clients to those whose affiliates are disproportionately poorer or sicker (including Belgium, France, Japan, and until recently, the Netherlands).

Managing such equalization mechanisms can be very difficult, since it is data-intensive and analytically complex to separate the financial effects of risk variation from inefficient management. Many countries have found that achieving equity is easier and more direct when individuals are grouped into fewer insurance pools because it facilitates cross-subsidies across individuals; simplifies eligibility criteria so that people do not find themselves moving from one scheme to another because of a change in income or employment; and reduces variations in benefits packages across population groups. For example, in the Netherlands, the population was segmented between people below a particular income level who were required to affiliate with a sickness fund and people above that income level who were ineligible and had to seek private coverage. The latest reform eliminated this distinction. In Chile, when FONASA was created, it subsumed a number of public insurance programs. Recent reforms in Taiwan (China), the Republic of Korea, and Tunisia explicitly combined multiple public insurance funds into a single scheme.

It appears that the advantages of scale, simplicity, and equity that come from having fewer insurers are quite strong, and countries that are considering health insurance reforms would be well advised to consider whether consolidation can and should be encouraged. There are certainly tradeoffs in having fewer or more insurance funds, but whichever choice is made, the system of governance needs to be consistent with that choice.

In countries with a single insurance fund, accountability mechanisms are likely to require much more extensive and direct government oversight concerned with promoting greater efficiency in management, avoiding capture by special interests and corruption, and generally assuring that the insurance scheme is managed in the best interests of its members. Estonia has followed this approach, in part, by giving Parliament and government an active role in many health insurance system decisions, such as premium levels and balanced scorecard targets. The contrast presented by Costa Rica's CCSS, which has "bounded" autonomy, shows the difficulties that can arise, particularly for addressing conflicts of interest, when direct government oversight is weak.

By contrast, in countries with multiple insurers, government regulation tends to be more indirect, concerned with preserving competition, controlling adverse selection and risk selection, and managing risk-equalization transfers. Where countries have a commitment to competition in health insurance markets, they have come to realize that the health insurance market needs to be structured if normal market mechanisms are going to function well.

Chile's experience is particularly noteworthy in this regard. Neither FONASA nor the ISAPREs were effectively subjected to oversight when they were created in the early 1980s, though FONASA was formally assigned responsibility for supervising its competitors in the private sector. A decade later, the Superintendancy of ISAPREs was established with limited powers, focused essentially on improved reporting of financial statements to monitor solvency and creating an avenue for consumer grievances to be reported. A major shift occurred during the 1990s as successive governments sought to use regulations not only to protect those affiliated with ISAPREs but to alter the role of ISAPREs. Eventually, regulations were put in place to expand and standardize information provided to regulators and consumers, to require ISAPREs to cover a minimum package of services, to prohibit denial of coverage or arbitrary cancellation of policies, and to constrain price setting.

The stories in the Netherlands, Colombia, and other countries with multiple insurers are very similar and strongly suggest that countries with multiple insurers could "leapfrog" a number of problems by addressing such regulatory issues as soon as possible. Experts in this area have come to agree that the benefits of competition in health insurance cannot be realized without explicit attention to structuring that market. People who are choosing health insurance need simple and clear information about benefits, prices, and quality of service if they are going to make informed decisions. In addition, the market needs to be structured so that insurers have incentives to attract clients by providing quality services at low prices, rather than using their ingenuity to attract low-risk low-cost clients at inflated prices. For countries with multiple competing insurers, reviewing the list of regulations that are in place in other countries and assessing their applicability is the best way to ensure that a comprehensive and consistent set of regulations for health insurance competition are put in place from the start.

Relationship between insurance funds and health care providers. The relationship between insurers and providers has a large impact on the kinds of choices that need to be made within all the governance dimensions. Although the original hypotheses related to the difference between cases of integrated provision and separation between financing and provision, in practice, the cases show that this structural difference does not necessarily have a large impact on governance. Rather, the features that seem to be more important are whether providers are strongly organized and whether the relationship between insurers and providers is driven by a search for consensus or by vigorous debate, conflict, and negotiation.

Providers who are well organized are likely to have a strong effect not only on the implementation but also on the design of any MHI system. The medical profession in the Netherlands played an important role in maintaining the split between public and private funds for decades while, in Estonia, they provided key inputs and advocacy for the very creation of the national health insurance system in the early 1990s. Significant reforms necessarily have implications for the livelihoods of health care providers and so, depending on how well organized they are, particularly in the political sphere, their interests and expertise will have to be incorporated and addressed.

In the regular operation of MHI systems, many decisions will be made that also affect health care providers and for which they will push for influence through whatever channels are available. This is particularly notable in negotiations over salaries and working conditions (as in Costa Rica's CCSS) or in setting price and fee schedules (in Estonia, the Netherlands, and Chile). Looking at the experiences of the latter three countries, governing this process in a way that is aligned with good performance appears to involve a set of well-known procedures and rules that is informed as much as possible by technical considerations and with a balanced degree of openness to negotiations.

It is extremely difficult to find specific lessons in this regard except to emphasize the importance of this contextual feature. Countries that are designing governance for their MHI systems need to consider the strength and form of health care provider organization and take it into account. This is particularly true for choices regarding stakeholder participation because even without representation on supervisory boards, providers may exert influence in other ways—either politically or by popular appeals.

When designing the governance structures, countries would be well advised to examine their own experience with labor relations in both the private and public sector and look for examples that have been more collaborative than conflictual. Using those examples, and examining the current way that providers are organized and relate to insurers, may generate ideas for channeling the legitimate interests of insurers and providers in productive directions.

Unanswered questions

The foregoing discussion of trends and issues reflect areas of agreement among the case studies. But some very important questions remain unanswered by the case studies and require serious reflection for any country that is creating or reforming mandatory health insurers. Three of these questions are:

- How can countries assure solvency and balanced budgets?
- How can countries assure financial protection for the population?
- How can countries promote efficiency and raise productivity?

How can countries assure solvency and balanced budgets?

Financial supervision, audits, and oversight cannot, of themselves, ensure that health insurers remain solvent or balance their budgets. In addition, there have to be consequences for making decisions that jeopardize the health insurers' financial condition. With multiple insurers, bankruptcy provides the ultimate penalty for spending beyond revenues because consumers can be reallocated to other competing funds. With a single insurer, enforcing bankruptcy is not a viable option for public policymakers and alternative approaches to enforcing budget constraints or liquidity requirements are necessary. In such cases, the ability to discipline or fire managers and board members may be the only tool available—and this may be heavily constrained by legal separation of powers. An additional problem emerges when key decisions—contribution rates, benefits packages, and service volumes—are determined by political processes that are not disciplined by clear budget guidelines nor informed by accurate and reliable financial forecasts.

The health insurers studied here have all maintained solvency and balanced budgets, but the causes are not clear. For example, Estonia's EHIF has performed admirably, but in a context of rapid economic growth and a political system that is fiscally conservative. Without these contextual features, would the EHIF's governance mechanisms be strong enough to assure solvency and balanced budgets? The same question can be posed for each of the countries studied here. Every country has to propose governance mechanisms that increase the likelihood of solvency and balanced budgets, but ultimately these are assured only by the dynamics of actual behavior by political and economic actors.

How can countries assure financial protection for the population?

All the countries studied here have achieved universal coverage for their populations with a relatively comprehensive set of health services. However, in many low- and middle-income countries, MHI has not expanded beyond a small subset of the population or provides only limited benefits. For example, in the Dominican Republic, the Social Security Institute (Instituto Dominicana de Seguro Social) is responsible for insuring formal sector employees and reaches less than 10 percent of the population. It has few incentives to expand coverage beyond this relatively privileged segment of the population. In the Islamic Republic of Iran, health insurance coverage is more widespread, but claims that 90 percent of the population have health insurance are exaggerated and the true share is closer to 30 percent. In addition, the services that are covered are relatively limited, copayments are high, and policymakers have been surprised to discover that those affiliated with public health insurance still spend substantial amounts of their income on out-of-pocket medical expenses. Such expenses, overall, are about 53 percent in Iran (Drechsler and Jütting 2005).

Countries that are creating or reforming MHI need to consider the strategy for reaching universal coverage. Will they create specific insurance funds for different population segments and then try to unify them, as has occurred in the Republic of Korea, the Netherlands, and Taiwan (China)? Or will they begin with universal eligibility and deal with the costs and consequences of trying to provide such wide coverage? Strategies for linking the expansion of health insurance coverage to an expansion of health care services will also have to be considered.

How can countries promote efficiency and raise productivity?

Health care costs will continue to rise as populations become wealthier and demand more services, and as health care technology advances and offers more services and products. Introducing health insurance can exacerbate the effects of rising demand by raising prices (Gertler and Solon 2002) or by increasing utilization (Fuchs 1974). Insurers can also play a role in improving the efficiency and productivity of health care through the financial incentives they create, their negotiations with health care providers, any requirements on health care quality that they establish, and the structure of benefits that they cover.

A well-governed health insurer has strong incentives to increase its own efficiency (by, for example, reducing administrative costs) and to encourage health care providers to be more productive. When they function well, governance mechanisms hold the health insurer accountable for its use of revenues in terms of services provided to beneficiaries. The benefits of improved productivity can then be used to lower premiums or increase the number and quality of services that are offered. By contrast, poorly governed health insurers can find any number of ways to avoid the difficult task of increasing productivity. If they are poorly regulated, nonprofit or commercial funds can advertise to attract only low-risk clients, they can write misleading contracts that limit coverage, or cancel policies when clients become ill. If they are poorly governed public insurance funds, they can pressure the government to subsidize their deficits, raise contribution rates, or skimp on payments to providers.

None of the approaches to governance of MHI presented here will guarantee that insurers focus on improving efficiency and productivity. Yet every country has been concerned with increasing efficiency and productivity as part of its reform efforts. This is another area in which those countries creating or reforming MHI will have to draw from others' experiences, reflect on their own conditions, and experiment with new approaches.

Endnotes

1. This discussion of corporate codes draws on Savedoff and Fuenzalida, forthcoming. The Web site of the European Corporate Governance Institute (http://www.ecgi.org) contains the full texts of corporate governance codes, principles of corporate governance, and corporate governance reforms in Europe and elsewhere. The Core Principles issued by the International Association of Insurance Supervisors (http://www.iaisweb.org/) for insurance institutions constitute a particularly useful reference for addressing issues of financial management and integrity.

2. Information on advances in improving health care quality supervision can be found in many places, including the U.S. Agency for Healthcare Research and Quality (www.ahrq.gov), the Joint Commission on Accreditation of Healthcare Organizations (http://www.jointcommission.org/), and the OECD's Healthcare Quality Indicators Project (www.oecd.org).

Reference list

Drechsler D., and J. P. Jütting. 2005. "Private Health Insurance in Low- and Middle-Income Countries: Scope, Limitations, and Policy Responses." Organisation for Economic Co-operation and Development, Paris.

Fuchs, V.R. 1974. *Who Shall Live? Health, Economics, and Social Choice.* New York: Basic Books, Inc.

Gertler, P., and O. Solon. 2002. "Who Benefits From Social Insurance in Low Income Countries? Evidence from the Philippines." University of California, Berkeley.

Savedoff, William D., and Hernan Fuenzalida. Forthcoming. "Promoting Accountability in Health Care Financing Institutions." In Joseph Kutzin, Cheryl Cashin, and Reinhard Busse, eds., *Implementing Health Financing Reforms: Lessons from and for Countries in Transition.* Copenhagen: European Observatory on Health Care Systems Series, Buckingham and Philadelphia: Open University Press.

Index